The Jewish Family

Most of the chapters in this book were first presented as papers at the Conference on the Evolving Jewish Family held at Queens College on June 22–24, 1981. The editors wish to express their appreciation to the National Jewish Family Center of the American Jewish Committee and to Queens College for making that conference possible.

The Jewish Family
Myths and Reality

edited by
Steven M. Cohen and Paula E. Hyman

Holmes & Meier

New York / London

First published in the United States of America
1986 by

Holmes & Meier Publishers, Inc.
30 Irving Place
New York, NY 10003

Great Britain:
Holmes & Meier Publishers, Ltd.
Pindar Road
Hoddesdon, Hertfordshire EN11 0HF
England

Copyright © 1986 by Holmes & Meier
Publishers, Inc.

Book design by Ellen Foos

**Library of Congress Cataloging in
Publication Data**
  Main entry under title:

The Jewish family: myths and reality.

    Includes index.
    1. Jewish families—Addresses, essays,
lectures.
I. Cohen, Steven M. II. Hyman, Paula E.
HQ525.J4P47 1986   306.8'5'089924 84-27896
ISBN 0-8419-0860-5

Manufactured in the United States of America

For my son, Adam Wall
—S.M.C.

For my daughters, Judith and Adina
—P.E.H.

Acknowledgments

This volume grew out of a conference on the Jewish family held at Queens College, CUNY. The funding for that conference came in equal measure from two sources which we gratefully acknowledge.

One source of support was the William Petschek National Jewish Family Center of the American Jewish Committee, under the direction of Yehuda Rosenman. Since 1979, the Center has been involved in the study and support of the Jewish family through the sponsorship of research, publications, and action programs.

The other half of the funding was provided by the Queens College Office of Graduate Studies and Research under the direction of Dean Helen Cairns.

Both Dean Cairns and Mr. Rosenman contributed to the conceptualization and planning of the conference, for which we are also grateful.

Contents

The Jewish Family

1. Introduction: Perspectives on the Evolving Jewish Family

Paula E. Hyman

There has been a great deal of mythmaking but remarkably little scholarship about the Jewish family. In modern times, Jews and Gentiles alike have constructed and perpetuated a romantically idealized image of the Jewish family as warm, supportive, and ever-nurturing. In part this image derived from the nostalgia of Jews who had moved from the relatively insular communities of traditional Jewry into the anonymity and tension of modern Western society. Looking back, these Jews saw the families of their childhood as their refuge in a hostile and forbidding environment. Not only did these writers find the family personally supportive; they also attributed the long survival of Jews as a people to the special qualities of the Jewish family.[1] In part, this image resulted from a potent antidefamation campaign waged by Jews who felt that traditional Jewish family patterns meshed well with the modern glorification of family life. Jews could rightly take pride in being among the first to possess the attributes of bourgeois domesticity.

Gentile commentators contributed to this popular image of Jewish family life. Even those Gentile intellectuals, such as most Enlightenment writers, who found much to criticize in Jewish religious and economic practices, praised Jews for their admirable home life. To cite but one example: the Abbé Grégoire, a supporter of Jewish emancipation and critic of what he called Jewish superstition and exploitative behavior,

---

I would like to thank Marion Kaplan, Ivan Marcus, and Jack Wertheimer for their comments upon an earlier draft of this Introduction.

3

devoted considerable attention to the virtues of the Jewish hearth. In a famous 1789 essay, he declared of the Jews, "They have placed strong barriers against libertinism. Nothing is more rare among them than adultery; their marital union is truly edifying; they make good spouses and good parents."[2]

In the past two centuries Jewish communal leaders have been quick to celebrate the virtues of Jewish family life for purposes of self-gratification as well as apologetics, but they have been equally quick, in periods of rapid social change, to blame contemporary Jewish families for failing to live up to the standards of a noble past. In particular, they have attributed assimilation to the Jewish family's alleged failure to maintain its traditional strengths. In this Jewish communal literature an idealized version of the modern bourgeois family is the only acceptable Jewish family. In a different vein, American Jewish novelists and critics have lampooned the Jewish family, viewing its emotional intensity and balance of power between the sexes as inappropriate to the American WASP ideal. The romantic myth of the traditional Jewish family, along with the caricature of the twentieth-century American Jewish family, threatens to distort reality, rather than illuminate it. They mask the diversity of Jewish patterns within an all-embracing stereotype, be it favorable or grotesque.

Only through scholarly investigation of the Jewish family will myth and caricature give way to sophisticated understanding of a variegated historical and contemporary reality. Two broad fields of academic inquiry—Jewish social history and family history—are logical arenas for the study of the Jewish family. The emergence of family history as a subdiscipline within the social sciences provides a new opportunity to study the development of Jewish family patterns in different times and places. With its focus on the emergence of the modern family, family history has proposed an agenda and developed methodologies for studying the private behavior of family life. Interdisciplinary in scope, it has drawn upon the resources of demography, anthropology, sociology, and psychology to chart changes in family patterns over time. Concerned with the experiences of ordinary Jews, Jewish social history has defined the family as an appropriate subject of study and has adopted the methodologies of family history.

The scholarly investigation of the Jewish family is of interest not only to Jewish historians, sociologists, and family practitioners but also to all who are concerned with the contemporary Jewish community. The field of family history as a whole can only benefit from an interdisciplinary exploration of the family patterns of this geographically dispersed minority group with its own religious heritage, cultural values, and economic structure. Insofar as Jews have developed differently from the populations among which they have lived, they offer an unparalleled opportunity for "deviant case" analysis that would isolate the factors accounting for whatever distinctive characteristics Jews exhibit in their family patterns. Insofar as they have developed similarly to the majority cultures among which they live, they offer an opportunity for understanding the impact of those cultures upon the intimate sphere of the family and the effect of impersonal forces—both structural and political—upon a minority's ability to maintain its unique family traditions.

The essays collected in this book aim to bring the resources of Jewish scholarship and family history to bear upon the transformation of the Jewish family in modern times. Drawn primarily from papers delivered at a conference on the Jewish family held in June 1981, they apply the methodologies of social history, anthropology, sociology, literature, and demography to analyze the image and reality of the Jewish family in diverse settings. They seek to explore the role of the family in the reshaping of Jewish patterns of behavior and identity—cultural, religious, and socioeconomic—in the last two centuries. In doing so, they fill a gap in the literature of both family and Jewish history.

There exists little previous scholarship on the Jewish family. Whatever their interpretive framework, family historians have omitted the Jews from consideration. Lawrence Stone, whose monumental *The Family, Sex and Marriage in England 1500–1800* was a significant contribution to the understanding of the emergence of the modern family in the West, has stressed the impact of religious values upon family behavior. Yet his recent suggestion that scholars broaden their focus when investigating the role of religion in family development merely added Catholicism as a legitimate field of inquiry to a corpus of scholarship limited almost exclusively to Protestantism. Stone's comment that "we still know very little about the effects of . . . Catholicism [upon the family]"[3] applies equally well to Judaism.

Jewish scholars, too, have paid relatively little attention to the family. While there exists a modest sociological literature on the demography and social characteristics of contemporary American Jewish families,[4] the opportunities for exploring the historical evolution of the Jewish family as well as its role in the adaptation of Jews to a variety of environments have scarcely been exploited. Notable exceptions are the work of S. D. Goitein and Jacob Katz.

Goitein's third volume of *A Mediterranean Society*,[5] his magnum opus on Jewish life in the Mediterranean basin in the tenth to the thirteenth centuries, based on rich archival sources from the Cairo Geniza, is devoted entirely to the family. A major contribution to family history, Goitein's book presents a wealth of material under the rubrics of The

Extended Family, Marriage, The Nuclear Family, and The World of Women. Goitein emphasizes the importance of the extended family among Jews under medieval Islam. Even while couples established their own households, they commonly did so in the home of the husband's parents, whose authority was supreme. Extended kinship responsibilities, especially between brothers and sisters and their respective children, were the norm, and kinship ties were reinforced through familial business connections. Despite the prevailing myth of stability among traditional Jewish families, Goitein reveals that geographic mobility, death, and divorce frequently disrupted Jewish family life in medieval times. While premodern families are generally described as formal and lacking in affective relations between their members, Goitein shows the existence of strong emotional ties between parents and children in Mediterranean Jewish communities, and on occasion between spouses as well. Finally, he illuminates the ways in which the dowry and *ketubah,* the Jewish marriage contract, provided women a measure of security within the family and demonstrates how some women with economic resources could break through the restrictive conditions of medieval Islamic society to play a limited role in public economic and civil life.

Although Jacob Katz has not written an entire book on the Jewish family, his articles on the Ashkenazi family in the early modern period represent pioneering efforts to analyze the structure of the Jewish family, its method of establishment, and the constraints placed upon it by communal norms.[6] Katz points out that in early modern Europe the Jewish family unit was primarily the nuclear household but that extended kinship responsibilities were both strong and numerous. As was the case with most families in premodern times, the Jewish family was established on the basis of economic and status considerations and not through the personal choice of the prospective marriage partners. Indeed, Katz cites as an important aspect of the emergence of Jewish modernity the introduction of erotic considerations and autonomy of choice in the formation of family units.

If there are some similarities between Goitein's Mediterranean Jewish family in the Middle Ages and Katz's European Jewish family at the end of the Middle Ages, there are also important differences. In fact, it is difficult to speak about *the* Jewish family. The study of the Jewish family indicates that the practice of Judaism as well as Jewish survival have been consonant with any number of family structures. Just as there is a plurality of family types in the modern Western world, so there has existed at any one time, as well as through the generations, a variety of Jewish family patterns. Since Jews have been dispersed through so many lands, the diversity of their families has been greater than among territorially defined national groups. The Jewish family of nineteenth-century Berlin, of nineteenth-century Vilna, and of nineteenth-century Cairo differed according to local socioeconomic development, prevailing customs, and the economic role, level of acculturation, social class, and legal status of the Jews in each city. Class distinctions also affected the timing of marriage and household composition in each place. Yet the stereotype of the Jewish family derives primarily from the experience of Ashkenazi Jews of Eastern Europe and America in the nineteenth and twentieth centuries. It recognizes no diversity.

Still, for all their differences, Jews shared a common religious tradition, prescriptive literature, and minority status. Because Judaism considered marriage as more than a concession to human weakness and because so much of Jewish ritual was home centered, the family appears to have occupied a central role in Jewish life throughout history. All Jews accepted the importance of family and entry into marriage as a religious and social obligation. Nowhere did Jews legitimate celibacy as an alternative to married life. Nor were illegitimacy or premarital conception as prevalent among Jews as among many non-Jewish populations. Since Jews share a religious literature, sense of common fate, and legal status, it is possible to examine the interplay between religious culture and environment in the variety of social settings in which Jews have lived.

The chapters in this book highlight the diversity of Jewish family patterns in the modern world. Using a number of disciplines and methodologies, they reflect upon the changes that the Jewish family has undergone as Jews have integrated themselves into their host societies and adapted to the economic and social conditions of the modern world. They also explore the interaction of Jewish family and community and the relationship between family structure and expressions of Jewish identity.

The book begins with two studies of the traditional Jewish family. Building upon Jacob Katz's work on the Ashkenazi family, Gershon Hundert suggests how focusing upon issues of concern to family historians can illuminate the development of Polish Jewry in the early modern period. In particular, Hundert connects the demographic explosion of the seventeenth and eighteenth centuries and the consequent proliferation of the young with such phenomena as the rise of Hasidism and the strengthening of *yeshivot* (schools of higher Jewish learning). Similarly, he posits that the extension of communal controls was a direct response to demographic pressures.

In his study of the traditional Sephardi family in eighteenth- and nineteenth-century Morocco, Shlomo Deshen makes good use of responsa literature to illustrate the nuclear family's integral relation to the

8 Paula E. Hyman

broader kin network as well as the power relations within the family circle. Deshen reveals that the traditional Jewish family in eighteenth- and nineteenth-century Morocco was, like Goitein's medieval Egyptian Jewish family, both patriarchal and patrilocal: married sons established their households in close proximity to their fathers in extended family compounds. As other historical and anthropological studies have shown,[7] this type of family structure limited the power and status of wives, who were dependent upon the geographical proximity and influence of their parents and brothers.

Deshen's work also demonstrates the variety of patterns to be found among Jewish families commonly characterized as traditional. Thus, the Moroccan Jewish family differed substantially from other traditional Jewish families, both Ashkenazi and Sephardi. Like their Muslim counterparts, for example, Jewish women in Morocco were largely confined to the home. Jewish men were responsible for food shopping and were even involved in certain aspects of food preparation. The Jewish family in Morocco was also unusual in the relative unimportance of dowries in marriage arrangements.

The modernization of the Jewish family, which has occurred in a variety of contexts within the past two centuries, altered many features of traditional Jewish family life: family size, women's role, and parent-child relations among them. While Central and West European Jews began the processes of acculturation and integration into their societies at the end of the eighteenth and the beginning of the nineteenth centuries, the Jews of Eastern Europe lagged behind by two to three generations. Not until the twentieth century did the Jews of North Africa and the Levant begin to experience the effects of modernization.

David Biale's chapter investigates the new attitudes to early marriage and love that emerged among the modernized, intellectual elite of East European Jewry, the *maskilim,* in the second half of the nineteenth century. Biale argues that the opposition to early marriage was central to Haskalah ideology and derived from the social reality of the maskilim themselves. While the maskilim were few in number, they defined a social problem for a broader audience and provided a vocabulary for the discussion of that problem. They also formulated a vision of a modern family, which prolonged childhood and reserved for adulthood the responsibilities of sexual relations and of making a living.

Looking at the already bourgeois German Jewish family of the Second Empire (1871–1914), Marion Kaplan analyzes the role of women within the family and the function of family for Jewish women. Kaplan finds that Jewish women, while often blamed by communal leaders for the assimilation of German Jewry, were the ones who preserved religious tradition within the family. Indeed, she notes that middle-class women were less assimilated than were their husbands and brothers. Because their opportunities in the larger society were so circumscribed and because their religious responsibilities within Judaism had always been home centered, they linked religious ritual with their concern for family. Indeed, maintaining family ties became a form of religious expression for women. The sanctioning by German society of the home as the only legitimate sphere for women reinforced the familial role of Jewish women. In it, they found a source of self-respect.

For Moroccan Jews, it was primarily the act of migration to Israel that inserted them within a modern Western society. In his study of Moroccan Jews in Israeli agricultural villages, Moshe Shokeid investigates the synergistic effects of migration and modernization upon the Moroccan Jewish family. Shokeid has found that Moroccan Jews who were placed in villages, in contrast to those sent to development towns, were settled in extended family units. The retention of the extended family facilitated their transition to Israeli society; they could rely upon kinship ties in periods of stress. Indeed, the Moroccan Jews in these villages display little of the family pathology (e.g., delinquency) commonly associated with Moroccans in Israel. They adjusted with relative ease to the lifestyle of small farmers and adopted certain family characteristics that were prevalent in the Israeli villages: the nuclear household and the employment of wives on the family farm. They also loosened the control that the paterfamilias traditionally exercised over his children. In a situation where traditional family ties were preserved, they served as a resource for immigrant adaptation. The family was allowed to develop at its own pace, rather than being ruptured by external forces. Thus, Shokeid demonstrates how the village context enabled the Moroccan Jewish family to modernize and yet to retain such traditional norms as large family size and sense of responsibility to extended kin. His case study is suggestive of the type of investigation still needed of the function of the Jewish family and its adaptive capacity in different immigrant situations.

The modern Jewish family is most widely known not through scholarly studies but through the image disseminated in fiction and other forms of popular culture. Such images shape the perceptions of non-Jews and, when internalized, the self-perceptions of Jews. They also reveal attitudes that pervade circles much wider than those of the literary elite. In her study of the portrayal of the Jewish family in the British novel, Anita Norich surveys the growing presence of Jews in British fiction in the nineteenth century. It is no accident that the Jews who figure in the British novel often lack families, because it is as mysterious representatives of finance capital that they interest English writers. Norich points out the symbolic role of the Jew as a touchstone for British anxieties about loss of historical roots and the impact of financial power.

While the Jewish family is peripheral and exotic in the British novel, within Yiddish literature the family saga is a recognized subgenre of fiction. Susan Slotnick argues that the family saga uses the family as a symbol both of unity and of disintegration. Individuals struggle within the family circle, trapped in and supported by its embrace. At the same time, the families themselves suffer a decline—of power, integrity, and Jewish authenticity—as they confront the conditions of the modern world. Thus, Yiddish literature confirms the popular image of the fall from past strength of the Jewish family in the modern era.

Perhaps more influential than literature because of their broad audience, jokes also popularize stereotypes and express deeply held emotional attitudes. Of all members of the Jewish family, the Jewish mother figures most prominently in Jewish ethnic humor. As Gladys Rothbell points out, in the past thirty years Jewish men—novelists, comedians, and psychologists—have developed a new, negative stereotype of the Jewish mother as manipulative, self-centered, and domineering. The attack upon the Jewish mother, while couched in terms of humor, reflects an antipathy toward immigrant Jewish family patterns and a strong desire for merging with the majority culture. While Jewish-mother jokes are often depicted as inoffensive because they are created by Jews themselves, Rothbell persuasively argues that such jokes express deep animosity toward Jewish women, who become symbols of the incomplete assimilation of American Jews. Yet when Jewish men lampoon Jewish women, they do not see in their attack an offense against the ethnic group as a whole. Self-hatred is thus released through gender-specific humor.

If our perceptions of family life are often shaped by a combination of personal experience and internalized stereotype, we owe our knowledge of the reality of family size, household composition, family stability, and timing of marriage to demographers. Because many countries do not identify Jews in their censuses, research on Jewish demography is difficult to pursue. However, using a variety of sources, Calvin Goldscheider, Sergio DellaPergola, and Frances K. Goldscheider have identified the dimensions of the contemporary Jewish family in Israel, France, and the United States.

What is striking in these chapters is the emergence of two identifiable entities: the Jewish family of the West and the Israeli Jewish family. The former is characterized by late age at marriage, low fertility, and rising divorce rates; the latter, by relatively early marriage, lower rates of divorce, and higher fertility. Thus, the condition of living as a majority population in a modern but pronatalist society has reversed among Israeli Jews the trend, visible for several generations among Western Jews, toward smaller families and relatively late marriage. While Diaspora Jews as a whole are failing to reproduce their own numbers, Jews in Israel, whether Ashkenazi or Sephardi, religious or secular, display a higher birthrate than most residents of industrialized societies.

The concluding section of the book explores the interaction between Jewishness, family patterns, and community in a number of cultural contexts. The family has always served as a primary unit of the Jewish community. Indeed, the relationship between the family and the community is fundamental to any understanding of the changing nature of Jewish identity, the transmission of Jewish values, and the extent of communal control. In the preemancipation period, the tight-knit, autonomous Jewish community was able to regulate the number of marriages in a particular locale and to stipulate conditions for the marriage of the lower classes. It also restrained deviant behavior through a combination of formal and informal controls. The family and the community shared responsibility for the transmission of Jewish values as well as for Jewish survival; they were symbiotic institutions, reinforcing each other.

In the modern period, when communal affiliation has become voluntary and the power of the Jewish community reduced to moral suasion alone, the family and the community no longer necessarily operate in tandem. The community cannot compel behavior or membership as it did in the past. What kind of influence then, does the modern Jewish community or subcommunity wield over its members? How does the family view its relationship to the community? What impact does the interplay of family and community have upon Jewish behavior and identity?

Investigating a contemporary Jewish community that rejects both acculturation and modernity, William Shaffir offers an analysis of the current situation of the Hasidic family. While that family remains an effective agent of socialization, screening its children from larger societal influences and inculcating the patterns of observance of strict Orthodoxy, it has been touched, at least in part, by external trends. Exploring the four areas of women and work, materialism, marital stability, and family planning, Shaffir finds limited evidence of change alongside more widespread Hasidic perception of change. Although the mechanisms of social control employed by Hasidic families have been effective, Shaffir concludes that even the minor inroads made by secular influences within Hasidic communities, because they are perceived as dangerous, may promote a strengthening of social controls.

If the Hasidic family raises its children to conform to tradition in an environment free from tension between biological family and community, the *havurah* family chooses a style of Jewish observance and a set of Jewish values often at odds with the biological extended family. In her ethnographic study of a Bar Mitzvah celebration in an independent havurah, Chava Weissler examines the conflict between kin and community and shows how the havurah performs the functions of an extended family even when close biological relatives are available to its members. As a community where choice and personal satisfaction prevail over coercion and biological dictates with regard to the demands posed both by Judaism and by family, the havurah reflects the values of Jewish modernity.

Drawing upon a variety of survey data, Steven M. Cohen, the co-editor of this volume, argues that the recent rapid demographic changes in the American Jewish family do not necessarily portend serious injury to the vitality of the family and the American Jewish community. The postponement of marriage and child-bearing and the rise in divorce and intermarriage seem to have limited and contradictory effects on Jewish identity and continuity. He contends that Jewish communal institutions must adapt to new family patterns or run the risk of alienating large numbers of Jews living in nonconventional families.

This volume cannot claim to be a comprehensive study of the Jewish family in modern times. But its wide-ranging contributions are a first step toward such a history. They provide information about and analyses of Jewish family development in the United States, Western and Eastern Europe, North Africa, and Israel. They chart demographic and social change, as Jews have responded to the opportunities and demands of modernity; and they illustrate the adaptability of Jewish families to diverse economic and cultural conditions. This book is intended, however, not only to illuminate little-known aspects of Jewish family history in the past four centuries, but also to raise questions and to stimulate further research in this nascent field.[8] We hope that it will do so.

Notes

1. For examples of this popular view of the Jewish family, see Louis Wirth, *The Ghetto* (Chicago, 1928), pp. 26–27; and the description of a 1973 conference on the family cosponsored by the American Jewish Committee and B'nai B'rith, in Paula Hyman, "The Jewish Family: Looking for a Usable Past," *Congress Monthly*, October 1975, p. 10.

Introduction   13

2. Abbé Henri Grégoire, *Essai sur la régénération physique, morale et politique des Juifs* (Metz, 1789), p. 36.

3. Lawrence Stone, "Family History in the 1980's: Achievements and Future Trends," *Journal of Interdisciplinary History* XII: 1 (summer 1981), p. 84.

4. See, for example, Marshall Sklare, *America's Jews* (New York, 1971), pp. 73–103; Sergio DellaPergola, "Patterns of American Jewish Fertility," Sidney Goldstein, "Jews in the United States: Perspectives from Demography," *American Jewish Yearbook,* vol. 81 (1981), pp. 3–59; and Steven M. Cohen, "The American Jewish Family Today," *American Jewish Yearbook,* vol. 82 (1982), pp. 136–54. For a comprehensive bibliography that reveals the paucity of scholarly studies see Benjamin Schlesinger, *The Jewish Family* (Toronto, 1971).

5. S. D. Goitein, *A Mediterranean Society: The Jewish Communities of the Arab World as Portrayed in the Documents of the Cairo Geniza,* vol. 3, *The Family* (Berkeley and Los Angeles, 1978).

6. Jacob Katz, "Marriage and Sexual Life Among the Jews at the End of the Middle Ages" [Hebrew], *Zion* X (1944), pp. 21–54; "Family, Kinship, and Marriage among Ashkenazim in the 16th–18th Centuries," *Jewish Journal of Sociology* I (1959), pp. 4–22; as well as *Tradition and Crisis* (New York, 1961), pp. 135–56.

7. Rayna R. Reiter, ed., *Toward an Anthropology of Women* (New York and London, 1975); and Michelle Zimbalist Rosaldo and Louise Lamphere, eds., *Women, Culture, and Society* (Stanford, 1974).

8. For a stimulating article that suggests the important questions to be investigated in the study of the German Jewish family in the nineteenth and early twentieth centuries, see Marion Kaplan, "Family Structure and the Position of Jewish Women—A Comment" in *Revolution and Evolution: 1848 in German-Jewish History,* Werner E. Mosse, Arnold Paucker, and Reinhard Rürup, eds. (Tübingen, 1981), pp. 189–203.

JEWISH FAMILIES IN
TRADITIONAL SOCIETIES

2. Approaches to the History of the Jewish Family in Early Modern Poland-Lithuania

Gershon David Hundert

With only one important exception, nothing has been written specifically on the history of the Jewish family in early modern Poland-Lithuania. In Jacob Katz's *Tradition and Crisis* there is a chapter on "The Family" which also appeared earlier in somewhat different Hebrew and English articles.[1] Precisely because there is no body of literature it is well to stress both the importance of the subject and the tentative and exploratory nature of this chapter, which examines novel subjects and issues. I will suggest some possible connections between demographic conditions and important social and cultural developments, including Hasidism; I will raise some issues related to the history of children and childhood and of women; and I will discuss the relationship between communal institutions and the family. In doing so, I intend to expose the potentially rich veins that ought to be explored and mined by future researchers. Not only will such research shed much needed new light on the experience of East European Jews, it will also provide a historical context for understanding developments among their descendants, who include the vast majority of North American Jews.

Sources of Jewish provenance, including rabbinic responsa and communal minute books, provide most of the data for this essay. A computer search of the database of the Bar Ilan Responsa Project, which is under the auspices of Yeshiva University, was used in the collection of material from responsa literature. Unfortunately, at the time, that database included only a few East European authorities. Although it has not been done here, in the future it will be imperative to seek comparative data on Christians in Poland-Lithuania as well.

Demographic development is one of the most important yet least explored areas of Polish-Jewish history. There is an urgent need for reexamination of the few estimates and calculations that have been made in the past, particularly in view of recent work in the field of general Polish demographic history. Because church records of births, baptisms, weddings, and deaths, which are the most objective and reliable sources of information, are least useful in computing the Jewish population, estimates of Jewish numbers have been based mainly on fiscal records, especially "hearth" taxes, which are notoriously unreliable. In addition to the questionable nature of the lists of dwellings or hearths, there is no agreement whatsoever as to how many Jews, on average, lived in each house. As a result, estimates of the mid-seventeenth-century Jewish population range between 170,000 and 300,000; one historian put Jewish numbers in 1648 at 450,000. Estimates of the Polish Christian population for that time range between 10 million and 11 million.

It is asserted generally that there was a dramatic increase of Jewish numbers during the sixteenth century and in the first decades of the seventeenth century. During the twenty years following 1648, Poland suffered territorial losses and many deaths caused by war, fire, famine, and disease, and its population was reduced by at least one-third. Jewish losses during the same period are very difficult to estimate but are generally thought to have amounted to as much as one-fifth or even one-quarter of the Jewish population. The next date for which computations have been made is not earlier, unfortunately, than 1764–65. By that time the Polish population had reached 11 or 12 million, while the number of Jews in Poland was about 550,000. If these figures are correct, they indicate that the Jews recovered more rapidly from the disasters at mid-century than the rest of the Polish population. That is, the proportion of Jews increased from between 2.7 and 3 percent of the Polish population in 1648 to between 4.6 and 5 percent of the population in 1764–65. The disproportion in the rate of growth between the Jews and the rest of the Polish population may have been even greater than this, but it is unlikely that it was smaller. It is well known that this rapid expansion of Jewish numbers continued through the nineteenth century.[2]

These demographic factors suggest a number of important implications which warrant systematic research. The growth of the Jewish population occurred at a time when the Polish Commonwealth, at least until 1740, was experiencing severe economic difficulties. The dimensions and velocity of trade and commerce were reduced. More and more Christian town dwellers turned to agriculture; there is a literature on the "agrarianization" of the Polish towns in this period.[3] At the same time, more and more Jews turned to artisanry. The limited opportunities in the established communities, which were themselves a consequence of burgeoning Jewish numbers and the difficult economic situation, stimulated geographic mobility. Jews appeared in more and more and smaller and smaller settlements. The proportion of Jews living in villages in Eastern Europe was never greater than it was during the second half of the eighteenth century. At the same time, the main centers of Jewish population became more highly differentiated in terms of occupation and income. As the communities grew the ties between people weakened, as did the compelling power of social sanctions. And finally a constantly growing population, attributable probably to a relatively lower death rate, must have meant that the proportion of young people within the Jewish population was increasing constantly. Although one might think that early marriage was the main reason for this rapid growth, it seems likely that that practice, by its very nature, was limited to the upper stratum of East European Jewish society.

The continuous increase in the number of young people may have been the reason for the very frequent repetition, in the enactments of the councils and in sermons, of demands for the establishment of *yeshivot,* for the acceptance of as many students as possible, and for their support by individuals. Rulings to this effect were enacted by the Lithuanian Council more than seven times during the second half of the seventeenth century.[4] The reason given in the enactment of 1662 is characteristic: "Boys and youths turn to idleness," therefore each community must establish a yeshiva and support two boys and one youth for every ten taxpayers.[5] Also, the continuing increase in the proportion of young people has never been taken into consideration in discussions of the revolts of the artisan guilds, or in the attempts to account for the rise of Hasidism. Although it is, at this point, only conjecture, surely the following question warrants further study: Is it not likely that there was some connection between the rapidly growing Jewish population, the high rate of unemployment, and the increasing numbers of young people and the appearance of a popular revivalist movement in Poland-Lithuania in the middle of the eighteenth century? This movement, after all, was characterized initially by a mocking attitude toward the learned; energetic dancing, singing, and drinking; turning somersaults in the streets, and so on. In a word, was Hasidism generational at its inception? This is a legitimate question despite the methodological difficulties inherent in the term "generation"; the issue warrants careful analysis.[6]

To be sure, other inferences could be drawn from these speculations about the demographic history of East European Jews, but in the absence of rigorous research it would be well to turn to some other, equally unexplored, questions related to the history of the Jewish family in East Central Europe. What, for example, were the implications of the authoritarian, patriarchal nature of that family? This conception seems to have included the notion that a man's wife and children were his property. One of the most frequently quoted pieces of legislation of the Lithuanian Council is the following:

> Whoever shall commit the following evil, enslaving his wife, son or daughter in a debt to a non-Jew and even more, whoever actually hands over his wife or daughters to a non-Jew because of a debt—his blood is on his head. . . .[7]

This passage is cited usually as an example of the oppression of the Jews by the nobility. However, in the same year, 1623, one community actually requested permission to negotiate loans in this way:

> The heads of the land of Grodno requested, in behalf of some residents of Grodno, permission to "enslave" their wives [in promissory notes] to non-Jews. It was agreed to take up the matter . . . and it was agreed to grant permission. . . . [But] the Council has no responsibility for the consequences which might arise; these rest with the community of Grodno. . . . In 1626 the heads of . . . Grodno relieved themselves of this responsibility. From now on they are included in the prohibition.[8]

Child-rearing practices and their consequences also merit investigation. Consider, for example, the following passage in the child-rearing instructions of one of the most popular manuals of practical morality of the period, the *Lev tov* by Yiṣḥaq ben Eliakim of Poznań, first published in 1620:

> Each father and mother must love his children with all his soul and all his might. But they must not reveal their love in the presence [of the children], because then the children would not fear them and would not obey them. Every man must teach his children to fear him.[9]

It would be feasible to collect data from manuals like the *Lev tov* and from other sources sufficient for informed speculation on the psychosocial consequences of parenting practices characteristic of East European Jews in·this period.

In general, the history of children and of childhood awaits exploration. What, for example, was the practical age of majority? Marriage before age thirteen for a boy and twelve for a girl was forbidden by the councils;[10] poor girls were considered ready for domestic service at twelve and for marriage at age fifteen.[11] Early marriage, however, was a religious ideal and need not necessarily indicate that either partner was considered independent or autonomous.[12] Consider the fact that if a young man under eighteen, according to the Lithuanian Council, or under twenty according to the Council of Four Lands, contracted a marriage without the knowledge of his parents, his actions were considered to have no legal validity.[13] According to the Council of Four Lands, no note signed by a man within two years after his marriage had any validity.[14] This was in 1624, but in 1635 and in 1644 the same edict was repeated, with the period of unreliability extended to three years after marriage.[15] Also, in 1624, a further enactment read:

> Whoever extends a loan to someone who is under twenty-five years of age or has not been married at least two years, even if the father or father-in-law cosigns, the note is invalid.[16]

The age of majority, then, was not necessarily related to marriage, and seems to have ranged between eighteen and twenty-five, even though marriage would occur years earlier.

What was the actual sexual morality of Polish Jews in this period? Even a cursory survey of the responsa literature turns up numerous references to behavior that did not conform to the ideal described in the *Shulḥan arukh*. Questions addressed to Rabbi Joel Sirkes (1561–1640) mentioned a woman who remarried in time to cover up an adulterously conceived pregnancy; a married man living openly with another woman; a man who seduced an apparently retarded girl; and a woman who induced an abortion to cover up an adulterous relationship.[17] In the responsa literature searched by computer for this paper, there was no reference to contemporary use of contraception of any kind. The issue of abortion merits further study, but the arbitrariness with which matters appear in responsa must be kept in mind.

In the homiletical literature and even in the legal writings of this period there was almost an obsession with the sinfulness of masturbation and nocturnal emission. According to Jacob Katz, this was a consequence of the influence of Kabbalistic literature, which stressed the gravity of sins of this kind and the extreme difficulty of atoning for them.[18] Could it perhaps also have been partly a consequence of the demographic developments mentioned earlier? Solomon Luria (1510–1574), in his commentary on Yebamot, remarked:

> Especially in these lands where there are bachelors who are not occupied with the study of Torah, nor are they above suspicion, it were indeed proper to coerce them to marry. Inasmuch, however, as times are hard and large dowries are expected of them. . . .[19]

There is also a series of questions related to the history of women which merit investigation. It would seem, for example, that the characteristic image of the woman who worked to support her family while her husband studied does not apply to the period in question here. I analyzed the uses of the municipal scale in Lublin for the period from October 1671 to March 1673, about 1,250 transactions. A total of 46 percent of the transactions involved Jews. The overall proportion of women was almost 10 percent (9.7), but the number of transactions in which women participated was lower for Jews (8.1 percent) than for non-Jews (10.9 percent). A total of nine Jewish women appear in the records by name. Of these, seven were known by their husband's names—Iczkowa, Jakubowa, etc.— and were presumably widows, but two were listed by their own names— Fegela and Golda. Another woman is identified by her trade as a soap-maker *(mydlarka)*. In fact, she was the most active of the Jewish women, participating in seventeen transactions. It may be, of course, that more than one Jewish woman was designated in this way.[20] Despite these indications from Lublin in the latter half of the seventeenth century that the proportion of women working in commerce was rather low, it would seem that in some circles the notion of the woman being the breadwinner was an ideal. Ephraim of Lęczyce (1550–1619) remarked that marriage was important for a scholar, "for only if he takes a wife shall she assume responsibility for the household, so that he may study the Torah of the Lord, day and night." Also various communities regulated female ped-dlers and "the women who sit in the marketplace." On the other hand, a book of sermons published in 1714 includes the passing remark that "women are always at home," while their husbands go to the mar-ketplace.[21]

I recently found a document that I think can be ascribed to the end of the third quarter of the eighteenth century. It indicates the existence of an *organization* of Jewish women, peddlers, in the Jewish town of Kazimierz, next to Cracow. The manuscript is a copy of a petition submitted to the Cracow municipal authorities and because it is a copy, the signatures, which would have been interesting to see and might have permitted some estimate of the size of the group, are absent. In the petition, which begins "We, poor women," they request that the municipality permit their trade because

> we cause no harm to the burghers of Cracow. We sell only old corals. Therefore we submit this supplication to be permitted to continue in accordance with old agreements . . . because we do not belong to the elders of the synagogue of Kazimierz but only to the treasury of the city of Cracow. . . ."[22]

The municipality at the time was seeking to eliminate the competition of Jewish merchants, and this group of women wished to be assured that they would be exempted from the restrictive legislation. This is a tantalizing text, alluding as it does to the deterioration of the *qahal*'s (community's) authority as well as, apparently, to independent initiative on the part of a group of women. Much further study will be required before the implications of the document can be assessed properly.

The history of female communal officials also merits investigation. In Poznań, for example, there were collectors of charity in the women's galleries in the synagogues who were cautioned frequently not to be overzealous in their efforts and not to collect more than was collected in the men's section.[23] The Lithuanian Council, at least twice, enjoined the appointment of *gabba'ot* (supervisors) "to attend to the poor women who wear coarse linen garments, the appearance of which was not white enough to distinguish the stain of menstrual blood. There is danger," the enactment continued, "that she may become impure unawares. Therefore the *gabba'ot* should, with charity money, prepare two fine white linen [under]garments for each to wear during her menstrual period." The enactment of eleven years later (1639) specified that these officials should supervise the common wives *(neshei am ha-ares)* and teach them the laws concerning menstruation.[24]

A striking feature of marriage among the Jews of the Polish Commonwealth is the degree to which it was a public act, properly within the supervision and control of communal elders and officials. This is particularly true of the poor and indigent members of the community. At each stage of the betrothal process, for everyone, there had to be witnesses from the community at large. Joel Sirkes, for example, described the betrothal of a poor young man in the presence of "the Rabbi of the town and other important men."[25] There were sumptuary regulations governing the celebrations, including how many guests could be invited to the various festive meals, what the bride and other relatives could wear, and how many celebrations could be held; there was even a requirement that the wedding jester *(badhan)* be properly licensed.[26] The close regulation of marriages of the poor, however, most clearly demonstrates the degree of communal control.

In Cracow, the 1595 communal regulations specified that

> no betrothal may take place in which the bride gives under 150 zloties before there has been an investigation establishing that they will not become a burden to the community, even when the householder has the right of settlement and is neither a widow nor an orphan.[27]

In 1632, an entry was recorded in the Cracow communal minute book to the effect that the elders had ruled regarding the daughter of Reuven Ṣoref (Smith), who was to be betrothed to a certain artisan youth—his name is not recorded—that the betrothal could not take place in their community,

> lest they become dependent, God forbid, immediately on charity. There-fore Reuven has undertaken that for at least five years after the wedding this couple will receive nothing from charity, not even a farthing. . . .[28]

In 1629 the elders of the Poznań community forbade the marriage of servants without the permission of the *qahal*.[29] In 1679 and 1681 the same community enacted the following regulation:

> In view of the great poverty . . . not more than six marriages of those whose dowry does not exceed four hundred zloties will be permitted in a year. That is, four marriages in which one side is from our community, and two in which both sides are from our community.[30]

In 1623 the Lithuanian Council enjoined that twelve poor young girls could marry each year in Brześć, ten in Grodno, and eight in Pińsk. Each would receive twenty-five (thirty) zloties and each must be at least fifteen years old. The brides would be chosen by lot. Those not chosen were to be married the next year without having to be chosen by lot.[31] In 1628 the issue was taken up again. The number of brides and the amount of the dowry remained unchanged, but a new dimension was added:

> Nothing should be given to them until each holds written permission and proof from the communal elders to the effect that she was a domestic servant of a householder living in the community for three years from the day that she turned twelve; and that she is suited to domestic service; and that she is fifteen years old. The salary of the girl who performs such service . . . will be ten zloties per year, and the salary will be given to a communal official, not to her father. And if he wishes to have Sabbath clothing made for her with this money he may do nothing without permission from the communal official. . . . From the adoption of this rule the heads of the lands must have it announced in all the synagogues of the communities and the regions and they must see to it that this ordinance is enforced. At future meetings the representatives of each region must bring a list, endorsed by the *av beit din,* of the young girls who have married in accordance with these regulations. The assignments will be made to the highest taxpayer who has a separate dwelling and then to the next highest taxpayer who has a separate dwelling and so on.[32]

In his explanation of why the communities were prepared to supply dowries for the poor, Jacob Katz suggested three factors: it is an indica-tion of the religious importance of early marriage; it was based on the self-evident, at the time, assumption that marriage required the means necessary to establish a household and to begin independent economic activity; and the limitations on the number of marriages of the poor were enacted out of a desire to limit the number of breadwinners.[33]

There is, however, more to be said about these regulations. Aside from suggesting that they may be a response to the demographic pressures noted earlier, I should like to raise the issue of justification. The fact is that these regulations were manifestations of a particular worldview espoused by the upper strata of Polish-Lithuanian Jewish society and intended to justify the standing of those at the top of a stratified society. The forms this justification took have been analyzed extensively by Haim Hillel Ben-Sasson. I shall quote only the critical passage from the writings of Moses Isserles (1525–1572):

> "Life, children and sustenance depend not on merit but on *mazal*" (Mo'ed katan 28a). Indeed, it appears to me . . . that everything depends on *mazal*, that is, the moment and hour of a man's birth. For . . . this determines his nature in the world. If the Lord knows that his nature is such that he will be unable to suffer great wealth and will be led to sin by it, then his merit leads to denying him wealth lest he be prideful with it. . . . He will never be wealthy . . . unless the Lord were to change his nature and his *mazal*.[34]

This was a novel idea; earlier literature contained not a hint that something in the nature of the poor was imperfect. Here, Isserles asserted that wealth was an indication of a good sign and a refined nature able to overcome pride. This is the heart of a conservative ideology of the elite seeking to justify its position in society. The passage quoted ends with the conclusion that "wealth is given to a man according to his worth." This is an ideology of social stasis which clearly justified sumptuary laws prohibiting people from dressing or celebrating in ways not in accordance with their station in life. It also justified attempting to limit the number of poor lest they become a burden to the community.

By the eighteenth century, however, social and economic conditions overtook this ideology. The good, upstanding householder whose life and values found justification in the teachings of Isserles and others had virtually disappeared. The economic decline, burgeoning Jewish numbers, and Polish political disarray combined to undermine the social stability of the Jewish community. Power in the *qehillot* (communities) flowed increasingly to those associated with the magnate-aristocrats who wielded power in the Commonwealth. Jewish artisans conspired and even openly rebelled against *qahal* elders. This shattering of the patterns of deference in Jewish society very likely extended to family life as well. Hasidism may have been one expression of youthful rebellion. This, like all of the issues raised here, demands further study.

Despite the brevity of this discussion, it must be apparent that the recovery of the neglected history of the Jewish family may well result in fundamental revisions of our understanding of the nature of East European Jewish society.

Notes

1. Jacob Katz, *Masoret u-mashber* (Jerusalem, 1958); also *Tradition and Crisis* (New York, 1971); also "Marriage and Sexual Life Among the Jews at the End of the Middle Ages" [Hebrew], *Zion* 10 (1944–45), 21–54; and "Family, Kinship and Marriage Among Ashkenazim in the 16th–18th Centuries," *Jewish Journal of Sociology* 1 (1959), 4–22. Compare the general remarks of Majer Balaban, "Obyczajowość i życie prywatne Żydów w dawnej Rzeczypospolitej," in *Żydzi w Polsce odrodzonej*, ed. Ignacy Schiper et al., vol. I (Warsaw, n.d.), pp. 345–74; also his "Jewish Life and Culture in the Sixteenth and Seventeenth Centuries" [Hebrew], in *Beit Yisra'el be-Folin*, ed. Israel Halpern, vol. I (Jerusalem, 1948), pp. 65–80. See also the chapter on "Social and Domestic Life" in Elijah Judah Schochet, *Bach: Rabbi Joel Sirkes, His Life, Works and Times* (Jerusalem–New York, 1971), pp. 176–89.

2. All of these figures are extremely tentative, particularly in light of the careful approach of Irena Gieysztorowa, *Wstęp do demografii staropolski* (Warsaw, 1976). Virtually all Jewish historians have accepted the figures for 1764–65 presented by Raphael Mahler in his *Yidn in amolikn Poyln* (Warsaw, 1958). See, however, the contradictions noticed by Tomasz Opas in his article "The Situation of the Jews in Towns Owned by Noblemen in the Lublin Województwo in the Eighteenth Century" [Polish], *Biuletyn Żydowskiego Instytutu Historycznego* 67 (1968), 11, 14. The most recent general evaluations of Polish-Jewish demographic history are by Bernard D. Weinryb, *The Jews of Poland* (Philadelphia, 1973), pp. 308–20; and by Salo W. Baron, *A Social and Religious History of the Jews*, vol. 16 (Philadelphia–New York, 1976), pp. 15–23, 192–211. And see the speculation mainly on the basis of nineteenth-century data of Zygmunt Suiowski, "The Mechanisms of Demographic Expansion of the Jews in Polish Cities in the 16th to 19th Centuries" [Polish], *Zeszyty Naukowe Katolickiego Uniwersytetu Lubelskiego* 17 (1974), 93–110.

Because the conditions in Kurland at the end of the eighteenth century (about 70 percent of the Jews in villages) oppositely mirror Polish conditions at the time (about 30 percent of the Jews in villages), and because the masses of Jewish poor characteristic of Poland were absent in Kurland, it will be difficult to generalize on the basis of the conclusions of Andrejs Plakans and Joel M. Halpern, "An Historical Perspective on Eighteenth-Century Jewish Family Households in Eastern Europe," in *Modern Jewish Fertility*, ed. Paul Ritterband (Leiden, 1981), pp. 18–32. Nevertheless, their work is an important contribution to the study of a subject that cries out for systematic reexamination.

3. Jacob Goldberg, *Stosunki agrarne w miastach ziemi wieluńskiej w drugiej poiowie XVII i w XVIII wieku* (Łódz, 1960).

4. Simon M. Dubnow, ed., *Pinqas ha-mdina* [*PML*] (Berlin, 1925), no. 355, p. 74 (1639); no. 513, p. 121 (1656); no. 528, p. 126 (1662); no. 557, p. 133 (1664); nos. 587, 588, 590, p. 143 (1667); no. 709, p. 174 (1676); no. 869, p. 230 (1695); no. 911, p. 243 (1720).

5. *PML*, no. 528, p. 126.

6. See Alan B. Spitzer, "The Historical Problem of Generations," *American Historical Review* 78 (1973), 1353–85.

7. *PML*, no. 44, pp. 9–10.

8. *PML*, no. 45, p. 10.

9. As quoted by Simhah Assaf, *Meqorot le-toledot ha-ḥinukh be-yisra'el*, vol. 1 (Tel Aviv, 1954), p. 75.

10. *PML*, no. 968, p. 266 (1761).

11. *PML*, no. 128, p. 32 (1628).

12. Katz, *Masoret*, p. 168.

13. *PML*, no. 32, p. 8 (1623); no. 430, p. 91 (1647); Israel Halpern, *Pinqas va'ad arba araṣot* [*PVAA*] (Jerusalem, 1945), no. 165, p. 59 (1634).

14. *PVAA*, no. 123, p. 47.

15. *PVAA*, no. 167, p. 59; no. 189, p. 70.

16. *PVAA*, no. 125, p. 48.

17. *She'elot u-teshuvot bayit ḥadash, ha-yeshanot* (Ostrów, 1834; reprint, Brooklyn, n.d.), qu. 100, p. 48b; qu. 70, p. 27b; qu. 99, p. 48a; *She'elot u-teshuvot me-ha-ge'onim ba-tra'i* (Czernowitz, 1860; reprint, Jerusalem, 1969), qu. 54, p. 38b.

18. Katz, *Masoret*, p. 166.

19. *Yam shel shelomoh*, Yebamot 6: 40b.

20. Lublin, Wojewódzkie Archiwum Państwowe, Księga miejska m. Lublina 189, passim.

21. *Olelot Efraim*, no. 338, as quoted in Salo W. Baron, *The Jewish Community* (reprint, Westport, Conn., 1972), vol. 3, p. 162; Solomon Buber, *Qirya nisgava* (Cracow, 1903), pp. 83, 110; Berakhia Beirakh of Klimontow, *Sefer zera berakh shelishi al ha-torah* (Halle, 1714), p. 4b.

22. Cracow, Archiwum Państwowe Miasta Krakowa i Województwa Krakowskiego, Akta Żydowskie III/11/8, unpaginated.

23. Dov Avron, ed., *Pinqas ha-kesherim shel qehillat Pozna* (Jerusalem, 1966), no. 224, p. 46 (1633); no. 456, p. 88 (1643); no. 590, p. 114 (1648); no. 822, pp. 151–52 (1656). See also no. 508, 509, 639, and 1298.

24. *PML*, no. 131, p. 33 (1628); no. 357, p. 74 (1639).

25. *She'elot u-teshuvot bayit ḥadash, ha-yeshanot*, qu. 10, p. 4b.

26. See, for example, *PML*, no. 42, p. 9; no. 314, p. 68; no. 316, p. 69; no. 469, p. 104; no. 669, p. 160; no. 670, p. 160; no. 722, p. 177; no. 884, p. 231; no. 962, p. 266; no. 972, p. 267; no. 976, p. 267; and no. 982, p. 268.

27. Majer Balaban, "Die Krakauer Judengemeinde-Ordnung von 1595," *Jahrbuch der jüdisch-literarischen Gesellschaft* 10 (1912), 43, pp. 328–29.

28. F. H. Wettstein, *Devarim attiqim mi-pinqes ei ha-qahal* (Cracow, 1900), pp. 8–9.

29. See B. D. Weinryb, "On the Attitude of the Communities in Poland to Artisans and Workers" [Hebrew], *Yedi'ot ha-arkheion ve-ha-muzeion shel tenu'at ha-avodah* 3–4 (1938), 15.

30. Ibid.

31. *PML*, no. 93, p. 20.

32. *PML*, no. 128, p. 32.

33. Katz, *Masoret*, p. 168.

34. *Torat ha-olah*, pt. 3, ch. 53, pp. 117a–117b. As quoted in Haim Hillel Ben-Sasson, *Hagut ve-hanhagah* (Jerusalem, 1959), p. 78.

3. The Jewish Family in Traditional Morocco

Shlomo Deshen

The Jewish family in precolonial Morocco can be conceptualized as a traditional family, having many of the features of traditional families everywhere. These include extended kin ties, marked inequality between males and females, clearly delimited division of labor between the sexes, and clearly structured mores pertinent to age and sex. These features, however, being so general, tell us little more than what a sociologically informed imagination might have guessed. Actual cases of family systems require specification as to the detailed arrangements in the aforementioned areas: what kind and range of extended kin ties the family maintains, what is the precise nature of sexual inequality, how systematic is the division of labor, and so on.

The explication of such questions is especially called for when studying the Moroccan field. Whereas many traditional societies in the Middle East and in Europe in preindustrial times comprised distinct and tightly knit corporate groups of a regional, tribal, or religious nature, the situation in Morocco was somewhat different. Recent anthropological research has uncovered a vigorous individualism deeply rooted in Moroccan culture. This individualism is coupled with the particular nature

The basic research for this paper was supported through a Hunt Fellowship from the Wenner-Gren Foundation for Anthropological Research in New York; in Israel, the Tel Aviv and Bar Ilan universities offered assistance. This study is part of a project on the social structure of Jewish societies in the traditional Orient, on which I have been engaged for many years; some points alluded to here are treated there in detail.

The secretarial help of Hadassah Raab is gratefully acknowledged.

of Moroccan Islam, highly articulate in abstract formulations and commanding widespread popular attention and devotion. These features of Moroccan culture lead to shifting group formations and multiple individual loyalties that mutate according to situational contexts. Men are not conceived of in given social terms, dictated by ascribed attributes, but instead in terms of the specific social contexts in which they interact. The studies that led us to this view of Moroccan society were conducted in our times, mainly during the 1960s, and not in precolonial times (see Evans-Pritchard 1949; Gellner 1969; Geertz 1968, 1973; Rosen 1972, 1973; Waterbury 1970; Eickelman 1976; Brown 1976; Rabinow 1976; Burke 1972, 1976; Geertz et al. 1979). But since they are all based on fieldwork in remote provincial towns and villages and not in the main urban centers, it is reasonable to assume that they do indeed reflect the traditional culture of Morocco, not a recent development.

As for the study of the Moroccan Jewish family in precolonial Morocco, it would now seem that the crude concept of "the traditional family," implying a tightly knit social group, is of even more limited use than in societies that encourage individualism to a lesser extent. We therefore need to clarify, in the Moroccan-Jewish context, the nature of the group that constitutes a family. Specifically, we must approach such questions as the nature of the boundaries that enclose the family and the hold of the family group over its individual members of various age and sex. I have sought to approach the problem through materials preserved in rabbinical responsa of eighteenth- and nineteenth-century Moroccan sages. There are case histories of issues that came to the rabbinical courts, or about which individual rabbis expressed formal opinions. Important data are often also embedded in cases that do not overtly concern family issues. Obviously sources of this kind are of prime value to the social historian, and constitute the next best thing to participant observation of the social anthropologist. However, the use of rabbinical responsa material is fraught with serious problems of interpretation, aside from the pertinent linguistic and literary skills that are called for, lack of which have hindered their use for sociological purposes.

The responsa are replete with phrases that superficially seem to express particular circumstances in time and place. However, many such phrases, and sometimes whole sections of case material, are taken from legal and literary precedents. The writers of responsa are often so immersed in their culture that they have absorbed the turns of phrase and expression of their antecedents and have made them their own. The social historian now reading this material must be able to recognize the various historical layers that compose the text written by the eighteenth- or nineteenth-century sage. Failing that, one is prone to mistake early materials for contemporary ones. Another, even more common pitfall of responsa research is the failure to recognize the appearance of stylized stock phrases and literary expressions. Such phrases, while often vivid and evocative, may in certain contexts be virtually meaningless. Obviously, conclusions drawn from misreadings lead to confusion, and responsa research does not lack examples (see Katz 1960).

During the eighteenth and nineteenth centuries, Moroccan Jewry, particularly in the communities of the center and north, such as Meknes, Fez, Tetuan, and Sefrou, was highly productive in various areas of traditional Jewish activity. The writers of the period, following the classical rabbinic tradition, did not specialize. Typically a sage would produce both religious hymns and talmudic commentaries, biblical homiletics, and halakhic treatises. The authors of the period have left voluminous writings, of which many have appeared in print (see Amar 1980). In this preliminary search of Moroccan responsa material pertinent to the study of the family I have made use only of the published tomes, numbering about twenty. I have also made use of an extensive collection of private letters that has been published in recent years (Ovadia 1975/78).

Independence and Enclosure

The nuclear family in traditional Moroccan Jewry was part of a wider net of kin, but at the same time it enjoyed a measure of independence. The tension between independence and enclosure within a broader family system was a matter of concern and sometimes came to court. People felt some responsibility toward their extended kin.

Lack of differentiation between the nuclear family and wider circles of kin is evident in the following case: A man wanted to break his engagement to his bride, without having to pay a penalty. He argued that after the engagement he had discovered than an aunt of the bride had given birth out of wedlock, and the family of the bride was therefore tainted. The explicit reasoning of the judge in this case is illuminating. He called upon a precedent in which the sister of a bride had converted to Islam and in which case the ruling had been in favor of the groom. In the present case also, the judge ruled in favor of the groom, because "what does it matter if an aunt of the bride or a sister of the bride is involved?" (Ibn-Zur 1894–1903; 1:75). The two degrees of kinship were considered as one.

A similar atmosphere pervades another case involving Jewish-Muslim relationships. A man, Abraham, was pressed for money by a Muslim. After a time, and for a reason not given to us, another man, Simeon, paid the Muslim on behalf of Abraham the sum that he was demanding. Simeon now requested that Abraham repay him his expense. The latter however refused, and among the arguments he made in court he said: I have relatives; and they would have paid for me, and then I would not have had to spend anything (Abihatzera 1885, 62). The judge did not reject the argument. Evidently the incident expresses a common feeling that a person in trouble could seriously rely on his kin to help him. This particular case does not include detailed information on the scope of the circle of relatives who are considered obliged to help an individual.

Light on this question is shed through another case: Again a man was being pressed by Muslims for money. During the course of this extortion the man was thrown into prison. The problem that came to the sage concerned the issue of which relatives were obliged to pay the necessary sums for extortion and bribes, in order to obtain the prisoner's release. The relatives involved were the man's wife, his wife's father, and his mother's brother. The sage ruled that the obligation of siblings precedes that of in-laws, and he placed prime responsibility on the mother's brother (Ibn-Walid 1855, 1:67). These data confirm that family responsibility was not restricted to the nuclear family, but extended at least to the range of siblings of the parents.

The nuclear family was not clearly distinct from other family members, and usually its independence, both as an economic and as a domestic unit, was limited. Adult sons often shared businesses and homes with fathers and brothers, and together participated in patriarchal types of arrangements. Typically men blessed each other that they should be "surrounded with sons" (Ovadia 1975–78, 649). The patriarchal domestic arrangements of married adult sons living in proximity to their father probably became more common during the nineteenth century.

The sources report cases of promiscuity stemming from crowded conditions and lack of privacy. Apparently these were linked with population increase in the *mellahs* (the Jewish quarters) due to worldwide improvements in public health. Some rabbis sought to prohibit different couples from living in close proximity (Berdugo 1910; Even Ha'ezer 84; and others), but judging from the high density of population that struck all European visitors to the mellahs, these attempts were probably ineffectual. Most commonly, extended families, composed of married brothers, lived in compounds that centered on a common courtyard—the preferred way of living in which the blessing made itself visible.

Patriarchal Families, Patrilocal Living

Patriarchal and patrilocal living, however, caused hardship for the bride who came to live with the family of the groom. The brides were young, only a few years beyond maturity and sometimes much younger. They suffered from the natural difficulties that were involved in the abrupt move, without much preparatory adjustment, from their parental home. As a young wife the bride was subjected to the dominance both of her husband and of his parents. Adjustment was easier to the extent that there was prior neighborly and social contact between the two families. Neighborly contact enabled the young bride frequent visits to her parents, in particular to see her mother. The parental support gained through this contact presumably smoothed the adjustment problems of the bride in her new situation.

On the other hand, the bride's distance from her parental home probably was a source of much distress for her. A recurrent theme in disputes between spouses, as they appeared before the sages, was the adamant objections of women to the requests of husbands to move to other localities, away from their hometowns. Husbands, on the other hand, because of economic pressure and needs, to which they were more sensitive than wives, sometimes desired to move away (Ovadia 1975–78, 440; and others). We even have cases of couples who lived separately because the wives refused to follow their husbands, who themselves were driven by economic circumstances to distant places.

On the whole, attachment to the hometown on the part of both men and women was very strong. But this was particularly so with women who, not being involved in the pursuing of livelihood, did not feel so strongly the relative merits of various localities. In a rather moving correspondence between a man who made a living as an itinerant preacher and his father, the latter wrote to him: ". . . and every night I raise my eyes to heaven and beseech God that He should not take you away from your place, and that He should give you your needs in your hometown" (Ovadia 1975–78, 501). Among women these feelings were even stronger, and we find concerted efforts to prevent husbands from moving. Most likely the welfare of a woman depended to a considerable extent on the moral and sentimental support that she drew from her parents and brothers.

Not only physical proximity between families of the groom and bride helped the bride adjust to the patrilocal family, but also social ties. When such ties were absent, and particularly when the families resided in different communities, friction and prejudice between the bride and her in-laws were apt to develop. The concomitant of local patriotism was ambivalence toward residents of other localities. We have evidence of prejudices between such neighboring communities as Fez and Sefrou (Ovadia 1975–78, 401), and in particular on the part of town dwellers against residents of smaller communities (A. Anekawa 1869–71, 1:75).

When families were physically distant, support for the wife on the part of her natal family was naturally not very effectual. It seems therefore that the most common marriage tie was between local people, neighbors who arranged the matches of their children. The famous matchmaker (the *shadkhan*) of traditional Ashkenazi Jewry was a role quite unknown here, and understandably so. Marriages were predominantly local, between people who rubbed shoulders in one community for many generations, and who were most likely already related. As a result, a formal intermediary was not essential.

Marriage arrangements initiated by parents were accepted and stable. One court case offers evidence for this. The issue was the claim of a bride's father against a groom's father for payment of a penalty because the groom had broken the engagement upon which the parents had agreed. Against this the defendant pleaded that he was not responsible because this was a case of force majeure, "an exceptional accident, because all sons agree to the choice of their fathers" (Abitabul 1935, 2:4). Although the judge eventually supported the claim because of other considerations, this particular argument of the defendant is in itself illuminating.

The patrilocal system, whereby the bride came to live with the groom's family, was also problematic for the latter, and in particular for the groom's mother as well as for the bride. A mother, in a letter written or dictated by her concerning the selection of a wife for her son, wrote that she did not want a young bride for "I will not raise a little girl" (Ovadia 1975–78, 401). Child marriage added to the responsibility of the mother-in-law, who now had to see to the needs of her young daughter-in-law as well as to those of her own children.

The text of an agreement between disputing spouses reflects some of the problems that stem from the frivolity of a very young married girl living with her husband's parents. According to this document, the bride was ordered to obey her mother-in-law. She was also told "not to give away any of the belongings of her husband to neither relative nor stranger, except with the permission of her husband or of his mother" (Ovadia 1975–78, 581). The proximity of a married woman's natal home allowed the maintenance of ties and provided support, but by the same token this proximity could cause problems. The interference of the bride's natal family in the affairs of her own family and in her relations with her in-laws could seriously disrupt harmony.

In another agreement between disputing spouses, the bride's father committed himself to restrain his wife, the bride's mother, from creating strife in her daughter's home (Ovadia 1975–78, 400). Too strong a tie between a woman and her natal family was frowned upon because it was considered as potentially leading to discord. A sage, writing about a case of marital strife, summarized it as follows: ". . . she also does not spend time at home. During most of the day she is in her father's house, and as a result she does not do household chores for her husband" (Ovadia 1975–78, 374).

The fathers of grooms were apprehensive of such situations. Therefore many wedding contracts had clauses regulating the ties between the bride and her natal family. For instance, the contracts sought to limit the frequency of a bride's visits to her parents. In one such document the bride was ordered "not to go to her father's house more than once a week" (Ovadia 1975–78, 645). This particular contract preceded the marriage. It is phrased abstractly, before the young actually experienced married life. Therefore it expresses the desired norm of relationships and visiting patterns, namely that it is fine and accepted for a married daughter to visit her parents once a week (or on the Sabbath day—the text is ambiguously phrased, and both translations are possible), no more and no less.

That desideratum, however, did not constitute reality. For the latter we turn to agreements made by couples in conflict after experiencing married life. In one such case the sage ruled on the question of visiting frequency: "The wife should not leave her home often, even in order to go to her father's house. She may go there only two or three times weekly, for work that she does together with her mother" (Ovadia 1975–78, 374). This was a situation of relatively frequent visits with concrete content, and the husband's relatives sought, through the ruling of the sage, to control the tie between the wife and her natal family. Control pertains both to the frequency and to the content of the visits. Visits with concrete content, such as engaging in housework or handicraft, were permitted. This implies that socializing without such ulterior purpose was discouraged.

We hear of an extreme case, early in the twentieth century, of a husband who ordered his wife to promise by oath that she would leave the house only once or twice monthly, and even that only upon receiving his written permission (R. Anekawa 1910, 86). It is difficult to imagine that this was carried out in practice, but the incident illustrates in an exaggerated way the fundamental sentiment about proper domestic behavior. Later in the court decision involving this couple we hear more realistic details: "And at times when her husband is away from the city, and she will have to visit the sick, or her mother, or go to the house of the bereaved, or to a house of celebration—she may do so." Sociability was thus permitted in certain clearly delimited contexts, the common element of which was that they were all linked with *mitzvot*.

In contrast to the problematic nature of the tie of married women with their families of origin, the tie of both spouses with the relatives of the husband was straightforward. In the context of a patrilocal family that tie was self-evident, so much so that it was hardly mentioned in marriage contracts, and figured only rarely in disputes and jurisdiction. Since people usually lived patrilocally, visiting the husband's parents was not an issue.

There were cases of matrilocality, but it is clear that they were linked with exceptional circumstances. One case figures in a marriage agreement where matrilocality is coupled with an undertaking on the part of the bride's father to support the groom for as long as he devoted himself to Torah study (Ovadia 1975–78, 480). This kind of arrangement was standard in traditional Ashkenazi Jewry, but unusual in Morocco. It was understood that when a man undertook the heavy burden of supporting his son-in-law, he was entitled to the satisfaction, pleasure, and honor of having him in his entourage. People would see him deferred to by a scholarly son-in-law. The general conditions of marriage at a very young age—particularly of young girls—naturally led the young couple to be attached to an existing household. And in the present case the attachment was to the particular household that offered to free the groom altogether from material concerns. In another case of matrilocality preserved in the sources, the situation is explained by the particularly tender age of the bride. Because of that her parents were apparently reluctant to permit a patrilocal arrangement.

Women's Weak Position

Women living patrilocally were detached to a greater or lesser extent from their families of origin, and subject to the kin of the husband. Women were usually also removed from economic activities. They thus commanded few resources of their own, and their power in internal domestic politics was very limited. In struggles between the wife and her mother-in-law and other powerful domestic personages, the position of the former was usually weak. The protection of the woman's brothers and parents in such cases of conflict could theoretically be very important. Our sources, however, do not reflect such conditions. Only in one case of domestic conflict did the woman's relatives figure in the role of protectors. That case involved a man who desired to take a second wife against the wishes of his first wife; the man was afraid of the violent objections of his brothers-in-law, and therefore he married the second wife in secret (Ibn-Zur 1894–1903, 159). The dearth of such incidents, coupled with the commonplace occurrence of domestic problems in general, leads to the impression that conflict between spouses was generally contained in domestic privacy, and did not usually spill over into the public domain. In these circumstances the major kind of power resource that was available to women lay in the area of uxorial rights that concern husband and wife individually, particularly sexual relations and domestic services.

Household chores included primarily the preparation of food and the treatment of clothing. If one can postulate from the division of labor that was current among recently arrived traditional Moroccan immigrants in Israel to the situation of the past, it would seem that the domain of food preparation was not an exclusively female one. Men had an important role to play here, because the preparation of meat, a major item of nutrition, required particular ritual skills. Certain sinews and layers of fat were ritually prohibited and had to be removed; also the blood had to be totally drained. The execution of these tasks, while not relegated to professionals as in certain other Jewish culture areas, was nevertheless considered important, and preferably executed by adult males (Shokeid 1971, 166).

Certainly the purchasing of food for the household was a male task, because the market, in the Muslim world in general, is primarily a male arena. For women to leave the home was, as we have seen, altogether frowned upon. So it is inconceivable that women frequented the markets very often. The handling of clothes, in contrast, was a female activity, and the part of men was restricted to the purchasing of the material or the finished garment. Men did not engage in needlework at home, despite the fact that many made their living from the crafts associated with the garment trade.

On this point we have general evidence. A sage dealt with the question of the degree to which men who worked outside their homes (as was the practice of most men; for details see Deshen, 1983, chap. 2) were involved in and knowledgeable about the details of their domestic affairs. The sage wrote: "We see that a husband does not know what items he has in his home, except for some particular items." And the sage added a personal note: "And I myself am domiciled at home at all times, summer and winter, yet in spite of this I have no idea how many shirts and trousers I own" (Toledano 1939, 42). The sage argued that people generally, who were not as sedentary as scholarly rabbis, were not knowledgeable in these domestic matters.

In cases of domestic strife, women apparently were in a position to withhold personal services from their husbands. They could disrupt the routine treatment of clothing and, to a considerable extent, also the daily preparation of food. However, the major female potential in domestic strife was in the area of conjugal relations. Sexual relations between husband and wife throughout traditional Jewry are governed by norms of "family purity." These norms concern a cycle of separation and reunion in connection with the menses, and prior to reunion wives are required to immerse in a ritual bath. The correct time for immersion requires on the part of women constant attention to the calendar, and self-examination as to the state of personal purity. In Morocco, these matters were virtually completely governed by womenfolk, the wives personally involved and to a limited extent their elder female relatives. The norms of "family purity" obviously also concerned husbands, and theoretically could be monopolized by men, as many other areas of life were, yet this was not the case. In other times and places, these matters were governed by females to a lesser extent (as in parts of Eastern Europe and in southern Tunisia in recent times; see Deshen, 1982). As a result of well-nigh total female regulation of married sexuality in Moroccan Jewry, through female decision as to immersion time, women were afforded an outlet for self-assertion and power. "Family purity" became a power resource, manipulated by wives; it enabled women to disrupt or to permit sexual life.

The following case summary by a sage reflects a typical scenario where a wife engaged in sexual manipulation, the one major resource she had on hand: "She curses his parents in his presence, and he overcomes himself, and he does not curse her parents, because of his respect for them. But he cannot restrain himself and continue to bear her curses. So he struck her . . . and she does not go to immerse, or she does so at improper times" (Ovadia 1975–78, 406; also 374). Cases such as this came to the attention of the sages, and figure in divorce proceedings.

Extended Kinship and the Nuclear Family

Incidents in which relatives of spouses were involved, such as we just saw, are linked to patriarchal conditions, where the family life of spouses was embedded in a broader net of kin. Since the nuclear family was not fully independent, squabbling spouses typically involved relatives in their disputes and hurled suitable imprecations at each other. The limited differentiation of the nuclear family was also evident in the behavior of people trying to encourage others to take one kind of action or to desist from another. They invoked the person's ancestors, and suggested that complying with the request would be in keeping with their honored memory or would benefit their souls in paradise. Here is an example of a rebuke: ". . . you ought to have considered the reputation of your holy ancestors and [thought of] the shame that you brought on the family" (Ovadia 1975–78, 271).

The limited independence of the nuclear family shows itself also in the area of economic activities. Wedding gifts were usually offered to the father of the groom "in honor of the groom," not to the groom personally. This practice apparently parallels the donations that friends and relatives of the couple offered in the synagogue "in honor of the groom." Such donations were promised on the Sabbath following the wedding, when the groom was called on individually to read from the Torah. (I report on this practice from the latter-day Israeli experience, and have not seen mention of it in historical sources. But I assume that the custom is traditional.) In both these kinds of donations, gift making was enmeshed in community and family structure. Gift making bolstered these, and not necessarily the nuclear family that was being founded. As a rule, the father of the groom did not separate these gifts from his other property on behalf of his son. The married son used to participate in the economic activities of the father, in handicraft or business, as a junior partner, and benefited in general from the family property (Ovadia 1975–78, 508, 586).

For her part, the daughter-in-law built up her household as part of that of her in-laws and, to a considerable extent, under their control. Under these conditions the married son had no great need for much personal capital. The incorporation of the nuclear family within the extended patrilocal family extended both to consumption—within the domestic sphere that was mainly governed by women—and to production—within the sphere of handicrafts and commerce governed by men. We hear little of dowries, which apparently were of the trousseau type, constituting personal effects of the bride. Also of bridewealth, we hear only of the standard Jewish *ketubah* type. This in effect means that payment, if due at all, was delayed to a time when the wife lost her husband, either through death or divorce. In any event this kind of bridewealth was materially meaningless as far as the young bride and her nuclear family were concerned. Marriages clearly did not have wide material ramifications, as often was the case in certain other Jewish culture areas—in Europe, Turkey, and probably also Iraq.

The extended patriarchal family remained potent as long as the paterfamilias remained alive and also for some time after his death. Upon the death of the patriarch, the family property was only partly divided among the sons. Half the property was not divided and was formally owned by the widow, though in practice it was most likely managed jointly by the sons. The sociological implication of these inheritance arrangements is that full economic independence was attained by the nuclear family only upon the death of the widow of the patriarch. Demographic pressure on the extended household must have been considerable for many years before the decease of the parents, because of the growth of the constituent nuclear families. The extended household probably started to disintegrate much earlier, but the death of the remaining parent and the ultimate distribution of the joint property dissolved the household formally at a time when the constituent households were themselves already in the process of becoming extended patriarchal households. The family thus moved through a full developmental cycle, from the initial stage of incorporation within an existing patriarchal family unit to the evolution of a new, extended patriarchal unit.

References

Abihatzera, Y. 1885. *Yoru Mishpatekha Le'yaakov* [Hebrew]. Jerusalem.

Abitabul, S. Y. 1935. *Avne Shaish* [Hebrew]. 2 vols. Jerusalem.

Amar, M. 1980. "The Writings of Moroccan Jews of the Protectorate Period (1880–1960)." In *North African Jewry in the 19th and 20th Centuries* [Hebrew], M. Abitbol, ed., pp. 127–40. Jerusalem.

Anekawa, A. 1869–71. *Kerem Hemer* [Hebrew]. 2 vols. Leghorn.

Anekawa, R. 1910. *Karne Re'em* [Hebrew]. Jerusalem.

Berdugo, Y. 1910. *Shufrey de'ya'akov* [Hebrew]. Jerusalem.

Brown, K. L. 1976. *People of Sale: Tradition and Change in a Moroccan City 1830–1930*. Manchester.

Burke, E. 1972. "The Moroccan Ulema 1860–1912: An Introduction." In *Saints, Sufis and Scholars*. N. Keddie, ed., pp. 93–125. Berkeley.

———. 1976. *Prelude to Protectorate in Morocco*. Chicago.

Deshen, S. 1983. *Individuals and the Community: Social Life in 18th–19th Century Moroccan Jewry* [Hebrew]. Tel Aviv.

———. 1982. "The Social Structure of Southern Tunisian Jewry in the Late 19th and Early 20th Century." In *Jewish Societies in the Middle East*, S. Deshen and W. Zenner, eds., pp. 123–36. Washington.

Eickelman, D. F. 1976. *Moroccan Islam: Tradition and Society in a Pilgrimage Center*. Austin.

Evans-Pritchard, E. E. 1949. *The Sanusi of Cyrenaica*. Oxford.

Geertz, C. 1968. *Islam Observed*. Chicago.

————. 1973. *The Interpretation of Cultures*. New York.

Geertz, C., H. Geertz, and L. Rosen. 1979. *Meaning and Order in Moroccan Society: Three Essays in Cultural Analysis*. New York.

Gellner, E. 1969. *Saints of the Atlas*. London.

Ibn-Walid, Y. 1855. *Va'yomer Yitzhak* [Hebrew]. 2 vols. Leghorn.

Ibn-Zur, Y. 1894–1903. *Mishpat U'tzedaka Be'yaakov* [Hebrew]. 2 vols. Alexandria.

Katz, J. 1960. "On Halakha and Derush as Historical Sources" [Hebrew]. *Tarbiz* 30:62–68.

Ovadia, D., ed. 1975–78. *The Community of Sefrou* [Hebrew]. 3 vols. Jerusalem.

Rabinow, P. 1976. *Symbolic Domination*. Chicago.

Rosen, L. 1972. "Muslim-Jewish Relations in a Moroccan City." *International Journal of Middle Eastern Studies* 3:435–49.

————. 1973. "The Social and Conceptual Framework of Arab-Berber Relations in Central Morocco." In *Arabs and Berbers*, E. Gellner and C. Micaud, eds., 155–73. London.

Shokeid, M. 1971. *The Dual Heritage*. Manchester.

Toledana, M. 1939. *Ha'shamayim Ha'hadashim* [Hebrew]. Casablanca.

Waterbury, J. 1970. *Commander of the Faithful*. London.

JEWISH FAMILIES IN THE
TRANSITION TO MODERNITY

4. Childhood, Marriage and the Family in the Eastern European Jewish Enlightenment

David Biale

In 1945, Jacob Katz published his fundamental article on Jewish attitudes toward marital and family life in traditional society.[1] Katz concluded his study with reflections on the new, individualistic values introduced by Moses Mendelssohn and the German Haskalah (Enlightenment), values which ultimately came to revolutionize attitudes toward marriage and the family. The chapter presented here on the late eighteenth and early nineteenth centuries begins approximately where Professor Katz's leaves off and focuses primarily on Eastern Europe. Although this is a study of the new values of the Haskalah, we must be careful not to argue too clean a break with the past, for the new was often deeply entangled with the old. The norms of a new social order may germinate in a traditional society as forms of deviance. Certainly it appears that new sexual attitudes emerged in Central Europe a good century before they became widely accepted as norms.[2] The early Haskalah in Eastern Europe may have functioned in the same way. Moreover, the new attitudes we shall explore here may well have been not only the result of influence from European culture, but also the products of a dialectical dynamic *within* traditional Jewish society.

I shall address myself not to the development of a new social reality in Eastern Europe, but rather to new *mentalities* regarding the institutions of marriage and the family. We are concerned here with ideology in the broadest sense of the word. The attitudes and perceptions of very small groups came to shape those of society as a whole. Thus, even if Jewish society was much slower to change than the intellectual elite, the Haskalah perceptions of social problems gave a new vocabulary to reality and contributed to its transformation.

Our discussion cannot however ignore a fundamental fact of Jewish social history from the eighteenth century to the end of the nineteenth: the demographic explosion which was far greater for the Jews of Eastern Europe than for the European population as a whole.[3] From 1648 to 1765, the Jewish population of Poland increased by 3.2 times to more than half a million. By 1825, the Jews of that part of Poland partitioned to Russia totaled some 1,600,000. By the census of 1897, this number had risen again by 3.2 times to over 5 million. This extraordinary increase, which remains something of a puzzle to demographers, must have had a profound impact on our subject. For some two centuries, the Jewish youth cohort, as the sociologists like to call it, was enormous compared to older age groups. I mean primarily the group in the years we today label adolescence and early adulthood. Restless and searching, such youth groups typically fill the ranks of radical religious and political movements, as our own century attests.

Societies have always tried to control the potentially dangerous energies of their young. Natalie Davis and Richard Trexler have shown such mechanisms at work in Renaissance France and Italy.[4] As Professor Katz has argued, the institutions of early marriage and education served similar functions in the Jewish world.[5] But by the eighteenth century, the pressures of demography may have made such solutions by themselves inadequate. I would submit that the great religious and intellectual movements of the late eighteenth and early nineteenth centuries may have all been products of the youth explosion. I have in mind, first, Hasidism, second, the yeshiva movement, which began in Volozhin at the beginning of the nineteenth century, third, the numerically much smaller Musar movement of Israel Salant, and finally, Haskalah itself. All of these movements, regardless of their fundamental ideological differences, were initially either made up heavily of teenagers or largely aimed at teenagers. As such, they provided varying ideological solutions to what Erik Erikson has called the crisis of identity that afflicts the adolescent.[6] But if revolutionary in origin, these movements quickly became instruments for social control.

If we are to believe the psychologists, every generation experiences searchings for a viable adult identity which necessarily includes a certain rebellion and ambivalence toward its parents. Yet the development of ideologies as expressions of and solutions to the problem of identity occurs only at historical conjunctures when old identities are no longer satisfying. In quiet times, the problems of adolescence are resolved primarily as venerable institutions provide the young person with avenues for maturation. When these institutions no longer prove adequate— for whatever reasons—the question of identity becomes a public matter, generating the impetus for new ideologies and ultimately new institutions.

We should not assume that because there is little evidence of conflicts between parents and children among Jews before the eighteenth century in Eastern Europe that such conflicts did not exist. But it is only with the emergence of the new ideologies aimed toward the young that these conflicts took on a public dimension. I do not propose to settle the question of whether ideology is merely the reflection of a struggle for identity or if it is the cause of youthful disaffection. But whether we label ideology chicken or egg, we cannot escape the conclusion that the new ideologies were manifestly part of generational conflicts. Here is one example from memoirs of the Yiddish writer Yehezkel Kotik.[7] Kotik, who was born in 1847, describes how his father rebelled as a newly married thirteen-year-old against his grandfather by becoming a Hasid. Kotik himself took after his grandfather and became a *mitnagged* (opponent of Hasidism). His father then arranged a Hasidic bride for him and thus tried to win him back to the true religion. But Kotik, after two months of marriage, fled his wife and father to study at the yeshiva of Volozhin, a stronghold of the *mitnaggedim*. If Hasidism and *mitnagdut* served as the bones of contention between generations for Kotik, the same role was fulfilled by Haskalah for others and by assimilation, socialism, and Zionism for later generations.

Our focus here is the conjunction between ideology and identity in the early Eastern European Haskalah—that period up to around 1870 when the *maskilim* (followers of Haskalah) were still a persecuted minority. The ideology of the Haskalah has received considerable attention from historians.[8] Productivization of the Jews, especially through the creation of Jewish farm colonies, moderate religious reform, change in dress codes, and a new educational system emphasizing European languages and sciences, were all parts of the well-known program of the maskilim. Yet this ideology did not emerge out of a vacuum but was rather the product of the biographies of the maskilim and, specifically, of the struggles for identity that marked their adolescent years. For it was typically during these years that the maskilim became converts to the cause. While many of the ideas of the maskilim were taken over almost word for word from the European Enlightenment, they were absorbed into a particularly Jewish framework, that is, the reality experienced by the maskilim themselves. Therefore, what is most interesting in the ideology of the Haskalah is not so much the ideas themselves—which were for the most part derivative and not particularly original—but how they resonated against the problems of Jewish adolescence.

The most compelling and inescapable fact of life for any young maskil was early marriage. The educated elite from whose ranks the maskilim came were almost all married between the ages of thirteen and fifteen. Abraham Gottlober states flatly that everyone he knew was engaged by age eleven.[9] Even if the lower classes were marrying in their later teens (as evidence indicates), the average age of marriage among Jews was extraordinarily young compared to marriages in Western Europe at this time and even to non-Jews in Eastern Europe.[10] The early age of Jewish marriage attracted much attention by writers, such as Polish enlighteners from the late eighteenth century, seeking to reform the Jews. Even Central European rabbis such as Jacob Emden and Yehezkel Landau remark on the young marital ages of Eastern Jews as if they were commenting on some exotic African tribe.[11] As far as I have been able to determine, it was not until the 1870s that the age of marriage among the elite began to rise significantly beyond adolescence.[12]

What was the impact of marriage at the time of puberty? Here again we must emphasize that the observations of the maskilim probably do not reflect a new experience but rather give it, for the first time, a public meaning. That such marriage was a traumatic experience is attested by at least some of the traditional literature. For example, a celebrated case from the 1760s reported in Yehezkel Landau's responsa tells of a twelve-year-old boy married to an equally young girl and forced by family pressure to have sexual relations with her.[13] In the middle of the act, one of the family, who were presumably waiting with bated breath outside the room, knocked on the door, thus aborting the children's attempt to meet the expectations of their parents. From that point onward the two would not go near each other, and shortly after his fourteenth birthday the boy disappeared. Although reported in the terse style of the responsa literature, one cannot fail to read such a case without experiencing the pathos and humiliation that must have caused the boy to run away from his in-laws' home. The point, however, is that such a case remained an individual and private one which has only come down to us because of the legal question of aginut (grasswidowhood).

The maskilim, on the other hand, transformed their own biographies into public polemic. The memoirs of Mordechai Aaron Guenzburg, Abraham Ber Gottlober, and Moses Leib Lilienblum, to name but three, are all conscious attempts to define the personal problems of Jewish childhood and adolescence as social issues.[14] The memoirs follow certain conventions and must therefore be seen as works of literature as much as objective accounts. Indeed, we learn less from them about the reality of Jewish life than we do about the image of that life which the maskilim consciously created. But in imaginatively reconstructing their early lives through their memoirs, the maskilim gave the first definitions of childhood and adolescence in Jewish history. As Philippe Ariès has suggested in *Centuries of Childhood,* the definition of childhood is a cultural construct that changes historically.[15] Although a legal category of childhood in Judaism existed since the Talmud, it was the maskilim who gave the term its first social definition by rebelling against the traditional treatment of the child.

The beginning of adolescence is not determined solely by biology: cultural factors certainly play a role in determining the age of adolescent struggles. For traditional Jews in Eastern Europe, marriage at thirteen or fourteen marked the transition from childhood to a new stage of life which was neither adulthood nor childhood. The maskilim portray this Jewish form of adolescence as an extended death, rather like premature old age. Abraham Gottlober speaks of the child snatched out of the paradise of childhood and forced to eat the apple of love which is "honey mixed with poison."[16] In this version of Adam's fall, early marriage was the kiss of death. In Mordechai Aaron Guenzburg's memoir, early marriage causes sexual impotence, which is the main theme of the book. This impotence is the medical analogue of the philosophical impotence and confusion which Guenzburg experienced during the same years. Both conditions are temporarily cured by a doctor who is also a maskil.[17] In the juxtaposition of sexual and intellectual dysfunction, Guenzburg explicitly fuses the problems of personal identity and ideology. It is interesting that although Guenzburg sees these problems as a consequence of early marriage, he is equally opposed to the late age of marriage typical of the German Jews: by marrying only at thirty, the German Jews too often frequent prostitutes. Thus the proper age of marriage, says Guenzburg, is around eighteen, a piece of advice which can be found already in the Mishnah.

The maskilim see childhood as a period of naive innocence and unproblematic relationship to one's biological parents. In most of the memoirs, the parents are portrayed in unambivalent and thoroughly positive colors. Frequently the father is described as a maskil, although here the authors play with the traditional meaning of the word ("learned") which was only transformed by the Haskalah itself. An intimation that this idyllic relationship must end first comes when the young boy is sent off to the *heder* (one-room elementary school) at the age of five or six. In memoir after memoir, the heder and *melamed* (heder teacher) are presented as the very antithesis of home and parents. Here the boy is abused and beaten. Perhaps the most graphic portrait of the heder is in Shmarya Levin's autobiography in which the melamed is nothing short of a pathological sadist.[18] Yet the prevalence of this brutal figure suggests that we are not dealing here with just a literary stereotype but instead with a real figure drawn from life.

The experience of the heder clearly sharpened the contrast between home and outside world. It may well be that a kind of splitting occurred in the later memories of the maskilim in which the parents were seen as thoroughly positive figures when the reality may have been more complex. In the memoirs I have studied, the writers never admit to having been beaten by their parents, while the melamed invariably metes out corporal punishment. We may be justifiably skeptical of this image of reality. It is however significant that brutality is typically perceived as external to the family. This perception is quite a contrast to what historians of the European family have taught us about child rearing since early modern times; corporal punishment, although also administered in the schools, was typically the province of the father and must have played a role in the deep ambivalence toward the father which we find, for instance, in Erik Erikson's study of the young Luther.[19] In the Jewish experience, this sort of harsh discipline is associated with an agent outside the family. Thus when the father and mother support the melamed, the child feels a sense of betrayal, an emotion which all the memoirists later experience in their marriages. There is a persistent tension in these works between the "good parents" who protect the child against a cruel world and a seemingly inexplicable alliance of these parents with the hostile values of society.

The heder is the first experience of separation from the parents and the memoirs invariably describe it in such tragic terms. But this separation is only a premonition of the more traumatic separation that will come with marriage. Curiously, however, the period of engagement, which usually lasted two years, is treated as the culmination of the idyllic childhood. Some maskilim describe experiencing feelings similar to romantic love toward their prospective brides, usually before they actually met them.[20] It may well be that the social expectations placed on marriage were the causes of these seemingly premature feelings. And, in fact, the maskilim are quick to add that they themselves had no notions of love whatsoever at this age. Although the maskilim report these feelings many years after the event when they had already been exposed to a European vocabulary of love, they were not merely literary inventions since many of these marriages ultimately failed. A failed marriage would tend to sour one's memory of the engagement period, so the persistence of more positive memories suggests that they were genuine and not later retrojections. Here perhaps is some evidence that feelings of romantic attraction were permitted and even encouraged by traditional society as long as they took place within the framework of a *shiddukh* (engagement). Certainly the Yiddish chapbooks of this period support such an argument when they relate Jewish love stories between couples who are fated from birth to be united.[21] Instead of dismissing the existence of romantic love in traditional Jewish life, we might consider the possibility that it was allowed to flourish within certain definite constraints.

If the period of engagement lent itself to a kind of puerile romance at a safe distance, the marriage itself seemed literally a death knell to all erotic feelings. The maskilim report the understandable fear of the two barely pubescent or probably even prepubescent children forced into marital relations, frequently without the slightest knowledge of what was expected of them. Guenzburg relates how his grandfather used the sexual symbols of the Kabbalah to try to instruct him about the birds and the bees. In virtually all of the memoirs, the trauma of premature sexuality seems to have made a mature relationship with the new wife extraordinarily difficult, and in some cases paved the way to later divorce. The failure of eroticism in many of these marriages led to sexual dysfunction in some cases, such as Guenzburg's. When the maskilim came later to adopt European ideals of romantic love, their own premature encounter with eros created a bitter tension between ideology and reality.

Yet it was not only the problems of relating to their new wives that plagued these memoirists: equally difficult were the separation from parents and adaptation to the new in-laws. Here the problems of the heder were magnified manyfold. We have to remember that most wedding contracts stipulated a certain period during which the in-laws would support the young husband as a student. He would live in their house together with his new wife. The length of this period of *kest* varied according to the relative wealth of the parties, but it typically covered a substantial portion of adolescence. Thus, during this stormy stage of life, the boy lived not with his biological parents but with in-laws. We know from the literature on the English public school what it meant to spend one's adolescence out of the home or, closer to our situation, what was the historical experience of apprentices and house servants separated from parents at an early age. Young Jewish boys experienced much of this trauma, but as sons-in-law, their situation was at once better and worse. They could be treated as a prize possession and pampered. Or, as the cases of most of the maskilim, as Solomon Maimon, Guenzburg, and Lilienblum attest, the in-laws could take over the function of the melamed as a persecutor.

Maimon describes the brutal treatment he experienced at the hands of his mother-in-law (the memoirs frequently blame the mothers-in-law much more than fathers-in-law).[22] Here the domestic politics are characterized by quite a bit of physical violence, unlike the remembered childhoods of the authors. The young married man is treated like a child, although not as he was treated in his own childhood. The authors experience a distinct tension between their new status as married "adults" and infantilizing treatment at the hands of their in-laws.

The memoirs discussed here were all written by men so that we have ignored the problems which the young wives must have faced caught between their parents and their new husbands. The autobiography of Pauline Wengeroff, which is one of the very few we have that was written by a woman who grew up in the mid-nineteenth century, suggests that the problems of growing up Jewish in this family situation were perhaps as difficult for girls as for boys.[23] There is also a fascinating case from the nineteenth-century responsa literature of a young town girl who comes to live with her husband's family in the countryside (the reverse of the usual situation where the boy went into the girl's household).[24] Disconsolate at leaving her family and lonely in the rural setting, she was seduced by her father-in-law while her husband was off at school. Unfortunately, no such racy tale can be found in the reverse situation of the young maskilim.

Hence the natural conflicts which adolescents experience with their parents involved not the biological parents, but for most male Jews of traditional society, the in-laws. Once again, when the maskilim turn this situation into an ideological struggle, they bifurcate the family into the "good" biological family of their childhood and the "bad" family of their in-laws. It is their entrance into the latter which seems to cut off all hope and create feelings of despair and impotence. It is also typically during this period that they begin to discover Haskalah ideas and in most cases come into severe conflict with their in-laws. Thus it is not surprising that the polemic against early marriage which one finds in many Haskalah texts should have such a strong biographical dimension. The Haskalah represented an avenue of escape from the pressure-cooker of the adoptive family and it was an escape that allowed the maskilim to attack the very social system which had torn them out of their parents' arms, first to subject them to the heder and then to the prison of an early marriage. It might equally be argued that Hasidism and the yeshivot also offered avenues of escape from the life of the traditional family during adolescence, but they did not provide weapons of direct criticism. No wonder that some of the maskilim found their way to the Haskalah through the court of the Zaddik or the study hall of the yeshivah.

The system of controlled early marriage therefore naturally formed the focus of the Haskalah program of reform. It is impossible to understand the theory of productivization of the Jews without a new system of marriage. For the early maskilim, the old system of marriage put a premium on talmudic scholarship, both in its hierarchy of marital virtues and in the rewards of marriage. Instead of gaining a worthwhile profession, the young married man was expected to study. Financial support would come from his in-laws and later his wife. The maskilim focused on this practice in their critique of traditional society. For instance, in Smolenskin's *Ha-To'eh be-Darkhei ha-Hayyim,* a young Hasid proclaims to a maskil who wants to know how he supports himself: "Is my mother-in-law paralyzed that I should have to earn a living? Until the day the worms take up residence in her corpse, she will go on working and supplying our needs."[25] The maskilim advocated destroying this system by creating an adolescence to be dedicated to gaining an occupation. Marriage would come later, only when the boy could himself support his wife. Adolescence would thus become a time of some autonomy, or at least a period when the perceived constraints of family would be delayed.

It should be added that the Orthodox world was beginning to come to similar conclusions. Where the general belief in the Middle Ages was that a youth might devote himself more energetically to study if he was married, a number of rabbinic authorities such as the author of the *Arukh ha-shulḥan* argued that study must precede marriage (a position which has support in the talmudic dictum: "Can he have a millstone around his neck and study Torah?"[26] The age of marriage of yeshivah students at the great Lithuanian yeshivot rose to twenty-five toward the end of the nineteenth century. Perhaps the most important Rosh Yeshiva of the period, Naphtali Zvi Berlin of the Volozhin yeshivah, claimed that early marriage was medically unsound, even if earlier generations had been up to it (this is a view he probably got from Jacob Emden, who in turn may have had it from eighteenth-century medical treatises).[27]

The connection between productivization and marriage in Haskalah ideology had a further dimension. The maskilim saw traditional marriage as a commercial transaction unsuited to the modern world. Instead of making money by productive labor or capitalist initiative, the focus of Jewish financial transactions was the shiddukh. The maskilim were particularly hostile to the institution of the *shadkhan* (matchmaker), who represented for them a type of *batlan,* or unproductive parasite. This image of marriage as a financial transaction had considerable justification as we can see by referring to Jacob Emden's autobiography, one of the most candid personal sources from the traditional world.[28] Much of Emden's account is taken up with the tedious financial details of various shiddukhim, transactions which were frequently the largest in the life of the traditional Jew. One might note that despite the hostility of the maskilim toward the shadkhan and the public financial negotiations around the shiddukh, they themselves all too often resorted to the same practices. Thus, Y. L. Peretz's father, who was a maskil, arranged his son's marriage in the traditional fashion, and Abraham Mapu's letters to his brother are filled with descriptions of the wealth of various women he tried to marry off to his brother. Even Moses Mendelssohn, who boasted that his own marriage did not require a shadkhan, is said to have taken a shiddukh commission. [29]

But if the maskilim did not live up to their own ideology, they at least wanted to remove marriage from the marketplace. Let us look at two didactic Haskalah novels. Israel Aksenfeld's Yiddish novel *Dos Shterntikhl*[30] is all about the tensions between the old commercial values, represented by the marital headband with its valuable stones, and the new values of capitalist commerce. As Dan Miron has pointed out, the former is based on fixed wealth and the latter on liquid.[31] In this novel, women represent medieval values. The hero, Mikhl, overcomes these values by marrying the heroine but presenting her with a *shterntikhl* (headband) of false pearls. Once the shterntikhl and all the values it represents are shown to be bogus, the new capitalist spirit which Mikhl has acquired in Germany can emerge triumphant.

In a similar way, Mendele's first Hebrew novel, *Ha-Avot ve-ha-Banim* (1868), weds new commercial values with free choice in marriage. Women, says Mendele, should no longer be treated as commodities to be bought and sold by their parents; instead, Jews must learn to relate to true commodities. The novel, which is explicitly based on Turgenev's *Fathers and Sons,* is about the generational conflict instigated by the Haskalah. For Mendele, this conflict is an essential ingredient of progress. At the end of the novel, the hero and heroine are finally engaged after numerous misadventures and receive the blessings of the patriarch Ephraim. His death a symbolic eight days later is like an inverted *Brit Milah* (circumcision ceremony) which signifies the birth of a new set of values and the triumph of a new generation.

Influenced by the nascent movement of Russian feminism, the Jewish writers of the 1860s and 1870s, such as Y. L. Gordon and Lilienblum, tried to liberate the Jewish woman from the bonds of traditional marriage. Gordon's poem *Al Kozo Shel Yod* probably remains the most eloquent denunciation of the oppression of women by Jewish law and is certainly the first attempt to write from a woman's point of view—a stance that the earlier Haskalah was unable to adopt since it typically treated women as allegories for the medieval world it despised.

Lilienblum also wrote a number of bitter manifestos against the traditional view of women, denouncing in particular what he calls the wife as "chamberpot" *(avit shel shofkhin)*.[32] He argues that the functions traditional Judaism attributed to married women could as well be performed by a servant.

Just as the Haskalah advocated taking marriage out of the marketplace, so it preached taking women out of commerce. A moderate maskil like Mapu could still trumpet the business skills of prospective matches to his brother,[33] but more radical writers like Guenzburg and Ayzik Meyer Dik were not so compromising. In one of his didactic letter formularies, Guenzburg praises the customs of countries where men work and women stay at home; in his own country, he complains, the girls are active in business and their morals have deteriorated.[34] Similarly, Dik, the Yiddish pulp novelist, saw the marketplace as bad for feminine morals. In one of his novels he writes with a characteristic lack of subtlety: "The women of Israel and their daughters sit and sell all kinds of silk and linen and everyone who comes to buy wants to taste the taste of a virgin and possess her."[35] Commerce was the midwife of female promiscuity. Both marriage and women must be decommercialized.

Those familiar with the history of the European family will immediately recognize the bourgeois impulse in this view of women and the family. We have here a Jewish variant on the notion that a woman's place is in the home. If the maskilim directed their polemics against a specifically Jewish system of marriage and family, their goal was the same as that of other nineteenth-century writers on the family. They advocated such bourgeois values as privacy and chastity. Here we encounter an interesting tension in Haskalah thought: although the maskilim advocated romantic love and free choice in marriage, their erotic desires were severely curtailed by values of almost puritanical restraint.

It is worthwhile reflecting for a moment on the meaning of such a bourgeois family given the background of the maskilim. The position of women in this new family was clearly less powerful than in the traditional family, or at least in the *image* of the traditional family we find in the memoirs and fiction of the Haskalah. Where the maskilim experienced their mothers-in-law, and to a lesser extent wives, as powerful and domineering, they construct a family in which power implicitly lies in the hands of the husband. Their revolt against the traditional family is a revolt against matrilocality, or at least the version of matrilocality that they experienced as young husbands.

The maskilim contrasted their bourgeois aspirations with a peculiar vision of traditional Jewish life. Where the typical image of traditional Judaism is of strictly controlled sexuality, the maskilim describe it as shockingly promiscuous. Such accusations against traditional society were particularly common in the Haskalah attacks on Hasidism. Joseph Perl, perhaps the most abusive critic of Hasidism in the early nineteenth century, believed that because the Hasidim focused all their attention on God and the Zaddik, they had abandoned their families.[36] Perl was particularly critical of the allegedly pornographic language of Hasidic theology (he deliberately distorted Hasidic texts to make them much more explicitly erotic).[37] Moreover, in his *Megalleh Temirin* (1819), two of the many interwoven plots involve promiscuous behavior by the Hasidim (in one case, two Hasidim rape and impregnate a Gentile woman; in another, the son of the rebbe sleeps with a Jewish woman). What Perl seems to be suggesting is that Hasidism has broken the bounds of sexual propriety on two fronts: its theology is obscenely erotic and its followers' behavior is promiscuous. He implies that the first leads to the second. On both the religious and social planes, all morality has broken down and the family is on the road to destruction. The maskilim pose here not as the critics of the family but as its redeemers; what they really have in mind is the bourgeois and not the traditional family.

It is curious indeed that the maskilim should have attacked Hasidism, of all movements, for unbridled eroticism. If anything, Hasidism was much more puritanical than mainstream rabbinic Judaism, at least if one is to judge from such Hasidic writers as Elimelech of Lysensk and Nachman of Bratslav. Hasidism celebrated the emotions over the intellect but redirected erotic feelings toward God. Here is a classic case of control and displacement of eroticism through theology. It might not be idle to speculate that the maskilim saw in Hasidism something uncomfortably close to home. Adolescents from the same general background as the Hasidim, they no doubt experienced the same erotic tensions which Hasidism had rechanneled. Where Hasidism confined dangerous erotic impulses to the love of God, the maskilim tried to do the same in an idealized image of the chaste bourgeois family.

Yet the escape to the family ultimately proved a personal and intellectual failure for the maskilim. Analysis of the literature of the end of the nineteenth century would be the subject of another chapter, but we should at least remember Baruch Kurzweil's shrewd observation that the heroes of the stories of Berdichevsky, Brenner, Gneissin, and others seem caught in perpetual adolescence.[38] The *Lebensphilosophie* of the end of the century demanded that eros be regarded as the touchstone of life. Yet the tortured and unsuccessful attempts at love which one finds in this fiction belie the bombastic philosophy it sought to serve.

The themes of sexual frustration and alienation in this literature are reflected in the biographies of the maskilim throughout the nineteenth century. The trauma of adolescent marriage was all too frequently followed by divorce. Although I have not done a statistical study of the divorce rate among the maskilim, my impression from reading dozens of biographies and memoirs is that it was well above 30 percent.[39] In some cases, the frustrated youth left his wife in order to pursue Haskalah; in others, angry in-laws, upon discovering the boy's attraction to Haskalah, coerced a divorce. Yet the breakup of these marriages did not always lead to more successful second marriages. For these generations, mature eroticism often seemed unattainable. The only extramarital affair I know of from the Haskalah—that of Lilienblum—remained platonic and largely epistolary.

We cannot know whether the high divorce rate was a consequence of Haskalah or if, conversely, Haskalah may have been one result of unhappy marriages. One suspects that it was something of both. Yet the fact remains that in their literature as in their lives, the maskilim could not sustain the kind of family that was their ideal. Small wonder that Abraham Mapu, in a letter to his brother, decries family life. At a time when the myth of the Jewish family was becoming a stock in trade of Western European rabbis, he wrote: "Only one in a thousand will derive joy from family life and even that will only be a facade."[40]

Small wonder, too, that the maskilim should turn to male friendships to replace shattered personal lives. Mapu writes to his brother: "Yes, the love of women is strong but as its price it will take the souls of the husbands. . . . Not so is brotherhood whose candle will never be extinguished."[41] Time and again, Mapu, like other Haskalah writers, uses frankly erotic language to describe male friendships.[42] Would it be too bold to suggest that the erotic energies which the maskilim could not direct toward women found their objects in men? Perhaps this speculation may help us understand the almost sectarian comradeship which we find among the maskilim.

I have argued that the formation of a Haskalah ideology and identity must be seen as a consequence of the life experiences of the maskilim and, even more important, of their perceptions of those experiences. In their revolt against traditional society, they wanted to revolutionize the politics of marriage and the family along the lines of romantic love and bourgeois marital relations which they adopted from Western literature. We may conclude that in their personal lives they could never realize these ideals; like the generation of the desert, they were still trapped by the realities of their own childhoods and adolescences. But if they failed to successfully wed eros to enlightenment, they did radically alter the perception of the Jewish family and thus contributed mightily to the erotic sensibility of the modern Jew.

58   David Biale

Notes

1. Jacob Katz, "Marriage and Marital Relations at the End of the Middle Ages" [Hebrew], *Zion* 10 (1944–45), 21–54. In addition, see his "Family, Kinship, and Marriage Among Ashkenazim in the Sixteenth to Eighteenth Centuries," *Jewish Journal of Sociology* 1 (1959), 4–22. In this article, Katz extends the analysis of the 1945 essay to include Eastern Europe. A summary of these arguments can also be found in his *Tradition and Crisis: Jewish Society at the End of the Middle Ages* (New York, 1961), chaps. 14, 15.

2. See Azriel Shohat, *Im Hilufei Tekufot* (Jerusalem, 1960), pp. 162–73. There is a good deal of debate over Shohat's thesis. Katz has suggested that what Shohat found among German Jews in the late seventeenth century was no more than deviations from the rabbinic norms which only changed with the Mendelssohnian Enlightenment. A synthesis of the Katz and Shohat positions might argue that deviance is a necessary prerequisite to new norms.

3. "Population," *Encyclopedia Judaica*, vol. 13, cols. 866–903 and the bibliography found there.

4. Natalie Z. Davis, "The Reasons of Misrule," *Past and Present* 50 (1971), 41–75; Richard Trexler, "Ritual in Florence: Adolescence and Salvation in the Renaissance," in *The Pursuit of Holiness in Late Medieval and Renaissance Religion*, ed. Charles Trinkhaus (Leiden, 1974), pp. 200–64.

5. Katz, *Zion,* passim.

6. Erik Erikson, *Young Man Luther* (New York, 1958, 1962), pp. 14, 41–42.

7. Yehezkel Kotik, *Mayne Zichrones* (Warsaw, 1913), vol. 1, pp. 110ff.

8. For Eastern Europe, see primarily Mordechai Levin, *Arkhei Hevra ve-Kalkalah ba-Ideologiya shel Tekufat ha-Haskalah* (Jerusalem, 1975); J. S. Raisin, *The Haskalah Movement in Russia* (Philadelphia, 1913); and Rafael Mahler, *Ha-Hasidut ve-ha-Haskalah* (Merhaviya, 1961).

9. Abraham Gottlober, *Zikhronot u-Masa'ot*, ed. R. Goldberg (Jerusalem, 1976), vol. 1, p. 85. Gottlober describes how the marriage brokers acted to force a low marriage age by pressuring parents to accept matches. The typical goal was to celebrate the Bar Mitzvah and marriage at the same party. Since a two-year engagement was considered necessary, the *shiddukh* (engagement) was often concluded when the boy was eleven.

10. See Adrejs Plakans and Joel M. Halpern, "An Historical Perspective on Eighteenth Century Jewish Family Households in Eastern Europe," in Paul Ritterband, ed., *Modern Jewish Fertility* (Leiden, 1981), pp. 18–32. The classic model for age of marriage is J. Hajnal, "European Marriage Patterns in Perspective," in D. V. Glass and D. E. C. Eversley, eds., *Population in History* (Chicago, 1965). See also Peter Laslett, *The World We Have Lost* (2nd ed., New York, 1971), pp. 84–112.

11. On the Polish enlighteners, see Jacob Goldberg, "Jewish Marriages in Old Poland in the Public Opinion of the Enlightenment Period" [Hebrew], *Galed* 4–5 (1978), 25–33. On rabbinical opinion, see Ya'akov Emden, *She'elat Yavez* (Altona, 1738–59), Q. 14, p. 18; and Yehezkel Landau, *Noda be-Yehudah*, Part 2 (Prague, 1811), Q. 54, p. 63. Some of the early marriages in the eighteenth and nineteenth centuries may have been a result of "panics" *(bahalot)* caused by

rumors that the government was about to legislate minimum marriage ages. See Israel Halpern, "Panic Marriages in Eastern Europe" [Hebrew] in his *Yehudim ve-Yahadut be-Mizrah Eropa* (Jerusalem, 1969), pp. 289–309. Halpern probably exaggerates the number of very early marriages since the tendency of the sources is to inflate such figures. Early marriage was common even without externally induced panics, although the latter brought about marriages at the age of eight, which was normally unheard of. In any case, the children typically were not brought together until they reached legal maturity. Halpern also contends that governmental decrees may have played a role in the eventual rise in marital age. While this may have been true in Bohemia where such regulations went into effect in the eighteenth century, it was not true in Russia where age of nuptiality was influenced by other causes.

12. See Shaul Stampfer, *Shelosha Yeshivot Lita'iot be-Me'ah ha-19* (unpublished dissertation, Hebrew University, 1981), Appendix. Stampfer brings evidence of the age of yeshivah students during the nineteenth century, which is some measure of the intellectual elite. A broader analysis of age of marriage in Russia between 1867 and 1902 can be found in Jacques Silber, "Some Demographic Characteristics of the Jewish Population in Russia at the end of the Nineteenth Century," *Jewish Social Studies* 42 (summer–fall, 1980), 277–78.

13. Landau, *Noda be-Yehudah,* part 2, Q. 52, pp. 45–46.

14. Mordechai Aaron Guenzburg, *Aviezer* (Vilna, 1863); Abraham Ber Gottlober, *Zikhronot;* and M. L. Lilienblum, *Ketavim Autobiografiim,* 3 vols, ed. S. Breiman (Jerusalem, 1970). Guenzburg (1795–1846) began his memoir in 1828 but did not complete it. Gottlober (1810–1899) published the first part of his autobiography in 1881 and the second in 1886, but the section on his youth and marriage seems to have been written in 1854. Lilienblum (1843–1910) is a generation later. His *Hatte'ot Ne'urim* ("Sins of Youth"), which is the relevant part of his autobiography, appeared in 1876 and, as such, is the only one of these works to have been written close to the period of life described (Lilienblum actually wrote the work in 1872–73).

15. Philippe Ariès, *Centuries of Childhood,* trans. Robert Baldick (New York, 1962).

16. Gottlober, p. 93.

17. On Guenzburg, see Alan Mintz, "Guenzburg, Lilienblum and the Shape of Haskalah Autobiography," *AJS Review* 4 (1979), 71–110. Mintz mistakenly thinks that Guenzburg's work ends with a resolution, when in fact the cure breaks down in the last two pages. But Mintz's treatment of these two autobiographies is by far the best recognition of the deliberate literary character of these works. See additionally Samuel Werses, "The Patterns of Autobiography in the Period of the Haskalah" [Hebrew], *Gilyonot* 17 (1945), 175–83.

18. Shemarya Levin, *Forward from Exile,* trans. Maurice Samuel (Philadelphia, 1967), pp. 51–52. Levin (1867–1935) relates how this discipline created adultlike behavior. Children attended the heder for most of the day and saw their parents for only an hour or so in the evenings. Because the heder was for boys only, it sharpened the separation between boys and girls.

19. Erikson, 63–79. See also Lloyd deMause, "The Evolution of Childhood," in Lloyd deMause, ed., *The History of Childhood* (New York, 1974), pp. 1–74; and David Hunt, *Parents and Children in History* (New York, 1970), pp. 133–48.

60   David Biale

20. Guenzburg, 54; Gottlober, 94–95.

21. This literature is described in David Roskies, *Ayzik-Meyer Dik and the Rise of Yiddish Popular Literature* (unpublished Ph.D. dissertation, Brandeis University, 1975), chap. 1.

22. Solomon Maimon, *An Autobiography*, ed. Moses Hadas (New York, 1947), pp. 31–33. Maimon's autobiography was first published in 1792–93.

23. Pauline Wengeroff, *Memoiren einer Grossmutter* (Berlin, 1913), pp. 100ff. Wengeroff's own marriage was a combination of old and new value systems. Although she was engaged in the usual way, she wrote love letters to her fiancé and spent time with him unchaperoned. She speculates that Nicholas I's edicts of 1845 requiring Jews to adopt modern clothing had an influence on marriage customs. Wengeroff came from an already partially enlightened family and all her children went on to convert to Christianity. Thus her testimony cannot be regarded as representative for the maskilim, but should rather be seen as evidence of changes among the assimilating merchant class.

24. Haim Halbershtam, *Divrei Haim* (Lemberg, 1875), Q. 28, p. 97. Halbershtam (1793–1876) was the founder of a Hasidic dynasty in Zanz, Galicia, in the first half of the nineteenth century.

25. Smolenskin, *Ha-To'eh be-Darkhei ha-Hayyim* (Warsaw, 1905), part 3, pp. 22ff. Translated in David Patterson, "Hasidism in the Nineteenth-Century Novel," *Journal of Semitic Studies* 5 (1960), 367–68.

26. Yehiel Michael Epstein, *Arukh ha-Shulhan: Even ha-Ezer* (1905–6), Sec. 1, P. 11:3. Epstein claims that by his day (beginning of the twentieth century) the custom of child marriage had virtually disappeared. The main reason for early marriage was to prevent masturbation, but Epstein holds that "in these generations, the instincts have decreased" so that such preventive measures are no longer necessary.

27. Naphtali Zvi Berlin, *Ha'amek Davar* (Vilna, 1879–80), commentary on Exodus 1:7. For Emden's view, see the responsa cited in *n*. 11.

28. Jacob Emden, *Migilat Sefer*, ed. David Kahana (Warsaw, 1897). Emden wrote his autobiography around 1752.

29. Y. L. Peretz, "Zikhronot," in *Kol Kitvei Y. L. Peretz* (Tel Aviv, 1957), p. 146; Ben-Zion Dinur, ed., *Mikhtavei Avraham Mapu* (Jerusalem, 1970), pp. 184ff; and Katz, *Zion*, p. 50.

30. See the excellent translation by Joachim Neugroschel in his *The Shtetl* (New York, 1979), pp. 49–172. *Dos Shterntikhl* was probably written in the 1840s but was prevented from publication by Hasidic pressure. It was finally published in Leipzig in 1862.

31. Dan Miron, *Ben Hazon le-Emet* (Jerusalem, 1979), pp. 177–216.

32. Lilienblum, *Ketavim*, vol. 2, pp. 89–93.

33. Mapu, *Mikhtavim*, 5 August 1862, p. 185.

34. M. A. Guenzburg, *Kiryat Sefer* (Vilna, 1847), p. 59.

35. Quoted in Levin, *Arkhei Hevra*, p. 152. For a fuller treatment of this theme in Dik and other Yiddish authors, see David Roskies, "Yiddish Popular Literature and the Female Reader," *Journal of Popular Culture* 10:4 (1977), 852–58.

Roskies quotes a similar passage from Dik's *Royze Finkl* (1874): "Our Jews only consider it shameful for [a Jewish woman] to flirt with a young Jewish fellow, but not with a Christian, because in the latter case, it is a matter of business."

36. Joseph Perl, *Uiber das Wesen der Sekte Chassidim,* ed. Abraham Rubinstein (Jerusalem, 1977), pp. 125, 146.

37. Ibid., pp. 41–43.

38. Baruch Kurzweil, *Sifruteinu ha-Hadashah: Hemshekh o-Ma'apekhah?* (Tel Aviv, 1971), pp. 234ff.

39. Guenzburg claims that early marriage produced a very high rate of divorce: out of every two women, one has had two husbands. See *Aviezer,* 104. Because of his own unhappy marriage, Guenzburg's testimony is suspect, but if we look only at the biographies of the maskilim, we find that his observation is not far from the mark.

40. Mapu, *Mikhtavim,* 29 October 1860, p. 133.

41. Ibid., 12/26 January 1861, p. 138.

42. See ibid., letters to Shneur Sachs, 1843, pp. 3–7, which include a "love" poem to friendship. See also his letter to his brother of 7 November 1857, p. 23, in which he writes: "My right hand embraces you and my lips kiss your lips." One must be careful not to impute too much to these conventions of epistolary style. What is significant is that such language seems appropriate between men but not between men and women. The modern ideal of friendship owes much to the German Enlightenment, and the language of friendship we find here is no doubt borrowed and translated. Whatever the particular emotional valence of these friendships, it is clear that they provided emotional outlets inconceivable within marriage. A comprehensive study of this neglected theme would have to include such sources as literature and letter formularies, in both of which there seems to be an abundance of evidence for male friendship.

5. Priestess and Hausfrau: Women and Tradition in the German-Jewish Family

Marion A. Kaplan

Lay and religious spokesmen throughout the era of Imperial Germany reproached women for the decline of Judaism.[1] They argued that Judaism depended to a large extent on the role of women, because Jewish home life itself had a religious character:

> The *Hausfrau* emerges as a priestess *(Priesterin)* of the home. Women are giants who carry the world on their shoulders by caring for the home. . . . If the religious home falls, so does the world of religion.[2]

Since women were supposed to imbue the home with its piety, the decline of religion was their fault.[3] This chapter challenges this common belief, which persisted well into the twentieth century, and examines the actual role women played in the maintenance of Jewish tradition and the Jewish family. It also assesses the extent to which female-specific conditions—women's primary role in the home and family, as a result of their exclusion from politics, most forms of public employment, and higher education—influenced their behavior and attitudes. It posits that women, for reasons beyond their control, remained the guardians of Jewish traditions.

I wish to thank Jay Kaplan, John Foster, Paula Hyman, Karin Hausen, Norma Pratt, and the members of the German Women's History Study Group (New York) for their comments and suggestions on an earlier version of this essay.

Women's experience can sharpen our understanding of a past that has been interpreted with no reference to women at all. This chapter suggests that a gender analysis is an essential tool with which to understand the processes by which traditional religious and familial customs were maintained or transformed in the period before World War I. Without analyzing the behavior of both genders, we get a skewed impression of Jewish behavior, since women were the majority of Jews in Germany. By gender, I mean a "socially imposed division of the sexes . . . a product of the social relations of sexuality"[4] as compared to sex, a biological given. Gender is created by culture, changing over time and varying according to class, ethnicity, and locale. The gender system includes relations of production, reproduction (procreation and domestic labor), and the family as well as the enculturation of gender in childhood and adult life. When we pursue the question of Jewish religiosity with gender differences in mind, a more complicated picture than the usual "modernization" approach to nineteenth-century German-Jewish history emerges. By focusing on women, we begin to recognize the more traditional attitudes and institutions that persisted in dynamic tension with the forces of secularization and assimilation.

Women were not aware of the importance of their lives as individuals, thus they left few or no records. The sorts of records they did leave—letters, household accounts, diaries—were not recognized as being important by others. In order to find them within their social context, I have used a variety of sources. Jewish newspapers, organizational bulletins, and records provided useful, mostly prescriptive, information. Scattered statistical sources, at least on a national level, are also available. Memoirs—for all their obvious drawbacks, particularly their middle-class bias—come closest to presenting women as whole persons engaged in the private and public spheres. I have also used letters by and to women; diaries by women and men; rabbinical and educational essays; oral history; and assorted collections at the Leo Baeck Institute in New York. By combining the objective data with the more subjective material, it is possible to reconstruct certain aspects of women's private lives.

If there is one generalization that can be made about Jewish women in Imperial Germany, it is that the overwhelming majority of them were housewives or future housewives. Single, married, widowed, divorced, whether they held paid or unpaid jobs or not, they performed the tasks associated with running a home. Even if they hired other women to do the more menial chores, the responsibility of the home was theirs. The housewife's job was (and is) gender linked, and it is clear that any understanding of the actions of Jewish women must take this into account. Beyond this one characterization of woman as housewife, differentiated analyses of Jewish women are essential to an understanding of their roles. Such analyses should reflect upon class, geography, pace of modernization, age cohort, and life cycle. Historians must also be aware of gender-specific changes within any given time frame, because the periods commonly regarded as turning points by historians are not necessarily the same for women as for men.[5] Nor were economic mobility and urbanization experienced in the same way by Jewish men and women: there were often time lags in the way women and men adapted, resulting from the limitations imposed upon women as well as internalized values and self-images. Women have generally encountered transitional periods differently from men: they have had to "keep up" with the times, but not push too far ahead. In Germany, Jewish women were protected from the "front lines" of change and were expected to cushion the family from its shock waves. They were often blamed for the dislocations of modernity, even as their responsibilities in the home and to the family interfered with their exposure to the modernizing influences to which their husbands were subjected. Their psychosocial responses to these time lags were manifold: some never adjusted to the incongruities in their material and spiritual lives; others accommodated to secular, industrial society; still others sought compensation in religion as they adapted outwardly. Most acculturated eagerly to the dress, literature, manners, and mores of the bourgeois culture around them while they clung—often long after their husbands and children had ceased to care— to traditional familial religious customs, a source of prestige or former prestige in the private sphere of the home to which they were still confined. Women were more "traditional"—a term not intended as one of moral endorsement or disapproval—because they had to accommodate to new functions while maintaining old ones.

Jewish women's relationship to Jewish tradition and the family is a complex one. This chapter asks more questions than it answers and is not always true to the differentiated analyses for which it pleads, because we need far more research before conclusions can be drawn. It presents an overview of the role of bourgeois women in the family, the area of their predominant activity.

Germany, unlike France or England, experienced an extremely rapid and intense period of industrialization and urbanization between 1870 and 1913. Industrialization had come late to Germany, but once it got going, it developed at an exceptionally quick pace. The stages of social development were telescoped, and politics rapidly polarized. Men reacted to the strains and stresses of industrialization by, among other things, expecting wives to provide islands of serenity in a mad world.[6] The family as haven—a prescription achievable only by some—became an integral component of bourgeois class consciousness.[7] It was the place where men were to be consoled and refreshed and where children were educated and prepared to face the world. More than ever before, women were defined through the family. A value system which defined women as domestic, weak, modest, dependent, protective, self-denying, emotional, religious, and virtuous gained, rather than lost, attraction in a period in which these same qualities were viewed as encumbrances by men under pressure to succeed in the world outside.[8] Woman's "natural" profession was "the preservation and cultivation of traditional morality, the defense of the family, and the furtherance of a spirit of self-discipline, moderation and self-sacrifice. . . ."[9] The home was to be a "retreat, refueling station to which the family members return periodically for spiritual, physical and psychological sustenance."[10] In theory, and often in practice, the home was off limits to conflict. Of her childhood in the 1870s, one woman recalled:

> Father, who worked very hard, wanted to have peace and quiet in the family. Mother was not allowed to come to him with complaints about the children, servants, etc. "I have enough problems at work," he would say.[11]

The home would assuage the pain of men confronted by an aggressive, competitive, status-conscious, and achievement-oriented world. The wife and family would not only soothe and comfort, they would also be the reward—and excuse—for the battles of the day. As one male educator, a propagator of this ideology, noted: "On one side of the threshold of his house he belongs to work, on the other side is peaceful pleasure. His second life begins there, the rewards for his day."[12] Nor were men unique in accepting this idyll. Lina Morgenstern, a German-Jewish writer and one of the founders of German feminism, commented in 1886:

> Out of the whir of the marketplace and the restless wandering in strange places, one longs again and again . . . for home. Here the success of the enterprises is manifest. Family life is the sphere in which the extent of our economic success is presented. No one should control this sphere more than the wife.[13]

Not only the psychosocial but the economic functions of bourgeois women were redefined. Before, women's reproductive work, including all aspects of childbearing, child rearing, and housework, had been essential to the family economy, but by the period under study most bourgeois homes—as in other industrializing countries—had become consumption units removed from productive economic activity. Women's work became less physical and more administrative and cultural. The ideal of housewifery, of a spotless home run by a *tüchtig* (efficient and capable) home manager who carefully instructed and regulated her servants, came to replace women's former productive work. An English visitor (1908) was to note, "It was a new idea to me that any women in the world except the Germans kept house at all." She continued:

> The extreme tidiness of German rooms is a constant source of surprise. They are as guiltless of "litter" as the showrooms of a furniture emporium. . . . Every bit of embroidery has its use and its own corner. . . . Each chair has its place. . . . Even where there are children German rooms never look disarranged. . . .

Peeking into the husband's room in one house, she remarked to the wife, "He must be a very tidy man. Do you never have to set things to rights here?" "Every half hour," was the response.[14] Extra leisure could turn housewives into *Putznärrinnen* (mad housewives) who tidied the home from dawn to dusk. Such was the case among many Jewish women as well, whose relatives and neighbors recalled their incessant cleaning compulsion. "Our peasant women didn't have time for that," remarked one observer.[15]

Jewish women were affected by the dominant cultural attitudes toward women as well as by the embourgoisement of the great majority of German Jews. Moreover, by the 1880s Jews led the trend toward smaller families.[16] Jewish women thus experienced greater leisure and wealth than in previous generations. They also experienced the contradictions of their new positions: they were expected to reflect the status and wealth of their husbands, but were subject to accusations of frivolity and ostentation due to the hypersensitivity of an assimilating Jewish community and to frequent charges of materialism made by anti-Semites. They were to maintain the sanctity of the home in a period in which husbands and children were increasingly drawn outside: in which "home" and "world" were increasingly polarized. Finally, while they were expected to smooth the way for acculturation, they became the target of those Jews who sought to protect religious feelings and practice in the face of increasing secularization.

The development of the new bourgeois family occurred at the same time as trends toward secularization, modernization, and, for Jews, acculturation and integration. The nineteenth century witnessed the disengagement of society from religion, the "downgrading of religion to a denominational category and concomitantly the end of the primacy of Judaism and Jewishness as an all-embracing influence dominating both social life and the conduct of the individual."[17] Jews experienced the uneven and uneasy process of secularization along with other Germans. By 1900, the Liberal branch of German Jewry, which had grown out of the Reform movement led by Abraham Geiger in the mid-nineteenth century, was predominant. There is no doubt that Orthodox religious observance declined in the imperial period. (Only 15 percent of Jews could still be classified as Orthodox at the turn of the century.) Eager to acculturate, some Jews modernized their religious practice to minimize their embarrassment at non-Western customs. Others attempted to shed their ethnic, social, and, in some cases, religious distinctiveness entirely. The family, however, remained a central focus. This was because many Jews, like their Gentile counterparts, promoted the idea of the family to fill the void that their neglect of religious traditions had created.[18]

Jewish women experienced the effects of secularization from their primary position in the home. Jewish observance, more than that of other religions, took place in the home in a familial setting. For women, in fact, *religion and family were one totality.* Whereas Judaism relegated women to a peripheral role in the synagogue, it placed them on a pedestal in the home. While this perch kept them safely removed from the centers of public and religious life, it had its compensatory side. Family life and the religious observance of the Sabbath, holidays, and dietary laws were clearly women's domain. Women's relationship to their religion, then, should be measured differently from men's, that is, by the extent of their maintenance of "Jewishness" in the home, both in specific practices and in sentimental attachment.[19]

The extent of women's interest or participation in the *formal* transmission of Judaism to their children has yet to be discovered. Religion teachers did count on the mother to transmit by her example a moral and religious education. Mothers were expected to pray with their children and to tell them religious tales, while fathers who fulfilled their own religious duties were considered good examples. Thus women had to *actively transmit* Judaism, whereas fathers simply had to *be* religious.[20] Were women, actually, more active? Did mothers or fathers hire religious instructors for the home? Who provided for religious schooling? Was it of equal importance for girls and boys? Who took more interest in the children's progress and homework in these lessons? What was involved in the formal and informal transmission of religious knowledge and feeling and how was it divided between parents?

While formal transmission of Judaism took place within the institutional framework of the synagogue and school, *informal* transmission—affective, "ethnic," private, and personal, including foods, family, and hearth—was in large measure women's domain, and among traditional families women were accorded social power and status for their religious adherence. Women shaped the milieu in which traditional sentiments were reinforced. As mothers and grandmothers, they impressed their offspring as much with their feelings about their religion as with their loyalty to religious forms. Looking back over a lifetime, memoir writers seem to have been more affected by their mothers' attitudes to their religion as it was revealed in the home (whether positive or negative) than by their fathers' attendance at synagogue or their own religious instruction or synagogue participation.[21]

Rural Jews throughout the entire Imperial era waxed almost elegiac when they described the family Sabbaths and holidays.[22] Mothers and grandmothers (with the help of servants) prepared the home and cooked traditional meals. The distinctive Sabbath atmosphere—certain foods, white tablecloth and finer tableware, candles, special clothing, and family gatherings—was attributed to the hard work of the mother. Women and men *benscht* (blessed) the children, and the lighting of the candles by the women signified that the spirit of Sabbath was in the home. This spirit, again, had everything to do with family union:

> The peacefulness and ceremony of a traditional Friday evening . . . was unique. It was an evening in which the whole family sat together. The business and sorrows of the work week were forgotten. It was as if one had stepped into another world.[23]

Women also took special care in the arrangements for the major holidays.[24] The most strenuous of these was Passover.[25] Housecleaning often began in January, climaxing in March or April with an all-night exchange of kitchenware and a carefully executed replacement of the year-round dishes with the Passover ones. While both parents participated in the final ritual, the symbolic search for *chometz* (leaven), the women had actually prepared the family for the holiday.

These were not simply rural phenomena. In the cities, where secular culture predominated (by 1910, 58 percent of Jews lived in big cities), memoirs indicate that Jews—particularly women—were conscious of the Jewish calendar and the tradition of particular rituals and foods on holidays. They experienced the Sabbath and holidays as unified religious and familial celebrations. Both elements reinforced each other and were difficult to disentangle. In fact, even as the family functioned to maintain religious practice, religion functioned to affirm family connectedness. One woman wrote of the 1880s in Berlin: "Besides the ceremony of

Friday nights there was a strict rule [*ein strenges Gebot*] of family together-
ness [*Familienzusammengehörigkeit*]."²⁶ She continued: "This was not always easy, but proved itself to be the right thing to do." When it was
impossible for all of her siblings to appear on the Sabbath, the blessing
over bread was made for those children present at the table and for those
who were absent. The holidays and Sabbath were occasions to reaffirm
the family.

Urban Jews, especially second-generation city dwellers, often reduced the number of holidays they celebrated and minimized the religious content. Yet in all but a small minority of families (those notorious
for their Christmas trees and Easter egg hunts) Jews were aware of, and
attempted to commemorate, the major holidays, if only by a family
reunion and a traditional meal. Symbolically, the holidays meant family—a way perhaps of accommodating to a society still geared in large
part to Christian feast and holy days in which Jews represented such a
small minority. Whereas old rituals were slowly replaced or forgotten,
family ties—supported by Jewish heritage and minority status as well as
by the socioeconomic forces affecting most bourgeois Germans—were
reinforced. Thus, Jewish religious tradition and identity were married to
an urban, secular lifestyle with the result that the family became the
cornerstone of a more secular version of Judaism. For these Jews, family
provided the meaning that religion once had. Thus the family became
visible testimony to the "embourgeoisement of Jewish piety."²⁷ The
family was the cornerstone of a piety being transformed into middle-
class morality, a heightened national consciousness, and liberalism. According to George Mosse, "Religious feeling itself had become identified
with . . . the proper bourgeois morality. . . . This . . . Jewishness . . .
was set within an ideal of life that was shared by most Germans . . . a
bourgeois utopia."²⁸ I would suggest that the family was the concrete
embodiment of this bourgeois morality.

This was apparently also the case for the Protestant bourgeoisie.
Public celebrations, many of which had taken place in churches,²⁹ became privatized in this era. The German Christmas, for example, once
focused on the church, now became famous for its emphasis on familial
intimacy. Christmas evolved into a celebration *of* the family.³⁰ Beyond
celebrations, however, the mundane everyday also centered on the family. Weekends, vacations, and special outings were family occasions.
Entertainment, for which extra funds were rarely available, took place
primarily within the family. The German bourgeoisie carefully allocated
its limited resources: hikes on Sundays and regular gatherings with other
family members were interspersed with infrequent concert or theater
visits. While maintaining "appearances" (house, servant, yearly vacation,

membership in clubs and charities), these families demanded thrift and self-denial from their members. A family strategy, including "appearances" and long-term savings for a son's education or a daughter's dowry, took precedence over individuals' short-term desires. Intensive family ties were the reward for self-disciplining personal needs. These family ties were not only necessitated by the demands of the family economy, but required by the Prussian state. Civil servants, for example, had to demonstrate an irreproachable family life or face dismissal from their position.[31] The success of a "social collectivism" within the family, which allowed it to maintain its lifestyle and secure its future, attests not only to the exigencies but also to the ideology of "family solidarity." Intimate family life became a means as well as an end for bourgeois Germans and they endowed it with spiritual significance.

Among Germans, women were acknowledged to be the more religious sex. Women clung to religion longer, because they did not acquire either the advanced, scientific education or the substitute, secular power of men whose world views gradually rejected all or parts of spiritual thinking.[32] A rigid division of labor ascribed religiosity, spirituality, and emotionalism to women and knowledge, reason, and intellect to men.[33] Women attended church more readily than men, and among Catholics tended to home rituals, such as maintaining the home shrine and eternal light. Weeks in advance, women were also involved in extensive cleaning and baking preparations for major holidays—although these were prescribed not by the religion but by family tradition. Men were excluded from such activities. Observers of German peasant customs noted that those holidays which were family festivals, that is, where women participated, remained intact whereas predominantly male holidays fell into disuse.[34]

Ritual waned most slowly among Jewish women as well. First, they experienced less dissonance between religious practice and their daily routines than men. Their private world was more traditional than modern, timed to childbirth, anniversaries, deaths, and the rituals that went with these as well as to seasonal and sacred holidays. Second, women could exert some control in the privacy of the family and home, whereas Jewish men faced obstacles to the performance of their religious duties resulting from business obligations and travels. Women's control over their domestic environment could extend to the maintenance of kosher ritual even against a husband's preference: "What you do in the kitchen is your own business," declared one husband.[35] Third, popular ideology permitted, tolerated, or encouraged female religiosity and, among the traditionally religious, women's religiosity provided them with a measure of social power that they could achieve nowhere else. They were loath to give this up. Finally, it was easier for Jewish women to consider themselves religious than for Jewish men. Women were excluded from many public rituals to begin with—they had fewer positive commandments to fulfill—therefore their actions had less relationship to religious sentiment than those of men. For example, the daughter of the Orthodox leader Esriel Hildesheimer wrote that while the men prayed at sunset, the women read short stories to each other while finishing their mending.[36] When men began to neglect their observances, it may have indicated some degree of declining religiosity. Women, for whom religion was less formalized and more internalized, could continue their patterns of behavior without any break in their previous loyalties or feelings. Fritz Stern has reminded us that "a good deal of religious consciousness and sentiment can live on without necessarily finding expression in socially observable conduct."[37] This was especially so for Jewish women.

Women were the last holdouts in practicing laws and traditions in the home, even among secular Jews who no longer observed dietary laws or the Sabbath. The wealthy scion of a Berlin Jewish family, born in 1876, wrote that he had no religious schooling or training, but "it is true that my mother taught me to pray every night." And his grandmother, who lived with him, left him with memories of carefully observed religious practice and daily morning prayers.[38] Another young man (born 1876) noted the totally unreligious behavior of his *parents*. His father would not attend synagogue, and he knew when Christmas, not when Hanukkah, was to be celebrated. Yet, "every Friday night, I saw my mother praying conscientiously, standing at the prescribed passages . . ."[39] A woman (born 1880, Breslau) recalled that her *family* observed only Yom Kippur. Yet she remembered her mother praying at home every Saturday morning.[40] Memoirs typically skirt over women's private prayers. Thus the historian knows far more about the *perceived* inferiority of women's private rituals than about their actual neglect of them.

Even when women abandoned certain rituals, there seems to have been a time lag between when husbands and wives gave them up. One daughter (born 1862, Posen) noted that while her mother fasted and prayed on Yom Kippur, for her father "it was easier to fast after a hearty breakfast."[41] Another woman recalled that her father ate pork with no compunction while her mother prayed fervently that her daughters would not neglect their religion when they grew up.[42] Furthermore, even when a couple gave up certain practices at the same time, it seems as if women were more troubled by it. Freud, for example, persuaded his wife to drop all religious practice. She did so, but to the end of their days husband and wife were still bickering because Martha wished to light candles on the Sabbath.[43] These and many more examples suggest that women resisted the complete abandonment of their religious heritage—not always successfully—in the only acceptable manner of female opposition: quietly, within the shelter of the home. Such gender-specific private observance was probably perceived as less important by both women and men, since men defined status and prestige in terms of public observance.

Beyond women's involvement in the rituals of the weekly and annual Jewish calendar, we know from folklore studies of southern and western Germany that women were actively involved in rituals surrounding childbed and baby naming. These rituals often ran parallel to the public ceremonies which took place in the synagogue. Since women had traditionally been barred from leadership of public ritual and relegated to observer status in the synagogue, women's initiation of life-cycle ceremonies, such as those surrounding birth, indicated their determination to participate in a separate sphere. In the case of birth rituals, women would sew and hang amulets around the room where the baby was to be delivered. They believed these would ward off evil spirits which could hurt mother and child. A mother's return to the synagogue and baby naming were more elaborate ceremonies. On a Sabbath, approximately four weeks after the birth, when her state of "impurity" (postnatal bleeding) had drawn to a close, the mother could reenter the synagogue. Her female friends accompanied her on this day, guarding her from any danger while she was still impure. Once she was blessed in the synagogue, she was as safe as any "pure" woman and was reintegrated into the community. On the same day, her daughter or son (who would already have been circumcised) was then welcomed into the community through the baby-naming ceremony, *Holekrash*. The mother invited every child of the locality to her home. The children surrounded and lifted the cradle, calling "Holekrash, what should the child be named?" They then shouted its secular (as opposed to Hebrew) name, repeating this ceremony three times. They were rewarded with fruit or candy. To bring these rituals into line with official religion, the cantor or Jewish teacher was requested to read biblical verses during the event. Elements of Holekrash appear in rabbinical literature as early as 1100, but anthropologists dispute whether the ceremony was essentially a Jewish one or one that Jews picked up from pagan and Christian sources.[44] In terms of women's history, however, the important point is that women believed they were fulfilling religious prescripts by guarding mother and infant and welcoming them into the community. In terms of Jewish family history, we recognize women's agency in defining and enacting religious family rituals.

It would be useful to discover the extent to which other rites of passage were initiated or practiced by women. Did they perform private, ceremonial roles in confirmations or marriages? In the case of death rituals, for example, women (like men) formally and traditionally belonged to (sex-segregated) burial societies where they washed and dressed the deceased. They watched over the bodies before interment and offered aid and solace to the bereaved family.[45] Were there informal, female rituals which accompanied these activities? More research is necessary to determine where and how long traditional and/or folk rituals remained intact, among which classes and in which geographical areas, and the role of women in their maintenance or neglect.

Of course, there were women who dropped most rituals and observance. Some preferred a more secular approach, others a more convenient one. One woman found that "one could be religious selectively, according to convenience" and convinced her husband that it was foolish to forego lunch on Yom Kippur.[46] And there were women who for social reasons assumed that a denial of their Jewish identity—religious and otherwise—would improve their position in Gentile society. Yet these were a distinct minority. Conversion and intermarriage statistics for the Wilhelmine era, for example, show Jewish men to have been the group far more prone to cut their ties with Judaism and Jewish society. Between 1901 and 1904, 8.4 percent of Jewish men and 7.41 percent of women intermarried; between 1910 and 1913 these figures increased respectively to 13.15 percent and 10.92 percent; and the war years, 1914–1918, saw them leap to 29.86 percent and 21 percent respectively.[47]

When women intermarried, economic necessity and lack of available Jewish partners were primary causes. Thus one finds that more Jewish males in mixed marriages had middle-class incomes than Jewish females. And in Berlin (1910), for example, far more Jewish women who entered into mixed marriages had been employed before their marriage (attesting to their economic need) than Jewish women who married Jewish husbands. Jewish demographers noted that Jewish men chose wealthier Jewish women who did not have to work for a living.[48] In marriages between non-Jewish men and Jewish women, commentators remarked that the latter most often *("ausserordentlich oft")* came from the lower classes.[49] In Hamburg at the turn of the century, Jewish men who married non-Jewish women belonged to the middle classes, whereas among Jewish women who intermarried, "the Jewish cook who married the Christian guard" was typical.[50]

As in the case of intermarriage, female conversion was more often necessitated by serious economic need than was male conversion, which was a means toward achieving job promotion and social acceptance rather than assuring one's basic sustenance. Tax records of Berlin converts in the years 1873–1906, for example, indicate that 84 percent of female converts as compared to 44 percent of male converts fell in the lowest income categories.[51]

Despite increasing rates of conversions and intermarriages, most middle-class Jewish women associated with a small group of Jewish friends and were enclosed in a family circle. It has been suggested that the family was particularly important to Jews, an itinerant people, forced to move from country to country with no history of permanence or belonging. Heinrich Heine referred to it as the "portable homeland" of the Jew. Placed in a foreign culture, amid different religions, Jews looked toward the family to provide the roots and security they often lacked. Even Jewish feminists, who would seek the emancipation of women from traditional sociocultural constraints, clung to the notion of the family as the cornerstone of Judaism.[52]

Did Jewish families in fact provide stronger human ties and support than other families of similar class and place? If the family was more central, to what extent did wider family ties hamper contact with Germans and even with other Jews? And to what extent did the family serve as a buffer between Jews and an often unfriendly society? Did this lead to a more tenacious hold over the individuals, particularly the women, by the family? Was this hold more likely to force the acquiescence or foster the rebellion of women?

We have yet to discover in a comparative manner the importance of the family to Jews relative to their German bourgeois counterparts, or the degree to which the centrality of the Jewish family was a result of internal or external factors. The former include religious and cultural traditions and a positive group identity. The latter encompass class status and economic necessity (we do know, for example, that there was among many Jews a close connection between business life and family life), the pressures of an anti-Semitic environment, and the high moral value placed on family life by the German bourgeoisie. What is clear is that the *ideology* of the family was very important to all Jews. What role this ideology played, whose interests it served, and who was most affected by it are areas for further research.

For Jewish women it appears undeniable that the family was the crucial center of activity and one that they actively sought to maintain. It provided them with communality and sociability to fill their newly gained leisure time and to make up for their exclusion from many Gentile circles. Jewish women took responsibility for family networks; for the care of grandparents and orphans; in short, for the moral and material support, the continuity and organization, of an often geographically dispersed family system.[53] Frequently this was left to the oldest woman in the family until she was no longer able to fulfill the responsibilities.

When her grandmother died, a woman (born 1891, Frankfurt/Main) recalled her mother assuming the obligation of maintaining the family network: "so that the connections remain."[54] The aged were seen as family responsibilities, family assets. Grandparents often lived within walking distance of their grandchildren in towns and big cities alike. They frequently moved in with their children when they became widowed. Single women also lived with an aging mother or father, often giving up their own ambitions to care for a parent.[55]

Jewish women participated in *Kusinenkreise* (cousins clubs), initiated vacations or a *Kur* (a stay at a health resort) with other family members, and planned regular family gatherings to coincide with Jewish holidays or birthdays and anniversaries. Frequently, such meetings and celebrations led to discussions of possible marriage partners for the younger generation, with women considering the likelihood of two personalities meshing and men talking over the financial prerequisites. The *Kur,* too, served as a *Heiratsmarkt* (marriage market), and relatives took the lead in introducing eligible partners.[56]

Naturally it was easier to maintain contact in the towns. Yet when heightened mobility threatened to tear family ties apart, women in particular traveled to visit relatives. Families with the financial means to make both leisure time and travel possible for their daughters sent them to care for sick relatives, to help sisters who had just given birth, to spend vacation time with distant cousins, to meet prospective marriage partners, to learn how to run a household with an aunt, or to enjoy the "big city" while visiting a relative.[57] Whereas boys left home for an apprenticeship or the university, girls left home in order to maintain family connections. Even among the less well-to-do whose daughters had to be trained to earn their own living, it was common for girls to be sent to relatives to help out in the household or store rather than to strangers. Family ties were nourished in a society barely tolerant of Jews and Judaism and among a people who had become disproportionately mobile in a very short time.[58]

The family was both a richer field of activity and a more constricting boundary for women than for men. Men spent more of their time in non-Jewish surroundings, making acquaintances of a wider circle of Gentiles. They were often unable to fulfill religious obligations in the face of anti-Semitism or unwilling to fulfill them if they were to compete successfully. Ensconced in—and restricted to—the family, Jewish women had far less access to Gentile environments, less opportunity to meet non-Jews, and less occasion to experience anti-Semitism. When they did come face to face with anti-Semitism, the possibility remained for them to withdraw further into the family. Even for the few who ventured out into the new world of women's careers, the family remained an important haven. While class, geographical location, the bonds and vitality of the *Gemeinde* (community), the hostility of the non-Jewish world, and male attitudes surely played their part in shaping women's religious and ethnic identification, it may be suggested that women's socially reinforced familial preoccupations gave them the unique potential to maintain Jewish traditions as they acculturated to the norms of the German majority.

In conclusion, Jewish family rituals had given women a sense of importance and power. As their religious role eroded and their economic role in the family economy also shrank, women hung on—at the very least—to family gatherings and to their socially and culturally respected family position. As religious observance declined, Jews, like other bourgeois Germans, looked toward the family for celebrations and wider purpose to their lives. Family holidays, like the growth of national holidays in place of some religious ones, seem to have come about as substitutes for religious holidays in the German and Jewish bourgeoisies alike during this period. The family and secular holidays provided the meaning and centrality that had once been the domain of "religion." Public celebration in synagogue and church became private celebrations *en famille*. The family was a way of explaining a rapidly changing universe to themselves: it was a "reservoir of resistance to the complete dehumanization [*Entseelung*] of the world."[59]

In a period of rapid transition, Jewish women seem to have sensed that preserving the family would also preserve a traditionally respected position for themselves. In so doing, they acquiesced to a hardening of the bourgeois definition of "women's place" at precisely the time when structural changes would open the public sphere to them. This did not stop those who had to work outside the home from doing so—although it placed a formidable obstacle in the paths of those who chose this route. It simply underlined the significance of the family to women in the private and public spheres. Through the mediation of women, the family itself increasingly provided a replacement for religion. As time went on, particularly after World War I, it was the Jewish family and the Jewish community, rather than the strict observance of traditional Jewish customs, which served as a vehicle for Jewish identity in Germany.

Notes

1. David Leimdörfer, *Ein Wort zu unser Frauenfrage* (Berlin, 1900), p. 3.

2. *Die Laubhütte* (Regensburg) XII (18 July 1895), 335.

3. Examples abound. See *Jüdisher Volksbote* (Frankfurt/Main), November 1909, pp. 48–52; *Der Freitagabend* (Frankfurt/Main), 1859, pp. 37–373; *Israelitisches Gemeindeblatt* (Cologne) V (12 October 1892), 1, XVI (15 May 1903), (21 August 1903), XXI (24 July 1908), 1; *Schlemiel* II (1 January 1904), 3. In the United States, rabbis and male leaders also blamed women for religious decline: see Norma Fain Pratt, "Transitions in Judaism: The Jewish American Woman through the 1930s," in *American Quarterly* XXX: 5 (winter 1978), 694–95.

4. Gayle Rubin, "The Traffic in Women: Notes on the 'Political Economy' of Sex," in Rayna R. Reiter, ed., *Toward an Anthropology of Women* (New York, 1975), p. 179.

5. They are also often not the same for lower-class men as for the elite. Joan Kelly has challenged assessments of historical epochs based on only half a population. She noted that the Renaissance, for example, was a period in which women experienced a contraction of social and personal options that men of their classes did not. "To take the emancipation of women as a vantage point is to discover that events that further the historical development of men, liberating them from natural, social, or ideological constraints have quite different, even opposite, effects upon women." "Did Women have a Renaissance?" in Renate Bridenthal and Claudia Koonz, eds., *Becoming Visible: Women in European History* (Boston, 1977), pp. 137–64. See also Kelly, "The Social Relations of the Sexes: Methodological Implications of Women's History," *Signs* I (summer 1976), 809–23.

6. For urban, middle-class Americans in the 1880s, the family ("little islands of propriety"—Theodore Dreiser) also became the social focus of men's lives after work. See Richard Sennett, *Families Against the City* (Mass., 1970), pp. 47–53.

7. Rolf Engelsing, *Zur Sozialgeschichte deutscher Mittel- und Unterschichten* (Göttingen, 1973), pp. 225–61.

8. Karin Hausen, "Family and Role Division: The Polarisation of Sexual Stereotypes in the Nineteenth Century—An Aspect of the Dissociation of Work and Family Life," in Richard J. Evans and W. R. Lee, eds., *The German Family* (London, 1981), p. 66.

9. W. H. Riehl, *Die Familie,* 9th ed. (Stuttgart, 1882), p. 80.

10. Gerda Lerner, *The Majority Finds Its Past: Placing Women in History* (New York, 1979), p. 132.

11. Anna Kronthal, *Posner Mürbekuchen: Jugend Erinnerungen einer Posnerin* (Munich, 1932), p. 10.

12. L. v. Stein (1886), quoted by Jürgen Zinnecker in *Sozialgeschichte der Mädchenbildung* (Weinheim/Basel, 1973), pp. 116, 118.

13. Lina Morgenstern, *Deutsche Hausfrauenzeitung* (Berlin), 10 January 1886, p. 14.

78   *Marion A. Kaplan*

14. Mrs. Sidgwick, *Home Life in Germany* (New York, 1912), pp. 113, 129, 136.

15. Utz Jeggle, *Judendörfer in Württemberg* (Tübingen, 1969), p. 221. See also S. Moore, "The History of the Family Moos," memoir collection, Leo Baeck Institute, New York (LBI), p. 52.

16. According to John Knodel, Jews probably started to reduce their family size several decades prior to German unification. Throughout the Second Reich they were well ahead of the non-Jewish population in family planning, although the latter, too, reduced its family size. *The Decline of Fertility in Germany, 1871–1939* (Princton, 1974), pp. 136–47, 246–63. See also Steven Lowenstein, "The Pace of Modernization of German Jewry in the Nineteenth Century," in *LBI Year Book XXI* (1976), p. 56; Heinrich Silbergleit, *Die Bevölkerungs—und Berufsverhält—nisse der Juden im Deutschen Reich* (Berlin, 1930), pp. 14–15.

17. Hermann Greive, "Zionism and Jewish Orthodoxy," in *LBI Year Book XXV* (1980), p. 188.

18. The centrality of the family was noted by Hannah Arendt, who wrote: "In the preservation of the Jewish people the family had played a far greater role than in any Western political or social body except the nobility. Family ties were among the most potent and stubborn elements with which the Jewish people resisted assimilation and dissolution." *The Origins of Totalitarianism* (New York, 1966), p. 28. Despite this centrality, it should be understood that while many used the family as a way of filling a religious void and resisting assimilation, there were also those for whom the growing German idealization of the family and the increasing German tendency toward family rather than religious celebrations (from birthday parties to Sedan Day festivities) provided a means of leaving religion behind and integrating into the secularized Protestant mainstream more quickly.

19. Men's relationship would be measured by synagogue attendance, observance outside the home (e.g., not working on the Sabbath), and only lastly by ritual in the home.

20. Heinrich Berger, *Methodik des jüdischen Religionsunterrichtes* (Leipzig, 1911), p. 15.

21. The case of Julius Bleichröder is illustrative. His wife felt fewer ties to the religion than he. "Although Julius felt very close ties to Judaism, he was unable to transmit this enthusiasm to even one of his children." Charlotte Hamburger-Liepmann, "Geschichte der Familien Liepmann und Bleichröder," memoir collection, LBI, p. 67.

22. See, for example, Monika Richarz, ed., *Juedisches Leben in Deutschland, Selbstzeugnisse zur Sozialgeschichte im Kaiserreich* (Stuttgart, 1979), pp. 158–59.

23. Bruno Stern, *Meine Jugenderinnerungen an eine württembergische Kleinstadt und ihre jüdische Gemeinde* (Stuttgart, 1968), p. 93.

24. Esther Calvary, memoir collection, LBI, p. 11; Clara Geismar, memoir collection, LBI, pp. 20–23, 42–44.

25. Henriette Hirsch, memoir collection, LBI, p. 9.

26. Johanna Meyer Loevinson, memoirs, archives of LBI #7095, 85, p. 23.

27. George Mosse, "The Secularization of Jewish Theology," in *Masses and Man. Nationalist and Fascist Perceptions of Reality,* ed. George Mosse (New York, 1980), p. 258.

28. Ibid.

29. Hansjoachim Henning, *Das Westdeutsche Bürgertum in der Epoche der Hochindustrialisierung, 1860–1914: Soziales Verhalten und Soziale Strukturen, Teil I: Das Bildungsbürgertum in den Preussischen Westprovinzen* (Wiesbaden, 1972), p. 479. Henning suggests that the lack of interest of academically educated German bourgeois men had to do with the new critical spirit in which they had been educated. The more they saw their existence as rationally determined, the more they loosened their engagement to the church.

30. Ingeborg Weber-Kellermann, *Die deutsche Familie: Versuch einer Sozialgeschichte,* 4th ed. (Frankfurt/Main, 1978), pp. 112–13.

31. Henning, op. cit., pp. 302, 345–46, 393, 488–89. That the state's interest in an irreproachable family life was common knowledge can be seen in Georg Hermann's novel, *Jettchen Gebert.* In this story, a librarian (a lower-level civil servant) loses his position because the authorities suspect that a woman has left her husband for him. The novel was written in 1906 and went into its ninetieth reprinting in 1920.

32. See n. 29. Men's scientific and women's more religious approach are also highlighted by Bonnie G. Smith in *Ladies of the Leisure Class: The Bourgeoises of Northern France in the Nineteenth Century* (Princeton, 1981).

33. Hausen, op. cit., p. 56.

34. Riehl, op. cit., p. 13.

35. Interview with Mrs. L, by John Foster, in *Community of Fate: German Jews in Melbourne* (Melbourne, forthcoming). Born in 1905, Mrs. L was married in 1930. Her upbringing was typical of traditional Jews in Imperial Germany and thus the question of control over the domestic sphere is representative of an earlier era as well. Her experience with a less religious husband is also typical: "He once took me to a restaurant that was not kosher. 'You won't always be able to eat kosher,' he said to me, because he . . . liked to travel a lot. I thought the roof would fall in or the building would fall down; but it didn't, and the chicken that he ordered was not so very different from a kosher chicken. But I had to have a kosher home because I wanted my parents to be able to stay at my place." That is when her husband agreed that the kitchen was her domain.

36. Calvary, op. cit., p. 19.

37. "Comments on the Papers of Ismar Schorsch, Vernon Lidtke and Geoffrey G. Field," *LBI Year Book XXV* (1980), p. 73.

38. Adele Rosenzweig (born 1867, Ahlen, moved to Kassel in 1872) recalled that her family kept a kosher kitchen until her mother died. At that point, her grandmother refused to visit their home because it was no longer kosher. "Jugenderinnerungen," ed. Rivka Horwitz, *LBI Bulletin, XVI/XVII,* nos. 53/54 (1977/1978), p. 144. See also Richarz, op. cit., pp. 298–99.

39. Richarz, op. cit., p. 362.

40. Toni Ehrlich, memoir collection, LBI, pp. 6, 9–10, 61. Charlotte Wolff

(born 1901, Riesenburg) recalled similar situations. She described the excitement of Christmas, the "festive meal of goose, red cabbage and a heavy Christmas pudding," and then wrote of "a special day of the week to look forward to—the Sabbath. . . . On Friday evenings my mother put two silver candlesticks on the dinner table; food was special and plentiful, and we had a small glass of port wine afterwards." *Hindsight: An Autobiography* (London, 1980), pp. 6, 21.

41. Kronthal, op. cit., p. 27.

42. Antoinette Kahler, memoirs, archives of LBI #2142, 1, p. 53. Examples of this time lag are available in many memoirs. See, for example, those of Ernst Herzfeld (about his parents), Doris Davidsohn, and Josef Jaschuwi (on poor, rural Jews).

43. Quoted by David Aberbach, "Freud's Jewish Problem," *Commentary*, June 1980, p. 37.

44. For further information on *Holekrash (Holekreisch,* or *Holkrasch),* see Max Weinreich, "Holekrash: A Jewish Rite of Passage," in *Folklore International, essays in traditional literature, belief, and custom in honor of Wayland Debs Hand,* ed. D. K. Wilgus (Pennsylvania, 1967), pp. 243–53; A. Landau, "Holekreisch," *Zeitschrift des Vereins für Volkskunde,* Heft I (1899), pp. 72–73; Steven Lowenstein, "Results of Atlas Investigations among Jews of Germany," in *The Field of Yiddish: Studies in Language, Folklore, and Literature,* vol. III, ed. Marvin Herzog et al. (London, 1969), pp. 27–30. For memoirs of these events, see Jacob Picard, "Childhood in the Village," *LBI Year Book,* 1959, p. 280; Edmond Uhry, memoir collection, LBI. p. 111; Bruno Stern, op. cit., pp. 116–18; Phillipine Landau, memoir collection, LBI, pp. 90–91.

45. Most likely, these death rituals were maintained throughout the Imperial period, particularly in the villages. It is unclear when Jewish women began to abdicate to "professional" death watchers and preparers. It is known that in small protestant villages, *Totenfrauen,* women who washed and dressed the body, were replaced by the gravedigger in the 1920s. Gerhard Wilke and Kurt Wagner, "Family and Household: Social Structures in a German Village between the Two World Wars," in *The German Family,* op. cit., p. 141.

46. Richarz, op. cit., p. 346.

47. *Zeitschrift für Demographie und Statistik der Juden (ZDSJ)* (Berlin), January-February 1924, p. 25; October 1930, p. 54. These statistics tell us how many men and women were willing to marry out of their faith. They do not tell us how many of these people married *converted* Jews. Such a breakdown, if it were possible, would spotlight a group of only partly assimilated Jews and might also offer evidence on gender preferences in such alliances.

48. These statistics are for Frankfurt/Main for 1914. *ZDSJ,* February-March 1915, pp. 52–54. See also Felix A. Theilhaber, *Die Schädigung der Rasse durch soziales und wirtschaftliches Aufsteigen bewiesen an den Berliner Juden* (Berlin, 1914), pp. 87–88. His statistics show that of 563 Jewish women marrying Jews, 359 (or 63 percent) had never worked for a living. Of 116 Jewish women entering a mixed marriage, 37 (31 percent) had never been employed.

49. Max Marcuse, *Über die Fruchtbarkeit der Christlichjüdischen Mischehe* (Bonn, 1920), p. 16.

50. Ibid., p. 12.

51. *ZDSJ,* January 1908, p. 13.

52. Rahel Straus, "Ehe und Mutterschaft," in *Vom jüdischen Geiste: Ein Aufsatzreihe,* ed. Der Jüdische Frauenbund (Berlin, 1934), p. 21.

53. See, for example, Edmund G. Hadra, memoir collection, LBI, p. 89 (on family networks); Julie Braun Vogelstein, *Was Niemals Stirbt: Gestalten und Erinnerungen* (Stuttgart, 1966), p. 53 (on helping family members); Simon Bischheim, memoir collection, LBI, p. 4 (on parents living with married children); and Geismar, op. cit., pp. 30–40 (on family visits).

54. Eva Ehrenburg, *Sehnsucht—mein geliebtes Kind* (Frankfurt/Main, 1963), p. 24.

55. One such young woman who had turned down a good job abroad in order to stay with her aging father (ca. 1900, Berlin) told her sister: "One has to sacrifice with a smile." Hirsch, op. cit., p. 65. Sophie Diamant (born 1879, Mainz) lived with her aging mother well after her five brothers and sisters left home. At thirty-one, she married and her mother moved into her home shortly thereafter. "Familiengeschichte Schlesinger," memoir collection, LBI. See also "Tante Emma," Max Gruenewald collection, archives of LBI; and Manfred Sturmann, memoir collection, LBI, pp. 22–23 (on Tante Trude).

56. Phillipine Landau, *Kindheitserinnerungen: Bilder aus einer rheinischen Kleinstadt des vorigen Jahrhunderts* (Dietenheim, 1956), p. 30. For a perceptive description of a *Kur,* see Max Brod, *Jüdinnen* (Berlin, 1911). He depicts young women who only perk up at the word "engagement" and who understand the seriousness of the *Kur* as an opportunity to meet potential marriage partners.

57. See, for example, Adele Rosenzweig, op. cit. (on learning household skills from a distant aunt); Jacob Rosenheim, *Erinnerungen, 1870–1920* (Frankfurt/Main, 1970; on learning household skills from distant relatives); Geismar, op. cit. (on visiting relatives in a big city and helping out in their home).

58. In 1871 about 20 percent of Jews lived in big cities. By 1910 the percentage had catapulted to 58.3 percent. Of the Gentile population, 4.8 percent lived in big cities in 1871 compared to 21.3 percent in 1910.

59. M. Horkheimer, quoted by Hausen, op. cit., p. 65.

6. The Impact of Migration on the Moroccan Jewish Family in Israel

Moshe Shokeid

The analysis of various socioeconomic and cultural phenomena in Israel has usually been based on a comparison between Jews of European extraction ("Ashkenazim") and those of Asian and African extraction ("Sephardim" or "Orientals"). This method has also been employed in the study of family life in Israel, as evidenced for example in recent works by Friedlander and Goldscheider (1978), Peres and Katz (1981), and Goldscheider (1981). While most scientists posit the overall stability of the Israeli family, they all use as base line for their research the comparison of the European versus the Asian and African Jewish populations. Their main findings point, however, to the growing similarity of the rates of marriage and family size between these "two major ethnicities."[1]

I intend to examine a few patterns of family life in one particular ethnic group from among those aggregated in the category of Asian-African Jews. The Moroccan case discussed here suggests that similar examination of other specific groups may produce some more revealing conclusions concerning continuity and change in family life than do the all-embracing statistical averages which point, for example, to the apparently growing similarity of birthrates between Ashkenazi and Sephardi families.

This ongoing research was facilitated by a Ford Foundation grant received through the Israel Foundation Trustees, and by a fellowship at Manchester University, financed by the Bernstein Israeli Research Trust. I am grateful to Shlomo Deshen for his comments, and to Tamar Berkowitz for help with the editing.

Migration and Settlement

More than 200,000 Moroccan Jews have arrived in Israel since the mid-1950s. At present numbering more than 400,000, they represent the largest group of Middle Easterners in the country. The Moroccans are particularly noticeable in farming villages (*moshavim*, small-holders' co-operatives) and development towns which were set up during the period of their arrival. In the larger population centers they have been less noticeable as a group, having settled in the more ethnically mixed suburbs of immigrant residence.[2] However, a few urban slums, centers of social disturbance and political agitation, do carry the image of Moroccan neighborhoods.[3]

During the late 1950s and throughout the 1960s, Moroccan Jews in Israel carried a stigmatized public image. Often described as unadjustable and violent, they were also attributed with the signs of communal and family breakdown. Scientific research has apparently confirmed some elements of this stereotype. For instance, in studies of the distribution of delinquency and prostitution according to country of origin, Moroccans are highly represented.[4] Some studies have related these phenomena to the rapid social and cultural changes that they have undergone since the recent trend of urbanization in Morocco and with immigration to Israel.[5]

This chapter will examine the situational position of Moroccan Jews' family life, drawing upon a series of community studies I and others have conducted which explore patterns of family life as they emerged under different economic, social, and ecological circumstances. A few of the anthropological studies of Moroccan Jews, mainly in the villages and development towns, have already discussed the position of the family in these communities (in particular Shokeid 1971; Deshen and Shokeid 1974, 122–50, 210–36; Marx 1976; and Cooper 1978). My two decades of research on a community transplanted from the Atlas Mountains, and settled in the villages that I call Romema and Yashuv, conducted since the mid-1960s, introduces a dynamic element and a perspective of process to the study of Moroccan immigrants. In considering Moroccan family life in Israel I shall query the patterns of transformation of a number of major structural features, in particular the position of the extended and nuclear family, the division of labor between the sexes, and parental authority.

Family Life in Towns and Villages

The stigmatizing stereotype of Moroccans has emerged from reports on their poor economic accommodation and aggressive behavior in towns, witnessed mainly during the first years of settlement in Israel. Studies of those Moroccans living in urban slums and new development towns (most of which have remained underdeveloped to this day) describe isolated nuclear families, often with many small children. Their adult men—the breadwinners—are usually unskilled in terms of Western technology and science, poorly paid at their manual or semiskilled jobs, and often dependent on welfare.[6] These disadvantaged men express their frustration at bureaucrats who control such resources as employment, housing, and welfare, at themselves (in suicide attempts), and at other members of their nuclear family (their spouses in particular).

The studies that were carried out during the same period in villages present a radically different situation.[7] The immigrants' transformation from peddlers and craftsmen to farmers—however difficult and, at times, degrading—was not an impossible task. Intensive instruction and industry turned most settlers into competent farmers within a few years. Moreover, *moshav* farming offered economic independence and even affluence.

But settlement in villages also carried an important social characteristic absent in towns: according to the policy of settlement applied since the mid-1950s, which intended to establish homogeneous village communities, settlers were sent to their village of destination immediately upon disembarkation at Haifa port. Consequently, the settlers sent to a certain moshav often originated from the same village or town in Morocco, and therefore included many family members. Moreover, these settlers often reorganized family groups by recruiting their relatives who had been settled elsewhere, or established new groupings by contracting marriage ties with their new Moroccan neighbors (Shokeid 1968, 1982). These groups supported the individual in competition with members of other groups for the limited resources available in the economic and other spheres of the moshav organization (Weingrod 1966; Shokeid 1971). Thus, revival of familism helped to reinforce traditional patterns of relationships between close family members and among groups of relatives.

My later observations, however, made in the same villages during the 1970s, reveal a growing ambivalence toward family corporate action. Family groups no longer function as they did during the late 1950s and the 1960s. Many of the hesitant novices in agriculture have become competent and affluent farmers; they no longer need their relatives' support.[8] Furthermore, with the passage of time, another intrafamily development emerged: married brothers who in Morocco shared a joint household, organized according to seniority or age, now head independent households; their economic achievements and social standing in the community are rapidly growing apart. Moreover, close relatives may now compete for the same resources.

Nevertheless, the tension often observed in the relationships between relatives never caused the long-term deterioration of family relations, and those Moroccans who had no close relatives in the community felt themselves at a disadvantage: "I have here no one of my blood, no one from the main source; here I have only friends, and they might not recognize me tomorrow."[9] The villagers looked forward to visiting or hosting relatives settled elsewhere in the country. These visits carried the features of pilgrimages; the guests traveled long distances and once they arrived were continuously entertained and richly fed for days by their relatives, who pressed them to prolong their stay (Deshen and Shokeid 1974, 210–36). They were thus sustaining a noted characteristic of Moroccan culture (Geertz 1979).

In the meantime, however, the social composition of the development towns has been crystallized. With the withdrawal of many of the settlers from other ethnic groups, a considerable number of towns have become noticeably North African in their composition. In fact these towns have turned into "extended villages," exemplifying particular social characteristics that have been identified in Moroccan Israeli villages.

Demographic Stability of the Nuclear Family

Considerable demographic stability, if not expansion, of the Moroccan nuclear family has been observed both in villages and in development towns. The continuing tendency of a high fertility rate in the older generation of immigrants who were already married on arrival may be explained by their basically traditional orientation. The growing size of these families was also due to the improved medical and related social services which drastically reduced the high rate of infant mortality. However, there is clear evidence that this trend continues among those who married in Israel within the first decade after their arrival. Moreover, there are some indications that the pattern persists among many of those who married more recently as well. Those who married in Israel, many of whom served in the army and were educated in Israel, often criticized the older generation for their uncontrolled family size; nevertheless they have gradually increased their own families.

One woman who married in Israel, already mother of five children, who considers herself a modern woman and aspires to a better standard of living, claimed that she "never said that a new baby was the last one—

whoever comes be he blessed!" In fact, she had had her fifth child against strong medical advice to avoid another pregnancy. On the other hand, she criticized her neighbor, a woman in her early forties and mother of eight, including a few grownup children, who was looking for a remedy since she could not conceive more children. It appears that within a vague norm of "reasonable" family size, influenced in particular by the age of the eldest children, the continuing birth of children was as acceptable to men and women of the younger generation as it had been to their parents. Only when her eldest son was conscripted into the army (at age eighteen) or once her eldest daughter reached marriageable age (at about twenty), was it considered shameful for a woman to give birth.

We find substantial support for our observations in demographic research based on national surveys. The scientists who produced those data, however, did not consider country of origin separately and in fact neglected it altogether. Thus, according to data presented by Friedlander and Goldscheider (1978, 316) it appears that among immigrants from African countries (the majority of whom are Moroccans), the younger marriage cohorts have retained high fertility levels more than other ethnic groups (particularly in comparison with immigrants from Asian countries). For example, we find different patterns among Asian and African immigrants when the 1945–49 (immediate preimmigration) and 1960–64 marriage cohorts among immigrants from Asian countries are compared. Among Asian immigrants, 55 percent of the earlier cohort had large families (5 + children), while in the younger cohort only 20 percent had large families. Among immigrants from African countries, 61 percent in the earlier cohort and 49 percent among the younger cohort had large families.[10]

A similar finding appears in Goldscheider's more recent presentation in this volume; his evidence proves that North African urban women in Israel exhibit the highest rates of desired and achieved family size.[11] Another indication of the relatively high fertility rates among Moroccans in Israel is offered by Inbar and Adler (1977), who compared the status of Moroccan Jews who immigrated to France with that of their siblings in Israel and reported inter alia on family size. Thus, the average family size in France was 3.88, while in Israel it was 4.79 (p. 54). It is also interesting to note that the association for rights of large families—Zahavi—is led by Moroccans, and is city based.

While the frequency of large families is not considered a "social problem" in the relatively affluent situation of the moshav, it has often been perceived as one of the severe problems of development towns. However, Cooper's (1978) study among Moroccans in a poor development town demonstrates the economic viability if not the economic rationality of a large family in that environment. The accumulation of income from a large (though often low-salaried) labor force, as well as the possibility of home manufacture of various products, tax reductions, and other privileges granted by governmental authorities (including welfare support) contribute to the smooth, though not affluent, running of the large family enterprise.

In the village, the management of large families seems to be easier, even when economic circumstances are particularly difficult. An example is the case of the poorest family in Romema. In 1976, Mr. Elgazi was fifty-four years old and his wife, who married him in Morocco in her early teens, was forty. They had ten children, the three oldest married with children, living elsewhere in Israel, and the youngest a two-year-old girl. When they arrived in 1962, Mr. Elgazi, who was a silversmith in Morocco, refused to take on the responsibilities of an independent farmer. Expecting a transfer to an urban environment, he was employed as a daily laborer on his neighbors' farms. In 1972 he underwent a minor operation, after which he has never returned to normal functioning, going to work only occasionally. Mrs. Elgazi worked regularly, either on their neighbors' farms or at various manual jobs in the nearby school. The older children at home were also employed on their neighbors' farms. The family received some welfare assistance.

Eventually, Mr. Elgazi requested and received a farm and full membership in the moshav organization. Although he did not take on active farming, his nominal farming and the privileges accompanying the new status afforded him another modest contribution to his family's budget. Their table was regularly as abundant with meat, soft drinks, and alcohol as that observed in the wealthiest homes in the villages. The Ministry of Housing expanded and refurbished their house as part of a special project carried out in most villages; there is currently no equivalent kind of support in towns. While Mr. Elgazi appeared somewhat pathetic, his wife was usually convivial, looking forward to the available possibilities to benefit her family.[12]

Women's Involvement in Economic Activities

The Jews in Morocco, in line with the Muslim code of honor, segregated the women from the company of unrelated men; therefore, women did not participate in economic activities outside of the home. There is not sufficient information about the patterns of women's employment among North African immigrants in towns; in villages, Moroccans easily accommodated with the economic constraints which necessitated women's participation in outdoor farming activities. They were recruited to help on their family farms as well as on their relatives' farms. But women were also regularly employed as farming laborers regardless of family ties. Even the most traditionalist men eventually succumbed to economic pressures and came to accept the employment of their wives, mothers, sisters, and daughters (Shokeid 1971, 165–215).

In the 1960s, I was struck with the vast participation of women in most farming activities; ten years later, their withdrawal from farming was equally striking. Since 1967, with the growing affluence of farmers and the availability of cheap Arab labor from Gaza and the West Bank, the farmers could gradually manage without their women's labor. In some cases, however, women continued to participate in the farm's activities as overseers of its Arab employees.

Particularly illuminating was the reaction of a successful Romema farmer whose wife was regularly employed on their farm during the 1960s. An outspoken woman, I recorded her in 1966 commenting at a family gathering that "nowadays women are more important than men since they work both at home and on the farm" (Shokeid 1971, 176). However, during my stay in Romema in 1976, the farmer, while acknowledging the immense improvement in his economic and social position since he came from Morocco, categorically denied that his wife had ever worked on their farm. Thus, with the change in economic circumstances, some ideological elements of the traditional family patterns were cognitively reinstated.

The broader field of relationships between spouses is not considered here; I have dealt with it more extensively elsewhere (Shokeid 1971, 165–215; Deshen and Shokeid 1974, 122–50). My data do, however, point to the growing accommodation with the impact of Western norms of behavior concerning equality between the sexes.

Changing Patterns of Mate Selection

Most marriages in Morocco, as well as most of those contracted during the first decade in Israel, engaged close relatives or other members from the same community. However, no marriages since then have involved close relatives or members from the same community. Since the mid-1960s, Romema and Yashuv have been completely exogamous.[13] Moreover, a few girls have married men from other ethnic groups (Iranians in particular). It seems that this phenomenon is related to another change: engagements are no longer arranged by parents. Those girls who do not attract suitors by their own devices cannot rely on their parents' intervention. The implications of this new situation were clearly demonstrated in the case of an affluent and influential Romema farmer whose three daughters were approaching their mid-twenties with no husbands in sight. His wife suffered mental depression, attributed by relatives and neighbors to that family predicament.[14]

Most girls in the villages I studied met their future husbands in school, at work, and through friends. This rapid change of a basic aspect of family life was adopted relatively easily. The villager mentioned earlier, who denied that his wife ever worked on their farm, told me about the engagement of his daughter: she was employed as a nurse in a nearby development town where she met a local Moroccan boy. The boy's elder brother came with one of Romema's leading settlers to tell her parents about his brother's serious intentions. Since the girl consented to the marriage, the father accepted her wishes, but stipulated one condition: they should not meet outside the village until they got married. However, when the boy later asked permission to take his fiancée to visit relatives and spend a few days in another village, her parents discussed the matter and agreed that "things are no longer as they used to be in Morocco where the bride and groom did not meet until the wedding ceremony." As a matter of fact, they thought it might be an opportunity for their daughter to become better acquainted with her future husband. The girl was advised about proper conduct when she was away—particularly that she shouldn't let the boy touch her. Soon after the trip the young couple were married.

This phenomenon of parental tolerance toward the changing modes of relationships between boys and girls and the rapid accommodation with Israeli youth culture, which we observed in a prosperous and relatively cohesive Moroccan community, has been even more strongly demonstrated among Moroccans settled in the more heterogeneous urban environment.[15]

Changing Patterns of Intergenerational Relations

In Morocco, married sons usually shared the household with their parents and siblings; this pattern was given up immediately on arrival in Israel. The change was greatly encouraged by the policy employed by the Jewish Agency in villages and towns alike, which entitled all immigrant couples, young and old, to separate lodgings. Although most old couples in villages did not take up independent farming, they did receive their own homes and land. Those who had only one mature son (not uncommon, considering the high rate of infant mortality in Morocco) transferred their farms to them. Consequently, these sons became owners of two farms. Moreover, in these families the old couples generally worked on their children's farms. This generation of old parents adjusted easily to the reversal of roles and authority; it actually increased their involvement with their sons' families.

However, the parents of the younger generation in Israel (as observed since the late 1960s) refused to share their farms with their maturing sons, in spite of the absence of vacant farms in the village, which often forced the departure of a son. In reponse to the suggestion that he share his farm with his only son, an aging father replied: "Am I already dead?" This attitude prevailed in spite of the pressure exerted by the settlement authorities to involve young farmers in the farms of aging parents. The settlement authorities even offered generous financial support for construction of separate homes on the farm for a son's family, a pattern that has been institutionalized in more veteran—mostly Ashkenazi—moshavim.

In towns, the rapid breakdown of joint households is not surprising. Adult children could not usually stay in their parents' small, crowded apartments after marriage. Neither were they expected by governmental and municipal authorities to stay on with their parents. In the villages, on the other hand, one could expect as least a partial reconstruction of the traditional pattern of joint households. It seems however that Moroccan parents who have given up authority over their children's major decisions, as for example with mate selection, have refused to forfeit their economic independence and authority over their farm enterprise.

I should emphasize, however, the apparently paradoxical phenomenon of the overall muting of intergenerational conflicts as observed in villages. Parents seem to be remarkably permissive and tolerant toward their children's behavior, including minor forms of delinquency. They do not enforce their ideological convictions (such as religious conformity), nor do they often demonstrate parental authority in other spheres of daily life. Thus for example, when the son of a leading farmer insisted on driving his van although he did not yet have a driving license, the farmer commented ambivalently: "Here you can't say anything to children, but Shimon is a good boy—he does not surpass limits."[16]

Levy Biton, among the most successful men in Romema and uncompromising toward his opponents, did not contest his nineteen-year-old son who often hinted at the father's religious naiveté when Levy was performing or expressing traditional Moroccan practices and beliefs. But another Romema settler became the laughingstock of the community when he stubbornly nagged his rebellious teenage son to adhere to religion. It was amusingly related that he complained to the police about the boy's refusing to wear a skullcap.

The eldest son of my closest neighbor in Romema refused to help his father, a hard-working farmer with seven children at home, on the farm when he finished his army service. Likewise, he was unwilling to take a job as a mechanic, a skill he had acquired at school. Instead, he asked his father for a considerable loan, which he invested together with a friend in a secondhand van that they bought for their own business. Their venture failed and the boy returned home penniless. Still, the son would not consider helping out on the farm. The father related that recent calamity, which had cost him the bulk of his savings, with no recriminations against his son but with the notion of bad luck which struck his family.

The few cases of juvenile delinquency reported in Romema and Yashuv were usually attributed by the settlers to the parents' indulgence, thought to encourage the youths' demanding and unrestrained behavior. However, the attitudes of parents and siblings toward delinquent youth were akin to the attitude expressed toward the few cases of mentally disturbed adults. Searching for the particular circumstances that had made the victims gravitate to misfortune, they viewed them with pity rather than contempt or disdain. It was apparently bad luck rather than bad nature that caused misconduct and delinquency.

The loss of parental authority among immigrants has often been described as a grave phenomenon effected by their economic and social failures. In this study, however, the apparent loss of parental authority emerged as an accommodation achieved with no real battle between generations, in the framework of overall economic success and the particular conditions that were relatively congenial for social and cultural continuity.

The description of family life among the Moroccans presented here points to a few major—though sometimes apparently contradicting—findings. These include rapid accommodation with changing environmental conditions, as represented by emergent familism in villages during the first stage of settlement and the gradual decline of that type of intensive family cooperation. Similar are the relatively easy introduction of women into regular farming activities contrasted with their withdrawal from farming at a later stage. Rapid accommodation has also been observed in the confrontation with social and cultural pressures affecting intergenerational relationships. Old and young rapidly adapted to the Israeli norms of nuclear family independence as well as to the new modes of relationships between the sexes and the overall independence of youth from parental authority.

The tendency of rapid accommodation with environmental constraints and cultural pressures of the dominant group in society is not a new phenomenon among Moroccan Jews. Moroccan Jewry present a remarkable example of a large Jewish group that survived in spite of its accommodation and actual acculturation for many generations with social and cultural characteristics of the Muslim host society (Sharot 1976).

At the same time, there are indications of the persistent continuity of a family orientation. First, a relatively high birthrate has been maintained, even among the younger generation. Second, in spite of the decline of intensive family cooperation, family ties within large networks of relatives still carry much importance in the life of individuals. Third, severe tensions and conflicts do not characterize the relationships between parents and children. The widespread persistence of family orientation among Moroccans is also indicated by observations of religious behavior in these communites—a subject outside the scope of this chapter.[17] In stark contrast to the stereotype of family breakdown among Moroccan immigrants, my observations suggest that the Moroccan family has greatly preserved its position as the center for affective relationships in society.

My research was carried out mainly in the relatively affluent Moroccan farming communities; this may apparently explain both the viability of family organization and its apparently smooth transformation. Yet there are indications that this trend applies to other Moroccan groups in Israel as well. For example, the high birthrate among Moroccans has been confirmed in nationwide surveys. To the extent that the various Jewish ethnic groups carry particular primordial social paradigms, some elements of which survive under changing circumstances, Moroccan Jewry seems to transmit to its members a deep sense of family ascription and allegiance as well as a diffused commitment toward relatives. The Moroccan case demonstrates overall continuity of a family orientation which seems to have been relatively unaffected by the exigencies of immigration and the cultural pressures of the "melting pot" ideology (which actually presents as model the lifestyle of the veteran and secular Ashkenazi segment of the Israeli population).

This conclusion may appear to contradict the data concerning the high rates of delinquency and prostitution among Moroccan Jewry in Israel. However, as shown by Shtal (1978), a similar phenomenon, demonstrated by far more impressive figures on the rate of prostitution and illegal traffic of women by Jewish gangs and pimps, was observed among Eastern European Jews in Europe and America at the turn of the century. These figures were analyzed as the result of the social and economic difficulties which confronted Eastern European Jewry at that period. Do these figures, reliable as they seem to be, convince us about a tendancy of prostitution and the breakdown of family life among Eastern European Jews, either then or now? No doubt, the particular situation of the exodus of North African Jewry to Israel, which often entailed severe economic and social difficulties, for the older generation in particular, and which also often influenced the loss of parental authority, has produced the circumstances for various types of deviance. But the rates of deviance do not necessarily reflect the position of the family in society, or negate the viability of a strong family orientation.

Beyond that somewhat evaluative concern, it seems necessary to carry out more sensitive demographic surveys and to interest more sociologists and anthropologists in the study of Moroccan Jews under various conditions as much as of other groups which compose the undifferentiated category of Jews of Asian and African extraction. This may identify those groups which, similar to the Moroccans as here presented, do carry a strong family orientation, as compared to those groups which have experienced drastic changes in their traditional family life style. This approach will test the validity of the present use of the "Ashkenazi-Sephardi" ethnic dichotomy as major categories for demographic and sociological research. More important, it will help reveal the processes and the conditions that mold the patterns of family life in various groups.

Notes

1. Peres and Katz 1981, 701.

2. About a third (some 85,000) of all North African immigrants have been settled in development towns. About 50,000 have settled in villages and the rest, more than 80,000, have settled in the older and larger urban areas.

3. The best-known are Vadi Salib in Haifa, where violent demonstrations broke out during the late 1950s (see Bar Yosef 1959, 1970) and Musrara in Jerusalem, where the Black Panthers movement was established during the late 1960s (see Cohen 1972).

4. See, for example, Shoham and Rahav (1967) and Shtal (1978) concerning the high frequency of prostitution among North African Jews. For information about the high frequency of juvenile delinquency among North African Jews, see for example Amir and Shihor (1975) and publications of the Youth Probation Service (1977, 1978). For information about the high frequency of North African adults involved in criminal acts, see Statistical Abstract of Israel (1980, 565).

5. See, for example, Bar-Yosef (1959, 1970); Weingrod (1960); Palgi (1966).

6. For the situation of Moroccans in development towns in particular, see

Berler (1970), Deshen (1974), Marx (1976), and Spilerman and Habib (1976), Cooper (1978).

7. For the situation of Moroccans in villages, see Weingrod (1966); Willner (1969); and Shokeid (1971).

8. A clear indication of that change was observed in the 1975 elections to the village committee in Romema. For the first time, voting was done by ballot; consequently, for the first time, the committee did not represent family groups (Shokeid 1980).

9. For more details about these modes of behavior see Shokeid 1982.

10. Friedlander and Goldscheider (1978, 316, Appendix Table 3).

11. Goldscheider (1981).

12. In fact, Mrs. Elgazi refused to let the work be finished in their house until she convinced the officials at the ministry that they were entitled to a larger house, although she was only in the first months of her last pregnancy. Sarcastic about the ministry's rules, she was also critical about the architects it employed, who designed large living rooms with no separating corridors and doors from the entrance to the house and other rooms. She exclaimed jokingly: "This is nice for the Ashkenazim who have two kids at most, but we Moroccans have at least ten children who roam around all the time."

13. This tendency of marrying out of the community negates Matras's (1973) findings in other ethnic groups and his conclusion that endogamy may continue in transplanted communities.

14. The eldest daughter, who was not considered particularly bright, refused any kind of matchmaking. The second daughter was not good-looking but was considered clever; her occasional suitors made great financial demands on her father, who therefore suspected their motives. The third girl refused to marry a cousin from another village who had asked for her, apparently because of medical apprehension about offspring of closely related parents. Eventually, the two younger girls married just before they were considered too old for a normal first marriage.

15. In a study of Arabs and Jews in an Israeli mixed city, I observed inter alia the freedom gained by Middle Eastern Jewish girls among whom Moroccans were particularly noticeable. The situation probably represents the more extreme circumstances of parental loss of authority (Shokeid 1980b, and Deshen 1982: 35, 40).

16. He went on in a pleased mood to tell about his reaction when he was informed that Shimon was playing soccer on the Sabbath. He immediately went to the playground and shouted at him: "Shimon, why don't you throw away your skullcap and leave school?" With that he turned away. Shimon ran after him, stopped him, and swore that he was only playing basketball. (Soccer players, though unintentionally, apparently perform acts that resemble work religiously forbidden on the Sabbath, such as digging and weeding.) The father was obviously extremely satisfied with his son's reaction, which apparently proved his obliging character.

17. My observations among Moroccans in villages and in a Tel Aviv suburb, as well as information available in the mass media, identify a certain pattern of religious behavior, anchored in the family life and family traditions. Many

Moroccans who do not consider themselves religious, and who are apparently nonobservant, nevertheless do attend synagogue quite often on Sabbath and the festivals, and practice some religious observances and ethnic traditions. The patterns of Ashkenazi Orthodoxy in Israel demand a full cycle of religious life; partial religiosity as observed among many Moroccans is at most attributed folkloric value. I suggest, however, that the religiosity of Moroccans in Israel, deficient as it may appear when considered in terms of Israeli Ashkenazi Orthodoxy, demonstrates the viability of Moroccan family characteristics and sentiments. For more details, see Shokeid (1980c).

References

Amir, M., and S. Shihor. 1975. "Ethnicity and Juvenile Delinquency in Israel" [Hebrew]. *Crime and Social Deviance,* 3:1–15.

Bar-Yosef, R. 1959. "The Moroccans: The Background of a Problem" [Hebrew]. *Molad* 17:247–51. Revised English version 1970, in *Integration and Development in Israel,* S. N. Eisenstadt et al., eds., pp. 419–28. Jerusalem: Israel Universities Press.

Berler, A. 1970. *New Towns in Israel* [Hebrew]. Jerusalem: Israel Universities Press.

Cohen, E. 1972. "The Black Panthers and Israeli Society." *Jewish Journal of Sociology* 14:93–109.

Cooper, S. 1978. *Newgate: An Old-New Town in the Negev.* Ph.D. dissertation, Catholic University of America.

Deshen, S., and M. Shokeid. 1974. *The Predicament of Homecoming: Cultural and Social Life of North African Immigrants in Israel.* Ithaca, N.Y.: Cornell University Press.

Friedlander, D., and C. Goldscheider. 1978. "Immigration, Social Change and Cohort Fertility in Israel." *Population Studies* 32:299–317.

Geertz, H. 1979. "The Meaning of Family Ties." In *Meaning and Order in Moroccan Society,* C. Geertz, H. Geertz, and L. Rosen (New York: Cambridge University Press), pp. 315–91.

Goldscheider, C. 1981. "Family Change and Variation Among Israeli Ethnic Groups." In this volume.

Inbar, M., and C. Adler. 1977. *Ethnic Integration in Israel.* New Brunswick, N.J.: Transaction Books.

Marx, E. 1976. *The Social Context of Violent Behavior: A Social Anthropological Study in an Israeli Immigrant Town.* London: Routledge & Kegan Paul.

Matras, J. 1973. "On Changing Matchmaking, Marriage, and Fertility in Israel: Some Findings, Problems, and Hypotheses." *American Journal of Sociology* 79:364–88.

Palgi, P. 1966. "Cultural Components of Immigrants' Adjustment." In H. P. David, ed., *Migration, Mental Health and Community Services* (Washington: International Research Institute), pp. 71–82.

96   *Moshe Shokeid*

Peres, Y., and R. Katz. 1981. "Stability and Centrality: The Nuclear Family in Modern Israel." *Social Forces* 59:687–704.

Sharot, S. 1976. *Judaism: A Sociology*. London: David & Charles.

Shoham, S., and G. Rahav. 1967. "Social Stigma and Prostitution." *Annales Internationales de Criminologie* 6:479–513.

Shokeid, M. 1968. "Immigration and Factionalism: An Analysis of Factions in Rural Israeli Communities of Immigrants." *British Journal of Sociology* 19:385–406; revised version 1982 in *Distant Relations,* M. Shokeid and S. Deshen, pp. 80–95.

———. 1971. *The Dual Heritage: Immigrants from the Atlas Mountains in an Israeli Village*. Manchester: Manchester University Press.

———. 1980a. "Reconciling with Bureaucracy: Middle Eastern Immigrants' Moshav in Transition." *Economic Development and Cultural Change* 29:187–205.

———. 1980b. "Ethnic Identity and the Position of Women Among Arabs in an Israeli Town." *Ethnic and Racial Studies* 3:188–206.

———. 1980c (n.d.). "Recent Trends in Sephardi Religious Life." Paper prepared for the Tenth International Seminar on Judaism and Secular Society, Bar Ilan University.

———. 1982. "The Regulation of Aggression in Daily Life: Aggressive Relationships among Moroccan Immigrants in Israel." *Ethnology* 21:271–81.

———. 1984. "Cultural Ethnicity in Israel: The Case of Middle Eastern Jews' Religiosity." *AJS Review.*

Shokeid, M., and S. Deshen. 1982. *Distant Relations: Ethnicity and Politics among Arabs and North African Jews in Israel*. New York: Bergin and Praeger.

Shtal, A., 1978. "Prostitution among Jews as a Sympton of Cultural Transition" [Hebrew].*Megamot.* 24:202–25.

Spilerman, S., and J. Habib. 1976. "Development Towns in Israel: The Role of Community in Creating Ethnic Disparities in Labor Force Characteristics." *American Journal of Sociology* 81:781–812.

Statistical Abstract of Israel. 1980. Jerusalem: Central Bureau of Statistics.

Weingrod, A. 1960. "Moroccan Jewry in Transition" [Hebrew].*Megamot* 10:193–208.

———. 1966. *Reluctant Pioneers: Village Development in Israel*. Ithaca: Cornell University Press.

Willner, D. 1969. *Nation-building and Community in Israel*. Princeton: Princeton University Press.

Youth Probation Service Annual Reports. 1977, 1978. Jerusalem: Ministry of Labor and Welfare.

IMAGES OF THE JEWISH FAMILY

7. Jewish Family Images in the English Novel

Anita Norich

The image of the Jewish family in English novels is rather like the position of the Jew within English society: met with no overt violence, subject to various forms of political and social prejudice, the Jew develops into a symbol. In the early English novel, the Jew is simply a literary convention presented in fairly predictable and, of course, stereotypical ways. A comparison of eighteenth- and nineteenth-century English novels is particularly interesting because it highlights this movement from literary convention to symbol. That is not to say that the image of the Jew ever breaks the boundaries of stereotype, but rather that the stereotype assumes a larger and more complex role. As the Jewish figure in English novels assumes this greater role, however, the portrayal of Jewish family relationships becomes increasingly problematic.

Several observations can be made with equal certainty about both the eighteenth- and the nineteenth-century novel. One may convincingly argue that neither period contains an artistically complete Jewish character. There are various sympathetic Jewish figures to offset the generally negative view taken of the Jews, but such characters attest to an author's liberal or reforming tendencies rather than to his or her realistic and aesthetically satisfying treatment of the Jews. Jews are, virtually without exception, seen in some relationship to financial dealings.[1] They are positive figures insofar as they are philanthropic, charitable to one another, or rebelling from the tainted money accumulated by their disreputable ancestors. They are, conversely, unsavory figures insofar as they are unscrupulous moneylenders, lying about the extent of their

99

wealth and the methods by which it was accumulated, attempting—often successfully—to buy their way into what the English like to call polite society.

One implication of this is that the Jew, even when seen in private relations, is primarily a public figure, a stock character representing a type or variations on the type, a spokesperson for tolerance or an excuse for prejudice. Jewish family relations thus become, at best, precarious. Family relationships, functioning within a private sphere where psychological motivation, interactions, and intimacy must be taken into account, are far removed from the public sphere of finance, stereotypes, and arguments for reform in which the Jewish character is normally to be found. Novelists' depictions of the Jewish family reflect this strain. These families are, for the most part, merely adumbrated. They are composed of one parent and one child, generally a father and daughter whose affections are strained by an improper (i.e., Christian) suitor for the girl's hand. Equally common is the solitary Jewish figure, lacking parents, siblings, spouse, children, family of any kind, and instead connected to other Jews by a mysterious financial empire modeled after the Rothschilds'. What we have are two predominating parallel strains which can be seen as different expressions of the prevalent image of the Jew. One strain presents us with the archetypal image of Shylock crying, "Oh my daughter! Oh my ducats!"—the Jew torn between concern for his child and his wealth, desperately lamenting the possibility that the daughter may be lost to him and to the Jewish people but always lamenting the equally tragic fate of his money. The other strain shows us the Wandering Jew, condemned to a nomadic existence, entirely severed from the family hearth, outside the limits of time and space, and yet, like some Romantic heroes, ennobled by the mystery surrounding him. This is the image that attracted the Romantic poets and that figures most prominently in Matthew G. Lewis's Gothic novel *The Monk* (1795). All the traits of such a character are heightened so that he becomes the symbol of all that is profoundly cursed and tortured, while yet possessed of demonic powers and knowledge.

We find the most straightforward representations of the Jew-as-usurer image in eighteenth-century novels. There is nothing in these novels quite as crass and evil as Chaucer's blood libel in *The Prioress's Tale,* but neither is there the complexity of Shakespeare's *Merchant of Venice.* The predominant Jewish image throughout the eighteenth-century novel is closest to a reductive *Jew of Malta.* Barabas, the title character of that play, is Christopher Marlowe's version of the medieval Jewish villain, a one-dimensional evil character. Shakespeare's later creation of Shylock would enlarge the image, humanize it, and make it much more complex than Marlowe allowed. The novelists of the eighteenth century return to Marlowe's presentation of Jews, invoking them only because they have become an easily recognized literary convention. Readers understand that "Jew" is equivalent to "immoral, ruthless usurer." The noun has, in effect, become an adjective requiring no further explication or description. This widely accepted conventional use of the Jew pervades the works of eighteenth-century novelists in a surprisingly uniform way. Certainly such writers as Defoe, Richardson, Fielding, and Smollett are distinct in their modes of presenting characters and have distinct interests in their development. And yet their portrayal of Jewish characters is quite uniform, employing as it does this conventional, flat depiction.

Even when a deliberate (and obviously strained) attempt is made to counterbalance the equation of Jew with evil usurer, authors only highlight the pervasiveness of the convention. Consider, for example, Tobias Smollett's novels, most of which present us with the stereotypical moneylender. In *Ferdinand Count Fathom* (1753) he explicitly attempts to reverse the image by creating a virtuous, benevolent Jew. Joshua Manessah is still a usurer, but now on superb terms with his Christian friends. He clearly serves as a spokesman for tolerance, yet the Jew is still an isolated figure and just as one-dimensional a character as the evil stereotype he is meant to negate. Although at the end of the novel we may assume that Joshua will remain the friend of the people he has helped, we have no clear sense of how he will fit into their society or their families. In later novels, Smollett returned to the minor and unsavory Jewish usurers who had preceded Joshua and who were even less integrated into any family or social structure. This use of reverse but basically similar images illustrates not only the indifference with which Jews were treated but also—and most significantly—the extent to which this literary convention of Jew as usurer was an accepted part of a novel's landscape. The reverse images are essentially interchangeable; neither the good nor evil usurer is integrated into the plot, contributes to the development of characters, or proves significant in the orderly endings of these novels.

The same can very rarely be said of nineteenth-century novels. In their transformation of the conventional use of the Jew into a symbol, later novelists attempt to broaden readers' understanding of Jewish characters as they broaden the parameters of the novel itself. Yet while the sheer number of Jewish characters and the increased significance they assume in nineteenth-century novels attempts to a greater interest, it fails to dispel the continuing haze through which the Jew is seen. Now, however, we also see Jews in varying relationships with others. Often, some part of a novel's Jewish concern is an attempt to resolve confusions about a prospective marriage between a Jew and a Christian and their families' responses to it. Such concern with individual Jews, their families, and marriages becomes more important not because there is a new perception of the Jew but rather because concern with individuality and social and familial relationships assumes a greater urgency for nineteenth-century novelists. In their works we see the intensity of such concerns rather than a new acknowledgment of Jew as private, personalized figure. If these works now suggest a greater tolerance for Jews, it is a tolerance limited to political and, at best, humanitarian considerations, but it still fails to integrate the Jew as a fully developed individual.

Consider, for example, two early nineteenth-century works, one now deemed minor and the other still popular: Maria Edgeworth's *Harrington* (1816) and Sir Walter Scott's *Ivanhoe* (1819). Both profess sympathy for Jews and are, in fact, specifically designed to justify the ways of Jews to Christians. For Edgeworth, *Harrington* is a conscious attempt to reverse the images of Jews presented by others and by herself in earlier works. The good Christian protagonist of this novel falls in love with a Jew and resolves to marry her, thus symbolically indicating his freedom from prejudice and the hope of assimilating Jews into English society. The Jewish girl, dramatically enough, is actually disclosed to be the baptized child of a Protestant mother. While this revelation is in no way meant to detract from the protagonist's selfless love, it obviously undercuts the radical stance toward which *Harrington* seemed to be moving.

Scott has equal difficulty with his Jewish marriage subplot. The Shylock figure, Isaac, and his beautiful, angelic daughter Rebecca are staunchly if inadequately defended by Scott. Here we do see family love and devotion or, rather, we hear protestations of it although there is absolutely no physical, intellectual, or spiritual similarity between these Jewish characters. Ivanhoe and his father, Cedric, are equally distinct from one another, but in his actions, emotions, sense of honor, and pride, Cedric is a far more worthy father for Ivanhoe than Isaac is for Rebecca. A marriage between Ivanhoe and Rebecca is inappropriate not because Scott's plot organically works toward a rejection of such an ending but rather because, as Scott himself explained, "the prejudices of the age rendered such a union almost impossible." While Ivanhoe marries Rowena, Rebecca is left to pursue a wandering life of devotion to others. She remains, through all, pure of mind and deed, resisting both the importunate advances of a sinful Christian religious figure and her own love for Ivanhoe. The price of purity and sympathy, however, is isolation. Scott endows her with some of the characteristics of the Wandering Jew: a lonely, mysterious figure who is not confined to base money interests or social connections. The symbolism is at the same time vague and heavy-handed, and Rebecca collapses into an unconvincingly mystical and, of course, unattainable being.

Impatience with the *Ivanhoe* story, and inversions of it, were predictable. William Makepeace Thackeray's manipulations of the plot and characters pointed farcically to the novel's many flaws and dismissed completely Scott's sympathy for the Jews. In *Rebecca and Rowena: A Romance Upon Romance* (1850), Thackeray's alternative ending is to convert Rowena into a shrew who obligingly dies, and then to convert Rebecca into a Christian who marries Ivanhoe for a brief and miserable time. In *Codlingsby* (1853), an attack on Disraeli's novels and ideas, we see for the first time a Christian conversion to Judaism. But Thackeray's heavily ironic presentation of Ivanhoe's conversion clearly shows how absurd are any implications of Jewish and Christian unions and also what wasted energies are spent on nonsensical defenses of the Jews. Thackeray also seems to have been reacting to the tenuousness of Scott's commitment to full-fledged portrayals of Jews. In these stories he points to the absurdities that would result from following Scott's implications to their conclusion. As he does throughout his works, Thackeray is reacting against hypocrisy. But in this reaction he is also legitimating the stereotypical English cool indifference to the others in their midst.

Like that most prolific Victorian novelist, Anthony Trollope, and other contemporaries, Thackeray could combine a political defense of the Jews with disinterest and an inability to come to terms with them imaginatively. In his novels, Trollope is more sympathetic than Thackeray but not more satisfactory. Whether a Jewish man marries a Christian woman, as in *Nina Balatka* (1867), or a Jewish man is an unsuccessful suitor for a Christian woman, as in *The Way We Live Now* (1875), the Jew continues to stand on the periphery of society. He mingles with the English; now it is even conceivable that he may marry an Englishwoman. He continues, however, as a public mouthpiece for tolerance, an isolated representative of the group as a whole, and a figure whose Jewishness consists of nothing more than financial dealings. Again: Jew as adjective. The appellation "Jew" further begins to refer to anyone with unclear origins and financial dealings. Thus, such diverse characters as Madame Goestler, Mr. Emilius, and Ferdinand Lopez in Trollope's Palliser series all bear the taint of Jewishness. Nor is this use of Jew as epithet limited to Trollope's novels. Even Will Ladislaw in George Eliot's *Middlemarch* (1872) bears the taint of Jewish associations because of his unclear affiliations with financial dealings. Whether or not these characters are Jewish is an entirely insignificant point since the term "Jew" is only intended to signify certain characteristics.[2]

Charles Dickens offers us the most explicit recognition of such reductive perceptions of Jews. After all, as Dickens often pointed out, designating Fagin "the Jew" was simply meant to convey a particular idea of him with which readers would be immediately familiar. In that memorable scene where Fagin is introduced in *Oliver Twist* (1839), calling him the Jew is synonymous with portraying his greasy presence, cooking sausages, brandishing a toasting fork. Fagin, presiding over a parody of family life, mentor and father figure to precocious, quite mature little thieves, undergoes a process of degenerative alienation. It is not the character who changes but rather the artistic conception of him. Rejected by his "family" with which he has never been convincingly integrated, he in turn rejects the Jews who come to pray with him on the eve of his execution, ending his life in a paroxysm of isolated horror.

As Smollett and Edgeworth had done before him, Dickens, in accordance with his role as social reformer, was deliberately to reverse this evil image of the Jew. In his last novel, *Our Mutual Friend* (1865), responding to a famous plea by Mrs. Eliza Davis, Dickens created the character of Riah. A virtuous Jew employed by a reprehensible Christian financier, Riah is the epitome of goodness. He glides through the London fog, staff in hand, blessing all around him, kissing the hem of his employer's garments as if to deprecate his blustering wrath. Yet for all his goodness, he is no more integral a part of proper English or any Jewish world than was Fagin. Questions of marriage or family can never enter into the consideration of either character. When Riah provides a haven for the troubled Lizzie Hexam and the crippled, poignantly disturbed Jenny Wren, we fully understand that he cannot serve as a replacement for the fathers who have caused these girls so much pain. At the end of the novel he is presumably united with his good Christian friends, but he is—atypically within the structure of this novel—assigned no clear conclusion.

To find Jewish characters who are more fully realized and essential to the structure and thematic development of a novel we must turn to George Eliot's last work, *Daniel Deronda* (1876). Here we have the widest spectrum of Jewish characters and English views of them. This final, most mature expression of Eliot's thought has been seen by many as consisting of two separable books: an effective half dealing with the trials and development of its heroine, Gwendolen Harleth, and a forced other half explicating, at much too great length, the dawning Jewish and Zionist commitments of Daniel Deronda.[3] Such a view distorts Eliot's intentions and success in the novel, pointing to sociological rather than aesthetic analyses by her critics. Invariably, English critics responded to this novel by discussing the political absurdities of Zionist preaching. But

Deronda's acceptance of a mission parallels Gwendolen's search for one, and neither character can be fully understood without the light cast by the other..

Eliot's extraordinary knowledge of Jewish ritual, religion, and history creates a sympathetic and fuller view of Jews than ever found in the English novel. We have Jews as artists, moneylenders, pious people, scholars, shopkeepers, gentlemen. We have charming, homey Jewish family scenes but also a worthless father, a dedicated daughter, loving siblings, a mother who renounces her son because she hates the limitations and stigma of Judaism, the son who joyously discovers his Jewish past, a perfect marriage between two Jews, and an equally perfect, if socially questionable, marriage between a supposedly Jewish musician and a genteel Englishwoman. The variety is endless and calls attention to itself, explicitly protesting against Jewish stereotypes by showing a range of very different Jews. The novel also shows the strain of Eliot's passionate defense. There are longer digressions, more convoluted speeches by minor characters, a wider and less fully integrated range of minor characters, particularly Jewish ones, and a greater self-consciousness about time than Eliot's novels generally contain. And even here, where Christians befriend Jews, where Christians are revealed to be Jews, the two groups remain perfectly separable and generally inaccessible to one another. The problem is not with Eliot's sympathetic imagination, or with the novel's structure, or the range of development. The problem of the novel is a historical one: that is, the aesthetic vision, the artistic possibilities, are constrained by the historical moment and by sociological realities. Eliot's artistic achievement is to force her way through these barriers to her imagination and to invite her readers to do the same.

Eliot, as I have suggested, engages in an assault on contemporary barriers. Another Victorian, Benjamin Disraeli, erects them, hides behind their rather flimsy walls, and then taunts his enemies to pursue him. His novels, views, and personality are undoubtedly the most peculiar of any we have considered. And their very peculiarity makes them fascinating. Disraeli's rise to political prominence despite his Jewish birth, his conversion at the ironically significant age of thirteen, his exploits as a dandy, and his wildly romantic novels make him a unique figure. Equally curious are his perversions of English and Jewish history, his search for aristocratic roots of both groups, and his discovery of them in the Disraeli family, culminating in himself. Christianity, Disraeli's novels insist, is the completion of Judaism, fulfilling the prophecies of the Old Testament. Judaism becomes a racial category superior because of the purity of its blood and its longevity. Disraeli always used his novels as extensions of his public personality, first as dandy and then, primarily, as politician. The arguments he presents in his novels are identical to and are meant to serve the political arguments he offered in Parliament and speeches. Often, the very language and tone are identical. We look to Disraeli's novels, then, not for compelling characterization or organic development, but rather for ideas. And his Jewish characters, like all others, are clear embodiments of such ideas.

Consider Sidonia, who appears in several Disraeli novels. He is, as Disraeli presents him, richer than any man in Europe, more brilliant, more handsome, certainly more interesting. He is the perfect example of the Wandering Jew as Rothschild. His empire is based on racial rather than family connections. He has no family, apparently having sprung fully developed from the seed of his superior race, and he can never marry for fear of sullying the purity of his race. David Alroy, Disraeli's version of the twelfth-century messianic leader, fights for the purity of his sister and the integrity of his people, but at the end of what we can only call a weak and insipid tale, he dies an honorable death. Disraeli can do nothing with such characters precisely because they serve the exact function Jewish characters always serve in the English novel: they are disembodied voices, public pronouncements, propaganda of one kind or another. Now, they clearly have greater significance than the stereo-typical moneylenders with which readers are familiar, but whether they are conventions or more complex symbols, they are never successful characters. They are, here as elsewhere, introduced because of sociological or historical considerations rather than aesthetic ones and thus, just as they can never be fully integrated into any social structure including the family, they can also never be fully integrated into the structure of the novels in which they appear.

Why, then, *do* they appear? What accounts for the increasing concern with Jewish characters in the nineteenth- as opposed to the eighteenth-century English novel? And why do Jews or the lack of Jewish families in these novels deserve our attention? The novels discussed here tell us virtually nothing about the Jewish family or the position of the Jew within English society at any period. That is, of course, only another way of making the obvious comment that novels cannot be taken as primary sociological documents. The novels do, however, tell us a great deal about the image of the Jew and imaginative, symbolic uses to which he could be put. Examining Jewish characters within these novels may tell us very little about the Jew but it does tell us a great deal about the English.[4] And what it tells us about them may also inform our understanding of recurrent literary images.

One of the most intriguing elements is that increased interest in the nineteenth century. There are several reasonable ways of accounting for it, quite apart from the increasing volume of English fiction in general.

Jewish figures are more visible in nineteenth-century novels because Jews were more visible in nineteenth-century England due to increased immigration and particularly urbanization. After the readmission of Jews into England in 1655 (following centuries of exile beginning with their official expulsion in 1290), they were very slowly politically reintegrated into English society, achieving full equality only late in the nineteenth century in the midst of reform agitation. But English political and social reforms are notoriously slow and it would be inaccurate to say that nineteenth-century novelists "discovered" the Jewish problem and sought reform. Victorian interest in the Jews is only secondarily due to these considerations.

Victorian novelists used the Jews because Jews represented for them the perfect symbol through which they could reflect their own profoundest concerns. The Victorians were concerned with interpretations of the past; they struggled with theories of race and nationalism, feared the social erosion brought about in the aftermath of industrialization, and were obsessed with money and its new power. In response to this they created historical myths pointing to a purer, more secure, religious, social, economic, and political past. The Oxford Movement, Carlyle's view of feudalism, new examinations of seventeenth-century English history, all point to this. Similarly, they lauded the virtues of moral earnestness, useful labor, family purity, religious adherence, and personal and social order. We should recognize that for all their insistence on these virtues the Victorians deeply feared their own distance from them and, in psychologically understandable ways, indicated that fear by displacing it into channels that could be appropriately removed from the perceived mainstream.

Consider, for example, their concern with sexual purity which marriage and the family unit was to safeguard. The popular image of the Victorians, indeed the very name "Victorian" has become (inappropriately) synonymous with sexual repression and an inability to deal personally or imaginatively with passion. And yet the Victorian era is also the one which saw the proliferation of an extraordinarily broad and popular pornographic literature and of prostitution. I would argue—if I may be pardoned the apparent crassness—that the Victorians used Jews in much the same way they used prostitutes. Both were highly visible, yet the existence of both could still be denied in appropriate circles; both could be imaginatively cast as being peripheral to polite society; and, most crucially, both had something the Victorians rather desperately wanted. In the case of the Jews this was a history, a past that must be honored, a strong group identity, and an informed involvement in financial enterprise. At the same time, albeit often against his own wish, the Jew was an independent figure, potentially unshackled by the strictures of English proscriptive society. Part of what his contemporaries found so objectionable about Disraeli was that he insisted on making these perceptions of the Jews explicit. In a very different, and far superior way, Eliot suggested similar reasons for her interest in the Jews. Other Victorian novelists were less explicit or less articulate about these views but were nonetheless influenced by them in their symbolic use of Jewish figures.[5]

Despite the early indications of family disruption, economic changes, and social unrest to which eighteenth-century novelists bore witness, they were nonetheless more secure in their sense of order and propriety than their nineteenth-century descendants. Pope's Chain of Being was, the clarity of hindsight suggests, inconceivable a century later. The eighteenth-century novelists, then, had less need of such symbolic uses of the Jew or the "others" in their midst. We should not be surprised that eighteenth- and nineteenth-century English novels contain no full view of Jewish family life, no artistically satisfactory marriages or integration of the Jew into larger structures. These were not the issues to concern eighteenth-century novelists. And the Victorians, for all their genuflections at the altar of family sanctity and group cohesiveness, were none too sure that they were in possession of its virtuous effects. The Jewish families—or lack of them—in the novels reflect these uncertainties.

It is useless to refer to the Jew as a scapegoat in the English novel since that term means very little in a literary context. But the Jew emerging from a literary convention used in its most limited ways into a symbol intended (although unable) to sustain greater weight does mean a great deal. Similar examinations can and should be made of any of the minor but recurrent figures in English novels, whether they are set off from the majority by a different nationality, race, religion, occupation, or age. By their very use of these categories as shibboleths, novelists tell us a great deal about their own worldviews and the major concerns of their culture.

Notes

1. For the most authoritative development of this thesis, see Edgar Rosenberg, *From Shylock to Svengali: Jewish Stereotypes in English Fiction* (California: Stanford University Press, 1960).

2. Thomas Pinney, in response to Jerome Beaty, makes a similar point about Eliot's novel. See Jerome Beaty, "The Forgotten Past of Will Ladislaw," *Nine-*

teenth-Century Fiction (NCF) XIII (1958), 159–62; and Thomas Pinney, "Another Note on the Forgotten Past of Will Ladislaw," *NCF* XVII (June 1962), 69–73.

3. F. R. Leavis is the most well-known exponent of this position, but he was later to modify it considerably. See *The Great Tradition* (1948); and "George Eliot's Zionist Novel," *Commentary* 30 (1960), 317–25, also reprinted as the introduction to the Harper Torchbook edition of *Daniel Deronda*.

4. Although he accounts for it differently, Lionel Trilling has made a similar observation. "The Jew in English fiction is a myth," he wrote. "And as with all myths, it tells us more of the hopes and fears of the people that needed it than of the Jews that figure in it." Lionel Trilling, "The Changing Myth of the Jew," *Commentary* (August 1978), 24–34.

5. I would go further and suggest that we can witness a similar phenomenon in contemporary American literature. Our social and personal concerns are different from those of the Victorians. Our society is obsessed with fears about the individual's inability to cope within a chaotic social structure, with emasculated power, with mediocrity, sexuality, effete intellectualism, fragmentation. And in our literature, the Jew has come to stand as modern man, representing all these fears. Thus we have the Jew as schlemiel, as mama's boy, as sexual machine, and as neurotic. But now it is Jewish writers who present the Jew in this way. Perhaps this points to the extent to which they have become acculturated into their society so that now it is Jews, and not others, who view themselves as symbols expressing the age. But that is the subject of quite a different study.

8. Charmed and Vicious Circles: The Study of the Yiddish Family Saga Novel

Susan A. Slotnick

The structure and development of the family is a subject that has been analyzed, examined, and interpreted by sociologists, psychologists, historians, even economists. In a very different way, novelists use this intriguing and complicated set of relationships and attitudes as the focus of novels, or series of novels, which follow generations of fictional families through years and decades of internal tension and external adversity. When we examine the dynamics of these fictional families, we find that they are inextricably bound up with the dynamics of the works in which they appear, works we call family saga novels. The present chapter is a discussion of this type of novel, as it appears in the tradition of Yiddish literature. While the generalizations made here may perhaps be extended to family saga novels of other languages and literatures, a demonstration of that application is beyond the scope of the present discussion.[1]

How do we recognize a family saga novel? It is a novel in which a family, or set of families, is the artistic focus, the structural and thematic center of the work. Thus the institution of the family in general, as well as the specific clan or clans depicted, is chosen by the author to be the unifying element on which the novel is based. In addition to providing

---

This paper is a summary in general terms of research during my tenure as a Mellon Postdoctorate Teaching Fellow at Cornell University.

this almost automatic unity, the focus on a particular family naturally delineates a set of characters, major and minor, with whom the novel will concern itself. The centrality of the family also facilitates an examination of social issues such as marriage, the raising of children, and the relationship between generations. Of course, these thematic characteristics are not limited to family sagas; they are the object of attention in many other types of works. What defines the books that we designate as family saga novels is the structural, artistic centrality of the family as unifying element and, at the same time, the paradoxical use of this same institution to portray breakup—decline, decay, disintegration, and destruction.

It is this tension between unity and chaos, continuity and disruption, that is the distinctive feature of the family saga novel. It is employed by different authors in different ways, toward different ends. And it is interesting, not only for the critics, as a hallmark of this kind of novel, but also for the writers, in the possibilities and difficulties that it presents and the diverse yet related variety of meanings that it enables them to convey in their artistic statements.

This tension, and its various realizations, have not been the focus of previous discussions of the family saga novel in the Yiddish tradition. These discussions tend to concentrate on the social aspects of the works: their relationship to, and judgment of, the societies which they depict; their relative accuracy as historical documents; and their general implications for Jewish life.[2] Other inquiries along the same lines include an investigation of the correlation between these fictional families and real ones, a study of the image of the Jewish family in these novels, or a look at the relationship between changes in fictional representation and historical changes (do the former reflect, predict, or distort the latter?). Of course, all of these socially oriented approaches must ultimately return to the works themselves. And so we may hope to illuminate the social, as well as other, aspects of these novels through an analysis of the artistic use of the family in them, with particular attention to the paradox formulated above: the tension between the vision of the family as synthesizing factor, and, simultaneously, as the symbol of disintegration.[3]

There are a number of ways in which these novels employ the family as structural center. The first model is the most straightforward: the novel portrays the members of a family from youth to old age, with the forward movement of their personal and public lives as the leading principle of construction of the work. This kind of novel divides typically into three parts: youth and early achievement, maturity, and the decline into old age. This three-part movement is usually correlated with the historical background of the novel, and may also be reflected in its geographical parameters. For instance, in Israel Joshua Singer's early novel *Di brider Ashkenazi* (*The Ashkenazi Brothers*, 1936), the careers of two brothers are contrasted, and juxtaposed with a specific bit of history: the economic growth, flourishing, and eventual decline of the industrial city of Lodz in the late nineteenth and early twentieth centuries. The author himself divides the work into three volumes, entitled: (1) Birth; (2) Chimneys in the Sky; (3) Cobwebs. In these very titles, he indicates his organic concept of this story of family and city.

In a later novel, *Di mishpokhe Karnovski* (*The Karnovski Family*, 1943), Singer employs a somewhat more involved version of this straightforward model. There are three generations of Karnovskis, whose careers are complicated by geographic as well as chronological movement. The novel is set in three countries: Poland, Germany, and the United States.[4] In each generation there is a twofold movement: rebellion against the parents, followed by eventual reconciliation. As the family migrates ever westward (as the author sees it, ever further from the Jewishness of Eastern Europe), the swings of the internal pendulum become wider. The first generation rebels by turning to the Mendelssohnian Enlightenment; the second, by discarding even the discrete, private Jewishness of that movement, espousing secular (German) values and culture, and marrying a non-Jew; in the third, most extreme case, by becoming an active anti-Semite (a member of the Nazi party in New York City). It is the radical nature of this last rebellion that finally brings the family back together, though its future is uncertain, since reconciliation is brought about by the ultimate act of self-hate—attempted suicide.

Though ten years, and some degree of artistic sophistication, separate these two novels, Singer's vision of the family as the center of personal strength and cultural vitality is constant and is underscored in both books by his straightforward use of the members of these families as the focal figures of the novels, figures who struggle against the external onslaught of historical forces. The author implies that those who survive will be the ones who keep in contact with their heritage, and who reach back to that heritage, the only dependable source of strength, in times of crisis.

In contrast to this straightforward model of the novel with the family as structural center, typically tripartite in construction, and viewing the family as adversary to history, is the second type of Yiddish family saga novel. Here the story begins, not with the biological initiation of birth and childhood, but at the height of family power. The course of the work follows its decline from that height. In this second type of novel, the force of the family is not one of energy and vitality; rather, it contains within itself the seeds of its own destruction.

Der Nister's unfinished novel *Di mishpokhe Mashber* (*The Mashber Family:* vol. 1, 1939; vol. 2, 1948) is such a work, in which the disintegration of power radiates from the weakness of the family itself. This book is not a sweeping saga, covering large spans of time and space; it is instead a work that reveals its scope in the wider implications of its specifics. *Di mishpokhe Mashber* takes place in one town, with a time span of less than a year. The novel centers around the downward-moving careers of three brothers of the Mashber family, each of whom represents one aspect of the failed potential of the clan: economic, intellectual, and spiritual. In general terms, the loss of power and status alludes to the failure of this aristocratic family to provide any meaningful leadership in a critical period of East European Jewish history (the end of the nineteenth century). And the threefold distribution of the attributes of the family among three brothers, whose individual careers slope downward toward death, insanity, and exile, suggests a more abstract level of meaning: a statement about messianism, redemption, and the potential of various systems of salvation.[5]

A third possibility in this catalog of models is that of parody. One of the best examples of this kind of work is Moyshe Kulbak's comic novel *Zelmenyaner* (*The Zelmenyaner Family:* vol. 1, 1931; vol. 2, 1935), which turns the traditions and conventions of the Yiddish family saga upside down. Though it is evident from the text that the action of the novel takes place in the Soviet Union in the years 1929 and 1930, the dimension of time—usually the chronological backbone of the family saga—refuses, in *Zelmenyaner,* to proceed in a straight line. It begins in the middle and constantly skips forward and backward, with a seeming capriciousness that is in harmony with the facetious tone of the narrator.

Similarly, the very structure of *Zelmenyaner* reveals its comic, satiric quality: the familiar pattern of the family confronted by history and responding with a series of rebellions and reconciliations becomes here a mockery of the "battle of the generations." Without really understanding what they are doing, the younger generation of Zelmenyaners play at rebellion, and their parents perform a charade of resistance and reaction. The external "invading forces" are, alternately, trivial or trivialized; the family goes through grotesquely comic convulsions over such issues as Bolshevism, free love versus arranged marriage, and the mysteries of electricity and radioelectronics. In each case, the mock synthesis of reconciliation results in an idiosyncratic Zelmenyaner version of reality. Most important, this family does *not* disintegrate—it survives by fragmenting reality (instead of itself) and recreating that reality in its own comic image. The erratic, labyrinthine structure of this book embodies

the essential nonmovement, nondevelopment, that Kulbak aims to portray, as it parodies the expected combination of straightforward and
cyclical movements of the family saga novel.

A very different kind of innovation within the Yiddish family saga
novel tradition is a combination of the straightforward organic and of the
cyclical internal models, one which may play without parody on the
expectations of this type of work and explode them in a noncomic
manner. A novel of this kind shows the family in a dual relation to
history. First, the degeneration of the family represents the disruption
and decay of its milieu, of a specific society, and of human life in general.
Second, the decline of the family, and of its individual members, is
reflected and magnified by the external spectacle of destruction and
chaos. A novel of this type has a twofold movement: a forward, chronological line and a circular movement of the generations—the members of
the family who try to break away from it, but are held in an uneasy orbit
by its gravitational pull. Combined, this produces a series of downward-
moving spirals, as the family loses inner vitality and outer power through
time.

Such a novel is Isaac Bashevis Singer's *Di familye Mushkat* (*The
Family Moskat,* 1950). This work focuses on a set of interrelated families
of Jewish Warsaw, from the beginning of the twentieth century to the eve
of the Second World War. Like his older brother, I. J. Singer (to whom *Di
familye Mushkat* is dedicated), Bashevis (as he is known to his Yiddish
readers) presents the family and its members in the grip of the forces of
history. Like Der Nister, he portrays the cycles of a cosmic tragedy in the
microcosmic world of the family. In *Di familye Mushkat,* the conflicts
between generations point up the overall weakening of the family and the
individual; those who instigate rebellions and innovations cannot cope
(any better than those who preserve the old ways) with a rapidly changing world.

The circular movement in this "combination" novel arises from the
senselessness and impotence of major and minor acts of rebellion, since
even (or particularly) those characters who try most desperately to liberate themselves from the old way of life—and from the family—become
the most entangled and trapped in its meshes. Different individuals
endeavor in different ways to break free from this pull; but even those
who intermarry, convert to Christianity, or immigrate to other continents are held by the power of the family, and return to Warsaw at the
end of the book, in 1939, to share in the final destruction of that family
and its world.[6]

Each of the types of family saga novels that we have considered so
far, as well as each of the specific examples, employs the characteristic

paradox of unity and disruption in a different way. The significance of each work is expressed in terms of this tension and its interpretation by each individual author. For I. J. Singer, the best-known writer of the "straightforward" type of family saga in Yiddish, the fate of the family is directly related to its struggles in the context of history; if it declines, it is because its members have been compelled or enticed away by outside forces, which sooner or later prove false and pernicious. The members of the Ashkenazi and Karnovski families also represent the societies of which they are a part; and their struggles and future are allusions to the struggles and future of the Jewish people.

Der Nister uses the Mashber family to show the end of an era in the history of the East European Jewish community. The internal disintegration of these characters has some relevance to the author's evaluation of what happened to the leaders of that Jewish community at the end of the nineteenth century. But this detailed portrayal of the fall of the house of Mashber goes beyond a social or historical critique; it ultimately alludes to the failure of various systems of salvation, on an individual as well as a universal basis. The powers of economic and social status, intellectual acumen and sincere spiritual striving, are all shown to be false paths, as the redemptive powers of the old generation are thoroughly discredited by the end of the first book of this unfinished work. In the context of this dominant downward trend, the only possibility for renewal lies with one of the Mashber grandsons, who, the author hints, represents a lone hope for the future of the family. But the sense of gloom and destruction is the overwhelming tone of the coda to the first (and only extant) movement of this work.

Kulbak's *Zelmenyaner* is a comic, and cruel, look at another time of crisis: the situation of provincial Jewish communities during the early years of the Soviet Union. Far from endorsing or condemning either the older or younger generation, Kulbak's satire is double-edged. And it transcends the topical, as the cycles of generational battles reveal not only the ridiculousness of the Zelmenyaner way of life but the general absurdity of human existence as well. The stubborn instinct for survival, one of the prime characteristics of the Zelmenyaner family, is both heroic and pathetic in the face of this larger absurdity.

Bashevis, too, transcends the specific social and historical parameters of the Warsaw Jewish community, to allude to the larger sphere of the modern world and the fate of the individual who must attempt to live in it. The futility of the quest of the individual for a meaningful existence, or even for a life without unbearable doses of violence and humiliation, demonstrates not just the impotence of the characters but also the arbitrary absurdity and fragmentation of the modern world.

116   *Susan A. Slotnick*

No matter how broad or narrow the scope of each work, a common element of these family saga novels is the way in which they deal with the universal issue of the individual's confrontation with the world. And it is with regard to this issue that we can understand the broadest implications of the paradox of unity and disruption that is central to these novels. On the one hand, the family, as well as being a protagonist in the greater world of history, is itself the first world with which the individual must struggle. In a modern view, it is a world in decline—it is always getting worse. On the other hand, the struggle of the individual for liberation from the family is essentially the struggle for identity and self-recognition—a kind of birth struggle. The climax of this battle is the moment of insight and self-discovery, when the individual has separated himself from the family, and only then can appreciate both himself and his origins. It is an indication of the modern vision, and the integrity, of most of these Yiddish authors that this moment of insight is usually either beyond the ken of the protagonist or is granted at the brink of destruction—at the moment of death.

The focus on the family, which gives unity and definition to novels like the ones we have looked at here, is much more than merely a convenient device for constructing a long piece of fiction. By recognizing the common elements of structural and thematic unity, and examining the works in the light of their similarities as well as their diversity, we can better understand the fascination, and significance, of the paradoxical view of the fictional family as paradigm of unity and symbol of fragmentation.

Notes

1. Even a brief look at the critical literature of other traditions reveals an interest in the issues dealt with here. See, for instance: G. Gersh, "The English Family Novel," *South Atlantic Quarterly* LVI (1957), 207–16; S. Manning, "Families in Dickens," in *Changing Images of the Family,* ed. V. Tufte and B. Myerhoff (New Haven: Yale University Press, 1979), pp. 141–53; D. Palamari, "The Shark Who Swallowed His Epoch: Family, Nature and Society in the Novels of Emile Zola," in *Changing Images of the Family,* pp. 155–72; T. Scanlan, *Family, Drama and American Dreams* (Westport, Conn.: Greenwood Press, 1978); P. Thody, "The Politics of the Family Novel: Is Conservatism Inevitable?", *Mosaic* III (fall 1969), 87–101.

2. There is no general study of family saga novels in Yiddish. Some exam-

ples of what the Yiddish critics have to say about these novels include: Sh. Niger, "Zingers *Di brider Ashkenazi*," *Di tsukunft* (December 1936); M. Ravitsh, "Y. Y. Zingers *Di mishpokhe Karnovski*," *Di tsukunft* (March 1944), pp. 155–58; Y. Y. Trunk, "Y. Y. Zinger," *Di tsukunft* (March 1944), pp. 149–54 (reprinted in Trunk's *Di yidishe proze in poyln in der tkufe tsvishn di beyde velt-milkhomes* [Buenos Aires: Tsentral Farlag, 1949], pp. 108–25); M. Ravitsh, "A khronik fun a mishpokhe—an epos fun a dor: Der Nisters *Di Mishpokhe Mashber*," *Di tsukunft* (July 1944), pp. 457–58; Sh. Bikl, "Natsyionale moments in der yidish-sovetisher literatur," *Di goldene keyt* 29 (1957), 46–49. There is one English article with a somewhat more general approach: M. Schulz, "The Family Chronicle as Paradigm of History: *The Brothers Ashkenazi* and *The Family Moskat*," in *The Achievement of Isaac Bashevis Singer,* ed. M. Allentuck (Carbondale: Southern Illinois University Press, 1969), pp. 77–83.

3. The following discussion is similar, though with a different emphasis, to the introductory section of my paper "*Di familye Mushkat* and the Tradition of the Yiddish Family Saga," in *Essays on Singer,* ed. David N. Miller (in press).

4. For a specific examination of the significance of place in this novel, see S. Slotnick, "Concepts of Space and Society: Melnits, Berlin and New York in I. J. Singer's Novel *Di mishpokhe Karnovski*," *The German Quarterly* LIV (January 1981), 33–43. For a more general discussion, see Y. Y. Trunk, "Y. Y. Zinger," and M. Ravitsh, "Y. Y. Zingers *Di mishpokhe Karnovski*" (cited in n. 2).

5. For a more detailed discussion, and additional critical bibliography on this novel, see Kh. Shmeruk, "Der Nister, hayav veyetsirato," in *Hanazir vehag-diyah* (Jerusalem: Mosad Bialik, 1963), pp. 9–52; and S. Slotnick, "Various Dimensions of a Family Saga: Der Nister's Novel *Di mishpokhe Mashber*," *Working Papers in Yiddish and East European Jewish Studies* (New York: Max Weinreich Center for Advanced Jewish Studies, forthcoming).

6. For a more detailed discussion of this novel, and some bibliography of previous articles, see S. Slotnick, "*Di familye Mushkat* and the Tradition of the Yiddish Family Saga."

9. The Jewish Mother: Social Construction of a Popular Image

Gladys Rothbell

The study of ethnic stereotyping in sociology has been primarily the study of ethnic stereotypes of men. The lazy Mexican, alcoholic Indian, mercenary Jew, dumb Pole, and shiftless black are all male images. While our theories of stereotyping recognize that ethnic stereotypes are created by ingroups about outgroups, we have not focused on the role of gender in the ethnic stereotyping process. We have not explored the question of the gender of ethnic stereotypes, nor have we examined the question of the gender of the creators of these stereotypes.

In this chapter I will use ethnic jokes as a database to explore the interaction between gender and ethnicity in the stereotyping process. The results reported represent preliminary findings from work in progress. My analysis of Jewish mother jokes indicates that they are created and disseminated by Jewish men. Since they are jokes by Jews about Jews, they *can* be viewed as nonhostile ingroup humor. However, I will argue that the evidence does not support this interpretation and points to gender rather than ethnicity as the primary butt of these jokes.

Findings

I examined a sample of twelve books of jokes spanning the period from 1920 through the 1970s. Six of these books, one per decade, were general American humor by non-Jewish authors, and six were compendia of Jewish humor by Jewish authors. This sample contained a total of 6,983 jokes. Of these, a total of 2,234 or 34 percent were about women.

In the books by non-Jewish authors there were 116 jokes about Jews, occurring almost entirely in the decades of the 1920s and 1930s. Of these, 101 or 87 percent were exclusively about Jewish males. The major theme was the Jewish man's extraordinary preoccupation with money, and his lack of scruples with regard to the methods by which the money was obtained.

The stereotypic Jewish mother does not appear at all in the books by non-Jewish men. In those few instances in which Jewish women were included in these jokes, they were either portrayed as promiscuous sex objects, passive vehicles for carrying the main point of the venality of Jewish men, or simply pawns in the male conflict. The latter is illustrated by the following joke (*Anecdota Americana* 1934, 71):

> Pat and Mike were united in one common sentiment, their hatred of Jews. Now it happened once that they parted, and when they met again two years later, Mike had married a Jewess. Pat looked woefully reproachful, but Mike anticipated him.
> "Never mind, Pat," he said, "I know what's on your mind. But you don't understand. That's really the only way to do it to the Jews."

In the Jewish-authored sample of jokes, jokes about Jewish mothers were practically nonexistent in the books from the 1920s and 1930s, and the few that appeared did not resemble the present popular image. The majority of jokes about women were not about mothers but about wives; these accounted for over 40 percent of all jokes about women. Most of these jokes about wives were moderately or extremely hostile, the most popular theme being wishing them dead. Interestingly, the Jewish wives in the Jewish-authored books were the obverse images of the Jewish wives in the books of jokes by non-Jewish authors. Whereas the within-group jokes refer to her ever-present headache to ward off sexual encounters, or her idea of foreplay being three hours of begging by her husband, the outgroup jokes view Jewesses as so sexual that, according to one joke, they aren't even *born* virgins!

Jokes about wives and women have been around for a long time, but jokes about mothers are relatively new. Mothers and virgins carried an aura of sacredness which was not true for wives and women in general. A typical example of the persistent wife/mother dichotomy can be seen in the story (Pollack 1979, 175) about a man who braved a terrible storm to buy two bagels. The baker was incredulous:

> "You came out on a night like this just for two bagels? That's all?"
> "Yes, that's all," answered the man. "Just one for me and one for Pauline."
> "Who's Pauline?"

"Oh what the hell difference is it to you?" answered the man. "Pauline is my wife. Who do you think she is? Would my mother send me out on a night like this?"

An analysis of the jokes in the Jewish-authored books of Jewish humor reveals 142 jokes about Jewish mothers. There were only two about Jewish mothers in the 1920s and only one in the 1930s, amounting to only 4 percent of the Jewish jokes about women in each of these decades. This increased to 11 percent of the Jewish jokes about women in the 1940s; 18 percent in the 1950s; 20 percent in the 1960s; and 21 percent in the 1970s.

These changes are not simply an increase in the same old jokes. The pre-1950 jokes about Jewish mothers are not only less frequent, but are also qualitatively different from the jokes that emerged in the mid-fifties and continued on to the present time. The early jokes paint a more positive picture of the Jewish mother than do the later ones. To the extent that it is possible to discern themes in the scant Jewish-mother jokes before 1950, there appear to be three of them. There is the mother who is self-sacrificing, poor, and pious; the immigrant mother who confronts new language, customs, and institutions; and the immigrant who is trying to socialize her children with respect to moral issues such as sex and gambling.

One such early joke (Richman 1926, 296) tells about a pious Jewish mother who:

> came home from shul on Yom Kippur for a brief respite. To her dismay she saw some chicken bones on the table, on this day of fasting. Her Max, a husky chap of about eighteen, was in the house and he looked too contented to be fasting. The evidence, though circumstantial, was strong against him.
> "Max," pleaded the haggard mother, "what does this mean? Did you eat on Yom Kippur? Woe unto me!"
> "No," said Max, "I did not eat and I am going to prove it to you."
> "He snatched a bottle of milk and in a moment gulped the contents thereof."
> "Now, you see?" said Max triumphantly. "If I had eaten the chicken I wouldn't have drunk the milk. You knew very well that as a Jew I wouldn't drink milk right after eating meat."

Such themes began to change in important ways in the mid-fifties. The new themes became overprotection, boasting about children, clannish ethnocentricism, and a general ignorance and incompetence about matters practical, political, ethnic, cultural, and sexual. In these new themes, normal parental behaviors of protecting children against illness, malnutrition, or physical danger, sacrificing oneself for one's children, and taking pride in their achievements are all made ridiculous by exaggeration to the point of absurdity. Thus we have the endless stories about "my son the doctor," such as the one where:

> Mama asks: "How much it costs to send a telegram?"
> The clerk replies, "Where to, Madam?"
> Mama answers, "To my son, the medical student."

The theme of overprotection is exemplified by the story about the two Jewish mothers who meet again after many years.

> Mrs. Isaacs has become wealthy in the interim, and she invites Mrs. Goldberg to her luxurious new home. The latter is impressed with the lavish surroundings and the many servants. Suddenly, however she sees Sammy, the son of Mrs. Isaacs, being brought into the room in a wheelchair. Mrs. Goldberg approaches Mrs. Isaacs and asks, "My god, what happened to poor Sammy that he can't walk?"
> "Who said he can't walk?" said Mrs. Isaacs. "Of course he can walk, but thanks be to God he doesn't have to."

Stuffing children with food is viewed as yet another manifestation of overprotection. The Jewish mother who will resort to anything to get her child to eat is one of the most popular images, played up in Dan Greenburg's *How to Be a Jewish Mother* (1964) and in the titles of such books as Harry Golden's *Ess Ess Mein Kind* (1966).

The theme of absurd self-sacrifice shows up in the light-bulb riddle:

> Question: How many Jewish mothers does it take to screw in a light bulb?
> Answer: None. She says, "For me I don't need lights."

The remaining themes in the popular Jewish-mother jokes point to her ethnocentricism, her general ignorance, particularly with regard to politics, and her asexuality. There is, for example, the story of:

> The young psychiatrist who had been studying Mrs. Margolis's case for some time, and had finally arrived at a strange conclusion.
> "I don't want to seem rude, Mrs. Margolis," he began somewhat hesitantly, "particularly since I know that you have had nine children and fifteen grandchildren. But—well, do you mind if I ask you an intimate question?"
> "Esk!"
> "Tell me, frankly, just what is your attitude toward sex?"
> "I love it," beamed Mrs. Margolis. "It's the finest store on Fift Evnoo."

In addition to the asexual Jewish mother, there is also the apolitical Jewish mother (Spaulding 1969, 166):

"What do I think of the Second World War?" asked Mama.
"To tell you the truth, I saw it in the movies and I didn't like it!"

This overprotective, self-martyring, boastful, ethnocentric, asexual, apolitical, rich, ignorant woman, who doesn't know the significance of World War II, is a postwar American creation. She is *not* the Yiddishe Mama of the twenties and thirties and forties. Moreover, she is the creation of Jewish men. Jewish mothers appear in only four jokes in the books written by Gentile men, and these four have significantly different themes.

These characteristics attributed to the postwar Jewish mother refer primarily to her behavior as a mother, and secondarily as a woman. They do not refer to her Jewishness per se. In fact, she is portrayed as ignorant of issues of major import for Jews. Thus, despite many Jewish immigrant women having suffered losses of close relatives in the Holocaust, we have a joke about one who is said to believe that the Second World War was a bad movie.

In one of the major collections of Jewish jokes (Spalding 1969), there is a chapter of jokes about anti-Semitism in Eastern Europe, the Third Reich, and the United States. These jokes are primarily confrontations between Jews and anti-Semites or Nazis, and they generally end with a clever retort by the Jew. Out of a total of eighty jokes in this chapter, there is only one joke in which a Jewish woman plays the part of the Jew.

In one of the rare jokes which does refer to Jewish women in connection with anti-Semitism, the Jewish woman does not respond as a Jew (Pollack 1979, 15):

> Natalia was at home in Russia with her elderly aunt when suddenly the door burst open and two burly Cossacks entered.
>
> "All right, you two. Any more at home? We intend to rape every woman in the house!" they announced.
>
> Natalia threw herself in front of her aunt and cried, "Do whatever you will with me, but please spare my aging aunt!"
>
> At this, the aunt pushed the young girl aside. "Why are you interfering, Natalia? A pogrom is a pogrom!"

What is notable about this joke is that the aging aunt does not respond as a Jew to the perpetrators of the pogrom. Even though pogroms were a significant factor in the major migration of Jews out of Russia, the aunt responds to the event as a woman who welcomes an opportunity for a sexual encounter.

These portrayals and nonportrayals of Jewish women in relation to significant Jewish political issues suggest that at least some Jewish men may tend to perceive their female ethnic counterparts less in terms of ethnicity than they perceive themselves. "A Jewess is not a Jew" is a common phrase among anti-Semites (Von Rezzori 1981). It may be that she is not fully a Jew among Jews either.

Discussion

Despite the non-Jewish character of the Jewish mother in these jokes, they are billed as sympathetic ingroup humor. Such an interpretation would require that we ignore psychological attributions of motivations, which are an integral part of the popular image (Jones and Davis 1965; Kelley 1973; Summers and Kiesler 1974; Ross 1977; Jones 1979).

These motivational attributions provide a basis for interpreting the behavior of Jewish mothers as an attempt to dominate their sons, to create dependency, and by self-martyrdom to instill guilt feelings. Such guilt feelings can then, allegedly, be manipulated for other purposes. This control through dependency and guilt then supposedly allows Jewish mothers to manipulate their sons into behaviors such as becoming "my son the doctor." The Jewish mother can then bask in the reflected glory of her son's achievements, while he spends all his money on visits to the psychiatrist because his mother had made him so crazy.

There is the story about the three Jewish mothers who are bragging to one another about their sons:

> The first two brag about the generosity of their sons who buy them the best of foods and send them to Florida every winter to the best hotels. The third mother then says, "What I'm going to tell you about my Irving you're not going to believe. He is going three times a week to see a man; he pays him sixty dollars an hour; and what do you think he does when he goes there? All he does is talk about me."

And what does this man, whom the son is talking to, believe about Jewish mothers? A noted psychiatrist, Theodore Reik (1962, 83), explains the motivations of the Jewish mother as follows:

> Jewish jokes ascribe to mothers an inclination to stuff their children, and worry that their sons do not eat enough or not the right food. *It is as if Jewish mothers tried to make the nutritional symbiosis of babyhood and with it the dependence of their children on them permanent.* [Emphasis added.]

Another psychotherapist, Maurice Temerlin (1972, 32), offers the following definition of the Jewish mother:

> The Jewish mother, as I am using the term, refers to a very primitive form of personality organization, the salient features of which are using guilt to

manipulate, speaking in double-binds . . . and masking hostility with self-deprecation and obsequiousness. . . . [It is] a mixture of sex, aggression, and hostility masked by sanctimony that is characteristic of the Jewish mothers when controlling by guilt.

Such conceptualizations of the psychological motivations of the Jewish mother make it difficult to view the stereotype as a sympathetic ingroup portrayal. Yet the joketellers as well as the psychiatrists have gone out of their way to make a special point of telling us how much they love and respect the Jewish mother (despite her shortcomings); about how these jokes are really expressions of love; and about how they're only kidding anyway.

Here are some examples of these protestations. From Temerlin (1972, xviii), whose definition of Jewish mothers we heard earlier:

I had anxiety lest this offend my mother, of whom I am fond. [A colleague] reassured me that " . . . mothers are always treated badly in books, and I am sure that your Jewish mother would rather be your Jewish mother than Philip Roth's . . ."

From Sam Levinson (1948, 99):

Although the stories in this section tend to "kid" the ladies, they are not to be taken as the accepted or acceptable Jewish attitude toward women . . .

From Spalding (1969, xvi), who has ninety-three Jewish-mother jokes in his books:

[These jokes] . . . are a kiss with salt on the lips, but a kiss nevertheless. . . . The Yiddishe Mama has become a stereotype, but, what lovely expressions of tenderness these stories convey.

From Theodore Reik (1962, 35), a psychoanalyst:

As for the sons, the fact that they sometimes make fun of their mothers' weaknesses and peculiarities, does not, of course, exclude their deep love for their mothers. . . . These jokes are never offensive, but only teasing and full of affectionate and protective compassion.

The gentlemen protest too much, displaying understandable discomfort with Jewish-mother jokes and concepts. Insofar as these jokes and concepts are hostile in intent and content, these men are helping to create a new negative Jewish stereotype.

Jewish sensitivity to stereotyping has a long history, and public sensitivity to the stereotyping of Jews increased after the Holocaust.

Under these circumstances, why did Jews create a new Jewish stereotype in the postwar period? And why was it focused on mothers?

One explanation is that the rules of morality regarding negative ethnic and racial stereotyping do not extend to women and to gender stereotyping. A book of jokes by Isaac Asimov (1971) provides a good case in point. Asimov, who is Jewish, declares that he finds ethnic jokes offensive. However, he does not refrain from telling Jewish-mother jokes. He prefaces these jokes with the following comments (p. 222):

> And this brings up the matter of the Jewish mother . . . with her over-solicitousness, her interfering ways, her selfish demands hidden under a strident appearance of sacrifice. Feh!
>
> I must say though, that the stereotype, like all stereotypes, is greatly exaggerated, and that Jewish *ladies* do not take kindly to it. [Emphasis added.]

Asimov's last sentence is telling. He does not expect Jewish *gentlemen* or anybody else to be particularly disturbed by the stereotype. No doubt he would expect all decent people to be disturbed by a similar new wave of stereotyping of Jewish men.

His first sentence is telling as well. It is difficult for me to imagine that he could write and publish similar hostile generalizations about Jews—that is, Jewish men. He speaks of "interfering ways," "selfish demands hidden under a strident appearance of sacrifice," and he polishes it off with an expression of general disgust: "Feh!" He is free from implication because while he is Jewish, he is not a mother. It is an issue for the "ladies."

Other possible contributing factors to the rise of this stereotype at this time suggest themselves when we examine the social context in which this image was created. In the interests of brevity, I list some of these without elaboration:

1. The popularization of the psychologistic perspective into the general culture after World War II laid the groundwork for the legitimization of the ridiculing of mothers.

2. Since virulent anti-Semitic stereotypes have always focused on Jewish men, with Jewish mothers notable by their absence, a Jewish *mother* stereotype would not call to mind prior hostile stereotypic images of Jews. The acceptability of the Jewish mother stereotype to those who find ethnic stereotyping offensive may rest on a basic (though often unconscious) perception of females as nonethnic.

3. There was a phenomenal rise in popularity of the Jewish comedian and novelist in the United States during the postwar period. These men, overrepresented on both sides of the psychiatric desk, quite naturally wrote about and joked about their own lives and families.

Conclusions

The popular image of the Jewish mother is based on the imagination and special perceptions of her sons acting in the roles of gag writers, novelists, comedians, and psychiatrists, among others. It would be difficult to gauge the extent to which the perceptions of the novelists and comedians were influenced by psychologistic conceptions of Jewish mothers; or the extent to which the psychiatrists and psychotherapists were influenced by *their* exposure to the one-sided reports about Jewish mothers presented to them by their clients, the Jewish sons, novelists, and comedians; or the extent to which they were influenced by their own filial prejudices.

The maintenance of distance and scientific objectivity with regard to the Jewish mother, therefore, presents a particularly difficult challenge for these providers of psychological services and theories. Confusion of subjective personal and client perceptions with objective scientific thinking is a constant danger. Theodore Reik (1962) falls into this trap. He uses jokes and client reports as if they were objective data on Jewish mothers. He views the jokes about food as evidence of a "domineering attitude that many Jewish mothers have towards their sons" (p. 83) and says that Jewish mothers "have some characteristic features of which the joke makes fun, for instance, their *primitive nature*" (p. 84). Reik makes no differentiation between the Jewish mother and the stereotype of the Jewish mother. Rather than analyzing wit in relation to the unconscious, he takes the manifest content of the joke as evidence for his theory of Jewish motherhood.

Entertainers, novelists, and psychologists, many of whom shared a common ethnic background, have reinforced one another in the social construction of the popular image of the Jewish mother. Once the image achieved popularity, it became not only a social construct but also a successful commercial commodity. This development placed pressure on the original creators of the image to protect themselves against charges of hostile intent or exploitation for personal gain.

They have argued that the Jewish-mother jokes are instances of sympathetic ingroup humor—Jews joking about Jews. This is a useful distinction for the examination of male ethnic stereotypes. The study of a *female* ethnic stereotype—in this case the Jewish mother—complicates the issue by introducing gender difference. When that occurs, the complexity of distinguishing between ingroup and outgroup stereotypes is very much increased. This problem is rare owing to the usual pattern of gender homogeneity among creators and objects of male ethnic stereotypes.

The unspoken rule of acceptability of ingroup humor presumes a homogeneity of interests and identities *within* ethnic groups (and hence between the creators and the objects of the jokes), which may be unwarranted. Common ethnicity can serve to obscure the basic classist, ageist, or sexist nature of a joke. This may well be the case in the social construction of the Jewish mother image.

General References

Anonymous. 1934. *Anecdota Americana*. New York: Nesor Publishing Company.

Asimov, Isaac. 1971. *Treasury of Humor*. Boston: Houghton Mifflin Company.

Golden, Harry. 1966. *Ess Ess Mein Kind*. New York: Putnam's.

Greenburg, Dan. 1964. *How to Be a Jewish Mother*. Los Angeles: Price/Stern/Sloan.

Jones, Edward E. 1979. "The Rocky Road from Acts to Dispositions." *American Psychologist* 34: 107–17.

Jones, Edward E., and Keith E. Davis. 1965. "From Acts to Dispositions: The Attribution Process in Person Perception." In L. Berkowitz, ed., *Advances in Experimental Social Psychology*, vol. 2. New York: Academic Press.

Kelley, Harold H. 1973. "The Processes of Causal Attribution." *American Psychologist* 28: 107–28.

Levinson, Sam. 1948. *Meet the Folks (A Session of American-Jewish Humor)*. New York: The Citadel Press.

Reik, Theodore. 1962. *Jewish Wit*. New York: Gamut Press.

Ross, Lee. 1977. "The Intuitive Psychologist and His Shortcomings: Distortions in the Attribution Process." In L. Berkowitz, ed., *Advances in Experimental Social Psychology*, vol. 10. New York: Academic Press, pp. 173–220.

Summers, Shirley Feldman, and Sara B. Kiesler. 1974. "Those Who Are Number Two Try Harder: The Effect of Sex on Attributions of Causality." *Journal of Personality and Social Psychology* 30: 846–55.

Temerlin, Maurice. 1972. *Lucy: Growing Up Human*. Palo Alto, Calif.: Science and Behavior Books.

Von Rezzori, Gregor. 1981. *Memoirs of An Anti-Semite*. New York: The Viking Press.

Joke Sample References

Books of Jokes by Non-Jewish Authors (listed in chronological order)

Cobb, Irvin S. 1923. *A Laugh a Day Keeps the Doctor Away*. Garden City Publishing Co.

Deponcet, Edwin Stanton. 1938. *Better Stories, Jokes and Toasts.* Boston: Meador Publishing Co.

McManus, George. 1947. *Fun for All (A Collection of Jokes, Anecdotes and Epigrams Without Moral or Serious Intent).* Cleveland: World Publishing Co.

Godfrey, Arthur. 1952. *Stories I Like to Tell (306 of the Best Jokes and Anecdotes I Have Heard in Twenty Years of Radio and TV).* New York: Simon & Schuster.

True, Dr. Herbert G. 1968. *Laugh Oil.* Indianapolis: The American Humor Guild, Miles Press.

Pendleton, Winston K. 1978. *505 Jokes You Can Tell.* St. Louis: The Bethany Press.

Books of Jokes by Jewish Authors (listed in chronological order)

Richman, Jacob. 1926. *Laughs from Jewish Lore.* New York: Funk & Wagnalls Co.

Hershfield, Harry. 1932. *Jewish Jokes.* New York: Simon & Schuster.

Mendelsohn, Felix S. 1941. *Let Laughter Ring.* Philadelphia: The Jewish Publication Society of America.

————. 1951. *The Merry Heart.* New York: Bookman Associates.

Spalding, Henry D. 1969. *Encyclopedia of Jewish Humor.* New York: Jonathan David Publishers.

Pollack, Simon. 1979. *Jewish Wit for All Occasions.* New York: A. & W. Publishers.

DEMOGRAPHIC VARIATIONS IN CONTEMPORARY JEWISH FAMILIES

10. Family Change and Variation Among Israeli Ethnic Groups

Calvin Goldscheider

Two major, interrelated themes dominate the analysis of Israeli society: (1) the analysis of rapid changes over time for a variety of immigrant groups from diverse countries of origin, particularly those from the less-developed societies of Asia and North Africa, and (2) variation among Israel's Jewish population along several dimensions of social life. Change—often extensive and concentrated in short time periods—and variations—often substantial and wide-ranging—reflect a complex set of structural and cultural conditions in Israel. These include: (a) demographic factors (immigration patterns, country of origin and time of arrival of immigrants, length of exposure to Israeli society, and generation); (b) social structural conditions (including residence patterns and regional location, education, occupation, and socioeconomic status); and (c) cultural values (religiosity, ideological issues, and the broad question of ethnic-cultural traditions and norms). In short, change and variation reflect the background baggage that groups of immigrants brought with them and their experiences in Israel.

These broad themes of change and variation apply clearly to the analysis of the changing family structure of Jews in Israel. Indeed, changes over time and heterogeneity at any point in the family structure of Jews in Israel are among the most salient and conspicuous features of Israeli society. An analysis of Jewish family patterns in Israel is therefore one key to understanding the broader patterns of change and variation in

This chapter was written while I was visiting professor of Contemporary Jewish studies, Center for Modern Jewish Studies, Brandeis University, and adjunct professor of sociology, Brown University.

Israel. To the extent that the family is central to a wide range of related social processes, the Jewish family in Israel may be the most fundamental and important unit of analysis of these broader processes. The diversity of Jewish family patterns in Israel reflects in microcosm the diversity of Jewish (and general) family patterns in countries outside of Israel over the last several decades. As has been noted many times, such diversity and change compressed in time make the analysis of family patterns in Israel valuable for the general analysis of family change and variation, and certainly for the analysis of Jewish patterns around the world.

The objective of this chapter is to review some of the major dimensions of these changes and variations in Jewish family structure in Israel and point to selected processes that may be generalized from these patterns. As we analyze these family patterns in Israel we need to bear in mind that diversity and change are set against the background of the socioeconomic transformation of immigrants to Israel from Asian and African countries, the socioeconomic dominance of European-American groups, and the general modernization of Israel society over time. In this regard we need to stress that Asian and African immigrants to Israel have been doubly disadvantaged. First, they came from countries of origin that were less developed economically and they in turn had lower levels of education and occupation than the society of destination. Second, Asian and African immigrants arrived in Israel in periods subsequent to the major waves of immigration of European migrants (see Friedlander and Goldscheider 1979). Hence, Asians and Africans in Israel were less able to take advantage of the initial socioeconomic opportunities available. Over time, they were unable to compete successfully with European control over economic and political resources. The timing of immigration and cultural differences among ethnics reinforced the structural background factors separating these ethnic Jewish communities (cf. Goldscheider 1983).

The focus of this chapter is on the impact of socioeconomic transformations in Israel on five specific family processes. These include changes and variations in (1) the proportion married, (2) the timing of marriage, (3) mate selection and ethnic intermarriage, (4) reproduction, and (5) divorce. Unless otherwise indicated, the data reviewed refer to the Jewish population of Israel, and were obtained from official census, registration, and vital statistics sources in Israel.

Marriage: Extent and Timing

An examination of the proportion married shows that an overwhelming proportion of Jewish men and women marry at least once. The pattern is simply one of universal marriages by age thirty-five with little ethnic or other systematic variation. The proportions are well over 95 percent. While it is problematic to infer norms from behavior, these data seem to reflect the enormous value placed on marriage, the emphasis on family within Israeli/Jewish culture, and the centrality of the family unit socially, economically, and culturally. This pattern of universal marriages is not surprising given the universality of marriage among Jews from Asian and African countries as well as among those from Eastern Europe. Although it is difficult to document empirically, the major change in the proportion married is for West European Jews who are likely to have increased their propensity to marry subsequent to immigration to Israel.

Recent evidence in Israel points to the emergence of some postponed marriage among young men and women. Annual marriage rates have been lower in 1974–78 than in previous periods. These new patterns are not fully documented or analyzed, and it is premature to conclude whether these are new trends or period effects that are transitory. These changes reflect some marriage-market problems related to cohort fertility declines and past immigration patterns as well as some sex-selective emigration from Israel. They may also reflect economic problems, housing costs, and some greater liberalization of living arrangements norms. Nevertheless, the overwhelming pattern remains, of high marriage rates and family formation, with small fluctuations and variations.

If Jews tend to marry at some time in the life cycle, when do they marry? Data in Table 1 show that age at marriage for those marrying in Israel *increased* for Asian-Africans (brides and grooms) and *decreased* for European-American grooms, remaining relatively stable for brides. Hence, by 1975 the average age at marriage of Asian-African brides and grooms was about the same as for European-American brides and grooms (age twenty-five for men and twenty-two for women). This contrasts with a decade and a half earlier when European-American brides and grooms married an average two years later than Asian-Africans. The Israeli-born category is too heterogeneous for analysis (no data are available by ethnic origin), but the important point to note is the difference between the Israeli and the foreign-born.

These data suggest (and other more detailed census data show) that over time a process of convergence in the timing of marriage has occurred for the two major Jewish ethnic groups. This convergence does not reflect changes in one group toward the other or toward some native-born Israeli model. Rather, the convergence has been the product of changes in *both* ethnic groups toward a *new* model. While no ethnic differences in age at marriage appear in recent years, the paths or processes toward that similarity have been very different. Convergence around a new, emerging model is different from both the European and

Table 1. MEDIAN AGE OF MARRIAGE OF SINGLE GROOMS AND BRIDES BY
PLACE OF BIRTH, JEWISH POPULATION, ISRAEL, 1960–75

	Asia-Africa	Europe-America	Israel
Grooms			
1960	24.7	27.1	24.2
1965	24.8	26.7	24.1
1970	24.6	23.6	23.6
1975	25.2	25.4	23.3
Brides			
1960	20.1	22.1	21.2
1965	20.9	20.5	21.6
1970	22.1	22.5	21.1
1975	22.7	22.4	21.5

Source: *Statistical Abstract of Israel,* various issues.

Asian-African communities of origin, reflecting, not surprisingly, the
social and economic conditions of Israeli society.

Interethnic Marriages

One context for examining ethnic continuity and change in Israel, and a
critical part of the analysis of family structure among ethnic groups, is
the issue of mate selection. Ethnic intermarriage has been viewed in Israel
largely in the context of the integration of immigrant groups into the
national Jewish society. Ideologically, ethnic origin is viewed primarily as
a Diaspora trait, at best a cultural legacy, and largely "transitional"—it
most likely will not persist beyond the second generation. As we shall
see, this is not necessarily the case empirically.

We begin with the changing levels of interethnic marriages. Overall,
the data available from marriage records in Israel show a slow but steady
increase in ethnic out-marriages. In 1955, less than 12 percent of the
marriages taking place in Israel were between persons of Asian-African
origins and persons of European-American origins. In the subsequent
two decades, the level increased to 19 percent. An index used to measure
the extent of endogamy prepared annually by the Central Bureau of
Statistics of Israel shows a steady decline from 0.81 to 0.64 in the years
1955–75.

The increase in ethnic intermarriage within the Jewish population is clearly a conservative indicator of the total range of ethnic intermarriages. The unit of analysis is "continent" of birth and origin and that is quite broad (although of enormous symbolic significance). Marriages between Asians and Africans and between Europeans and Americans, and between persons of different countries of origin within these broad continents, are defined as "homogamous" marriages. Nor are generational distinctions (foreign-born and Israeli-born) included in these data. Census data from 1961 and 1972 clearly show the increase in intermarriage levels by generation status (Matras 1973).

Increases in ethnic out-marriages reflect the loosening of ethnic constraints and the weakening of ethnic boundaries. In part, they reflect some patterns of ethnic integration. Very likely they also reflect the tensions between very strong norms that encourage marriage and family formation, on the one hand, and the limitations of small marriage markets or marriage "squeezes" on the other. For selected numbers of persons marrying in Israel, the choice has become to insist on intraethnic group marriages and face a limited market of choices (or no choice and hence nonmarriage) or to delay marriage or marry out of the ethnic group—i.e., to broaden the range of eligibles. As we have shown earlier, some delayed marriages have occurred as has a broadening of the pool of eligibles. In part, therefore, the increase of ethnic intermarriages in Israel is not only an indicator of the assimilation of ethnics but may also reflect a traditional response to the pressures of marriage and family.

Furthermore, whatever the determinants of intermarriages across ethnic lines, two facts are beyond dispute: (1) the level of ethnic intermarriages, however defined, has increased, and (2) there are implications of ethnic intermarriages for the strength and form of ethnic identity-continuity for the next generation. In this context, ethnic intermarriages are viewed not only as a consequence (or indicator) of assimilation but as a cause of ethnic changes as well.

The identification of the increased levels of interethnic marriages is only the first step, since issues of mate selection and exchanges are more complex. Detailed cross-sectional data in Table 2 divide the population into native and foreign born for the two broad ethnic groups and separate ethnic origin for brides and grooms. These data show that by the late 1970s the levels of ethnic homogamy are very high for all groups—80 percent of the foreign-born brides and grooms and 75 to 80 percent of the native-born marry within their own ethnic group. Ethnic homogamy is higher for Asian-Africans than for European-Americans and for foreign than native-born. Asian-African brides are slightly more likely to marry out of their ethnic group than are Asian-African grooms, indicating the possible connections between marriage and social mobility for women.

Table 2. INTER- AND INTRAETHNIC MARRIAGES IN ISRAEL, JEWISH BRIDES
AND GROOMS, 1977

Ethnic origin of groom	Total %	Ethnic origin of bride			
		Asia-Africa		Europe-America	
		Foreign	Israeli	Foreign	Israeli
Asia-Africa					
Foreign-born	100.0	46.1	38.5	7.5	7.8
Israeli-born	100.0	17.8	65.5	5.0	11.7
Europe-America					
Foreign-born	100.0	9.0	10.7	56.0	24.3
Israeli-born	100.0	7.9	20.5	16.1	55.5

Ethnic origin of bride	Total %	Ethnic origin of groom			
		Asia-Africa		Europe-America	
		Foreign	Israeli	Foreign	Israeli
Asia-Africa					
Foreign-born	100.0	58.3	23.7	8.7	9.3
Israeli-born	100.0	28.6	51.2	6.1	14.2
Europe-America					
Foreign-born	100.0	10.6	7 .5	60.6	21.3
Israeli-born	100.0	8.7	13.6	20.5	57.2

Calculated from Israel Central Bureau of Statistics, *Vital Statistics 1977*, Special Series No.
609 (Jerusalem, 1979), Table 19.

In contrast, European–American brides are more likely to marry homogamously than European–American grooms. Overall, however, differences by sex, ethnic origin, and nativity are relatively small.

The complexities increase when detailed country of origin is examined. The variations among countries and between men and women in
the extent of out-marriage are substantial (see Tables 3 and 4). The
proportion of foreign-born grooms marrying Israeli-born brides, for
example, ranges from 60 percent for grooms born in Libya to 15 percent
of grooms born in the Soviet Union. The proportion of grooms who
marry brides from different continents and different ethnic groups is
generally less than 10 percent except for grooms from Bulgaria-Greece,
Turkey, and Egypt. For these, the country classification may be less
indicative of cultural background (e.g., many Bulgarians may not be
European but "Sephardic").

With but one exception (brides born in Syria-Lebanon), the proportion of foreign-born brides marrying native-born grooms is lower than
the proportion of foreign-born grooms marrying Israeli-born brides.
With some exceptions, foreign-born grooms marry out of their ethnic
group more than foreign-born brides.

Table 3. MARRIAGE PATTERNS OF FOREIGN-BORN JEWISH GROOMS IN
ISRAEL BY COUNTRY OF BIRTH, 1977

Place of birth of groom	Bride Israeli-born	Same country	Same continent, different country	Different continent, same ethnic group	Different continent, different ethnic group
Asia					
Iraq (689)	56.5	16.5	4.8	13.6	8.3
Iran (508)	47.4	35.4	4.9	7.8	4.5
Turkey (273)	49.1	24.2	5.1	11.0	10.6
Yemen-Aden (195)	52.3	24.6	7.7	8.7	6.7
Syria-Lebanon (98)	42.9	18.4	13.3	17.3	8.2
Africa					
Morocco (2971)	46.6	39.6	4.6	2.7	6.5
Algeria-Tunisia (601)	47.4	19.8	23.1	4.5	5.2
Egypt (259)	54.1	9.7	17.8	5.4	13.1
Libya (159)	60.4	8.2	17.6	8.8	5.0
Europe					
USSR (1336)	15.5	72.0	7.4	1.9	3.1
Romania (1109)	42.6	31.7	14.1	2.5	9.2
Poland (637)	42.2	18.7	25.9	3.9	9.3
Germany-Austria (189)	59.3	8.5	23.8	2.6	5.8
Hungary (124)	53.2	5.6	27.4	6.5	7.3
Bulgaria-Greece (89)	49.4	6.7	18.0	1.1	24.7
Czechoslovakia (81)	42.0	9.9	38.3	2.5	7.4
America					
United States (380)	56.1	19.2	3.4	12.4	8.9
Argentina (207)	45.9	27.1	10.6	7.2	9.2

Calculated from Israel Central Bureau of Statistics, *Vital Statistics, 1977*, Special Series No.
609 (Jerusalem, 1979), Table 24.

Table 4. MARRIAGE PATTERNS OF FOREIGN-BORN JEWISH BRIDES IN ISRAEL
BY COUNTRY OF BIRTH, 1977

Place of birth of bride	Groom Israeli-born	Groom foreign-born			
		Same country	Same continent, different country	Different continent, same ethnic group	Different continent, different ethnic group
Asia					
Iraq (308)	26.0	37.0	9.7	11.0	16.2
Iran (494)	41.3	36.4	7.5	10.1	4.7
Turkey (205)	35.1	32.2	6.8	10.2	15.6
Yemen–Aden (124)	33.9	38.7	11.3	7.3	8.9
Syria–Lebanon (97)	51.5	18.6	11.3	12.4	6.2
Africa					
Morocco (2589)	34.4	45.5	17.7	15.7	7.2
Algeria–Tunisia (505)	37.0	23.6	27.1	5.3	6.9
Egypt (144)	41.0	17.4	16.7	8.3	16.7
Libya (72)	31.9	18.1	13.9	20.8	15.3
Europe					
USSR (1491)	13.3	64.5	14.8	1.4	6.0
Romania (893)	38.3	39.3	14.1	1.2	7.1
Poland (362)	31.8	32.9	22.1	2.5	10.8
Germany–Austria (118)	38.1	13.6	35.6	6.8	5.9
Hungary (63)	27.0	11.1	47.6	3.2	11.1
Bulgaria–Greece (38)	44.7	15.8	13.2	0.0	26.3
Czechoslovakia (50)	30.0	16.0	46.0	0.0	8.0
America					
United States (422)	50.2	17.3	4.3	12.3	15.9
-Argentina (200)	43.5	28.0	6.0	11.0	11.5

Compiled from Israel Central Bureau of Statistics, *Vital Statistics 1977*, Special Series No.
609 (Jerusalem, 1979), Table 24.

The variations reflected in these data are less suggestive of cultural determinants than factors associated with the size of the marriage market, length of time in the country, size of the ethnic group, residential-geographic distribution, and so forth. In short, demographic and social structural factors seem to be the most likely sources of variations rather than differential values associated with ethnic group cohesion or differential socioeconomic disadvantage. It seems unlikely that variations in ethnic intermarriage by sex and country of origin reflect differential preferences or "desires" for integration or different values associated with endogamy.

Reproduction

Fertility levels and variations in Israel have been studied extensively, and reinforce some of the major family patterns I have been describing. These include: (1) overall, relatively high levels of Jewish fertility in Israel relative to Jews elsewhere and to more developed nations; (2) the relationship of these fertility patterns (behaviors and norms) to family structure and familism; and (3) major ethnic convergences in fertility levels and norms. In particular, fertility reductions among Asian-Africans have been dramatic over the last several decades and the fertility gap between Asian-African and European-Americans has narrowed considerably. The reductions in Asian-African fertility have been compressed in a short time span, without government intervention, with the retention of relatively high fertility norms and the general absence of modern contraceptive usage (see Goldscheider and Friedlander 1981).

One aspect of this dramatic fertility reduction relates to the transformation of family structure among Asian-African immigrants, particularly the changing control of families over economic resources and the changing roles of women. The decline in Asian-African fertility preceded major socioeconomic mobility. Changes in family structure generated by the immigration process—the breakdown of the family-economic connection—and the exposure to an opportunity structure outside of the control of the extended family are among the critical processes that resulted in the sharp decline in family size among Asian-African immigrants (see Friedlander and Goldscheider 1978).

Several illustrative statistics reveal these changes among Asian-African women. Gross reproduction rates in the twenty-five years following 1951 fell steadily among Asian-African women, by 46 percent from 3.1 in 1951 to 1.7 in 1977; total fertility rates declined by about one child each decade, from 5.7 in 1955 to 4.6 in 1965 and 3.8 in 1975.

Fertility convergences between Asian-African and European-American women have occurred, but not all differences have been eliminated. In 1977, for example, the total fertility rate of Asian-African women was 3.4 compared to 2.8 among European-born women. An examination of the parity distribution of births in 1977 reinforces this point. Of the 71,809 Jewish births, 3,923 or 5.5 percent were of the sixth or higher birth order. Asian-African-born women accounted for 72 percent of these higher-order births while accounting for about 30 percent of all births. Viewed in another way, 12.5 percent of all births to Asian-African-born women in 1977 were higher-parity births compared to 3.5 percent of the births to European women.

A detailed study of cohort fertility patterns among Israel's Jewish ethnic subpopulations allowed for the examination of retrospective histories of Asian and African women of the first and second generations. These data document clearly the sharp decline in fertility for cohorts of women from Asian and African countries. For Asian migrants, for example, fertility fell by 50 percent for cohorts marrying twenty-five years apart—from 6.5 births to just over three births. This decline occurred ten to fifteen years later for Asian women who immigrated after 1948 when compared to those who immigrated before the establishment of the state. After twenty years of marriage, 75 percent of the Asian women from the marriage cohort 1930–34 had five or more births; only 17 percent of the women marrying 1950–54 cohort had five or more births. Identical patterns characterize African-born women. Differences between African and Asian women are in the initial levels of fertility (which have been higher for African women). However, when length of exposure to Israeli society is examined, African fertility levels declined in precisely the same way as Asian fertility levels (Friedlander and Goldscheider 1978).

The remarkable "fit" between exposure to Israel and fertility decline has resulted in clear convergence in the fertility patterns between Asian and African women and between Asian-African women and those born in Europe (both West and East). These convergence patterns are already evident for foreign-born women and reinforced among the second generation. Israeli-born women of Asian-African origins have lower fertility than their foreign-born mothers, while second-generation European-origin women have higher fertility than their first-generation European-born mothers. Fertility convergence between second-generation Israelis of Asian-African and European origins is, therefore, the result of generational declines for Asian-African women and generational increases for European women.

Further clarification of these fertility convergences may be obtained by examining fertility norms. Among older marriage cohorts of Asian and African women, family size desires tend to be lower than actual family size—i.e., fertility levels exceeded fertility desires. Among more recent marriage cohorts there is a congruence between family size desires and expectations. The data in Table 5 suggest that over time, family size norms among Asian and African women have changed *downward* and family size expectations have been reduced to fit into family size desires. In sharp contrast, both first- and second-generation European women have moved family size expectations *upward* to fit into desires which in the past have exceeded actual family size. Hence, the high fertility of Asian and African women of older cohorts was higher than they desired and higher than they considered ideal for the average Israeli family. With exposure to Israeli society, their reproductive norms and their fertility behavior changed in conjunction with the social and economic conditions and toward lower levels. Among second-generation Israelis, fertility expectations and desires are only slightly higher for those of Asian-African origins than those of European origins (Goldscheider and Friedlander 1981).

Two analytic themes need to be emphasized for these reproductive patterns. First, ethnic differences in fertility within the Asian-African and within the European-American groups are largely explainable by social-structural–demographic factors rather than values or cultural differences. Although we have noted continuing ethnic differences in fertility levels and norms among the most recent marriage cohorts, most of these differences reflect socioeconomic, educational, and residential differences

Table 5. EXPECTED AND DESIRED FAMILY SIZE BY ETHNIC ORIGIN AND TWO MARRIAGE COHORTS, URBAN JEWISH WOMEN: ISRAEL 1974–75

Ethnic Origin	Family Size			
	Expectations		Desires	
	Before 1955	1965–74	Before 1955	1965–74
East Europe	2.3	2.8	2.8	2.8
West Europe	2.8	3.1	3.1	3.1
Israel-Europe	2.8	3.3	3.3	3.2
Asia	5.0	3.5	4.5	3.5
Africa	6.2	3.6	5.8	3.6
Israel-Asia/Africa	4.0	3.4	4.5	3.3

Source: Calvin Goldscheider and Dov Friedlander, "Fertility Expectations, Desires and Ideals Among Jewish Women in Israel," in U.O. Schmelz et al., eds., *Papers in Jewish Demography: 1977* (Institute of Contemporary Jewry, The Hebrew University of Jerusalem, 1980), pp. 301–14.

among ethnic groups. A second theme that emerges from these data parallels the conclusions of the analysis of changes in age at marriage. Despite the major convergence over time in ethnic differences in fertility norms and behavior, the paths to this convergence have been significantly different. For European-Americans, the changes over time have been increases in family size; for Asian-Africans, declines in fertility behavior and norms. Hence, an examination of cross-sectional fertility measures may show ethnic similarities in fertility levels, but these similarities may not necessarily imply similar meanings at either the macro or micro levels.

Divorce

Divorce rates have been remarkably stable and low over time in Israel. The pattern contradicts the oversimplified expectation of increased levels of divorce in the process of modernization. The low level of divorce is consistent with the overall high marriage rates, and has been described in terms of the "stability and centrality" of the nuclear family in Israel (Peres and Katz 1981). Recent evidence suggests that in the period 1974–78 there has been an increase in divorce levels which have characterized recently married couples. Data show no increased rate of divorce among couples married for longer durations. Nevertheless, the overall level of divorce remains low.

Low and relatively stable divorce rates characterize both Asian-African and European-American ethnic groups. Some evidence suggests, as might be expected, that European-Americans have somewhat higher divorce rates than Asian-Africans. The margins in Table 6 show higher divorce-marriage ratios (the number of current divorces per current marriages) for foreign- and native-born European-Americans compared to Asian-Africans.

The divorce-marriage ratios (D-M) are crude measures since they do not take into account the population at risk and probably distort the absolute levels—particularly for the foreign-born. (The foreign-born are less likely to be marrying currently, while a larger proportion are exposed to the risk of divorce, having been married either at an earlier date or outside of Israel). It is nevertheless instructive to examine the divorce-marriage ratios for the native-born, particularly for interethnic marriages.

The divorce-marriage ratio for the Israeli-born of Asian-African origin homogamously married is 5.4; for the native-born European-American homogamously married the D-M ratio is 12.5. This pattern is consistent with other findings noted earlier, that divorce is higher among

European-American ethnics. These data, however, address a related issue
of divorce among interethnically married couples. The D-M ratio for
native-born Asian-African–origin husbands married to native-born European-American wives is 12.2—similar to the homogamously married
European-American Israelis. However, the D-M ratio for Israeli-born
European-American husbands married to Asian-African wives is 5.2—
similar to the homogamously married Asian-African Israelis.

These data show that interethnic marriages in Israel do not automat-
ically lead to higher divorce rates, but depend on the ethnic origin of
wives. Asian-African women may be less independent, whether married
to Asian-African men or to European-American men, and therefore their
divorce levels are lower. Whatever the reason, it is clear from these data
that interethnic marriages do not simply imply greater conflict and/or
greater independence of choice. That conclusion is consistent with the
earlier argument that ethnic intermarriages do not necessarily reflect
desires-preferences for integration, and are not simply an indicator of
greater freedom from the constraints of family-ethnic networks.

A final point relates to the relationship between interethnic marriages and fertility. Some previous research has indicated that, at least in
the United States, intermarriages across ethnic and religious lines tend to
be associated with lower fertility (see Goldstein and Goldscheider 1968).
The data for Israel indicate that no clear pattern of lower fertility among
the interethnically married emerges (Table 7). For example, among foreign-born couples where the husband was born in Asia and the wife in

Table 6. DIVORCE-MARRIAGE RATIOS BY ETHNIC ORIGIN OF MEN AND
WOMEN, JEWISH POPULATION OF ISRAEL, 1977

| Ethnic Origin of Husbands | | Ethnic Origin of Wives | | | |
| | | Asia-Africa | | Europe-America | |
	Total	Foreign	Israel	Foreign	Israel
Asia-Africa					
Foreign-born	18.2	25.4	9.9	25.4	15.3
Israel-born	7.1	8.6	5.4	19.0	12.2
Europe-America					
Foreign-born	23.2	27.6	12.8	28.7	18.2
Israel-born	10.4	10.6	5.2	17.1	12.5
Total	—	19.7	6.8	24.2	12.7

Source: Calculated from Israel Central Bureau of Statistics, *Vital Statistics 1977*, Special
Series No. 609 (Jerusalem, 1979), Tables 19 and 34.

Table 7. Average Live Births to Mothers Aged 30–34 by Ethnic Origins of Mothers and Fathers, Jewish Population of Israel, 1978

Ethnic Origin of Fathers	Total	Ethnic Origin of Mothers					
		Foreign-Born			Israel-Born		
		Asia	Africa	Europe-America	Asia	Africa	Europe-America
Foreign-Born							
Asia	3.6	3.8	3.7	2.8	3.3	3.1	2.9
Africa	4.1	3.3	4.4	3.1	3.3	3.3	2.8
Europe-America	2.8	2.6	2.8	2.8	2.4	2.8	2.9
Israel-Born							
Asia	3.0	2.9	3.2	2.8	3.3	2.9	2.8
Africa	2.9	2.7	3.3	2.8	2.9	2.5	2.4
Europe-America	3.0	2.6	2.7	3.0	2.8	2.8	3.1
Total	3.3	3.4	4.0	2.9	3.1	3.0	3.0

Source: Adapted from *Statistical Abstract of Israel, 1979*, No. 30, Table 3/27.

Africa, average family size was 3.7; among African-born husbands married to Asian-born wives, family size was 3.3. Both were lower than homogamously married Asian- and African-born couples. But for the second generation, parallel comparisons show that interethnic marriages between Asian- and African-origin persons are intermediate between homogamously Asian-origin and African-origin marriages. A somewhat different pattern emerges when Asian-European marriages—native and foreign born—are examined.

Hence, while there are no clear patterns to the fertility of interethnic marriages in Israel, the data available seem to suggest that fertility levels differ depending on the generation involved, the ethnic origin of husbands or wives, and related factors. It is not simply lower—often it is higher or the same. Again, this suggests that interethnic marriages are less reflective of preferences and desires, less indicative of "independence" and conflict, and may be more related to marriage-market constraints and squeezes.

Conclusions

This overview of family patterns among Israeli ethnic groups leads to several basic conclusions. First, there have been major ethnic convergences over time in family processes. These convergences are the result of changes among *all* ethnic groups—European and Asian-African. The convergence is not to a European pattern, nor to an Asian-African pattern, nor to a "Middle East" pattern, nor to some "Jewish" family pattern (that is largely nonexistent and certainly not universal). It is to an emerging Israeli pattern, reflecting in large part the social, economic, cultural, and political conditions of the emerging society in Israel. Indeed, it would be untenable sociologically if new family patterns did not evolve under the societal conditions emerging in Israel.

A second conclusion suggests that variations in family structure that remain are related in large part to structural variation rather than to major cultural differences. This does not imply that cultural variation does not exist among Israeli ethnic groups; indeed, there are major ethnic differences in values and norms. Nevertheless, variation in family patterns—at least those described here—seem to be related primarily to socioeconomic status, educational attainment, community, and place of residence. These structural features differentiate ethnic groups in significant ways. Thus it is the ethnic-socioeconomic-community connection that is of overwhelming importance for family variation in Israel rather than the ethnic-cultural connection. Perhaps the only major cultural division that relates to family variation among Jews in Israel is religiosity, and that is becoming less tied to ethnic variation (see Goldscheider and Friedlander 1983).

Third, there are strong indications of familism among Jews in Israel. The centrality of families is reflected in the high proportion who marry despite marriage-market problems, the emphasis on family formation, higher average fertility patterns than in comparable developed nations, and low rates of divorce. There are some indications of changes in these patterns. Over the last several years there appear to be some delayed marriage, lower birthrates, and increased divorce. All these indicators, plus the possibility of new, more liberated roles for women and the emergence of new living arrangement patterns, may be temporary or may be indicative of the onset of new long-term changes. It is premature to know the answer. We do know that continuing adjustment to new societal conditions is to be expected.

The convergences over time and the similarity in family patterns among ethnics do not imply identity in process. Indeed, all the evidence available points unmistakably to the different paths taken by the various ethnic populations. Since the process has been different, there is every indication that the consequences will be different and the strains will be greater for some ethnics compared to others.

Finally, there is strong evidence of ethnic-group continuity despite change and convergence. There is indeed no contradiction between ethnic convergence and ethnic continuity. The convergences in family processes reflect structural pressures toward similar but new patterns. Ethnic continuity manifests itself in some marriage patterns and in the broader realm of ethnic inequalities that are perpetuated.

Emerging in Israel are parallel ethnic communities with growing similarities in family patterns, separated geographically and ethnically. There are as in the other pluralistic societies emergent patterns of ethnicity (cf. Yancey et al. 1976). "Asian-African" and "European-American" ethnic categories have meaning only in Israel. Ethnic groups in Israel are significantly different from their communities at the places of origin. Moreover, ethnic differences in Israel do not reflect only cultural legacy or the vestigial, primordial identity of the past. Emergent ethnic communities in Israel are marked by differential advantage and access to resources. This pattern is reinforced by discrimination *and* culture, often united nationally by externals, related to other non-Jewish ethnics in Israel (cf. Smooha 1978). Within this context, family patterns illustrate the complex processes of ethnic change and continuity in Israeli society.

References

Friedlander, D., and C. Goldscheider. 1978. "Immigration, Social Change and Cohort Fertility in Israel." *Population Studies* 32 (July), 299–317.

———. 1979. *The Population of Israel*. New York: Columbia University Press.

Goldscheider, C. 1983. "The Demography of Asian and African Jews in Israel." In J. B. Maier and C. I. Waxman, eds., *Social History and Ethnicity*. Transaction Books.

———. 1981. "Patterns of Jewish Fertility in Israel." In P. Ritterband, ed., *Modern Jewish Fertility*. Leiden: Brill.

———. 1983. "Religiosity Patterns in Israel." *American Jewish Yearbook*.

Goldscheider, C., and D. Friedlander. 1979. "Fertility Expectations, Desires, and Ideals Among Jewish Women in Israel." In *Papers in Jewish Demography: 1977*. Institute of Contemporary Jewry.

Goldstein, S., and C. Goldscheider. 1968. *Jewish Americans*. Englewood Cliffs, N.J.: Prentice-Hall.

Matras, J. 1973. "Changing Matchmaking, Marriage and Fertility in Israel." *American Journal of Sociology* 79 (September), 364–88.

Peres, Y., and R. Katz. 1981. "Stability and Centrality: The Nuclear Family in Modern Israel." *Social Forces* 59 (March), 687–704.

Smooha, S. 1978. *Israel: Pluralism and Conflict*. London: Routledge & Kegan Paul.

Yancey, W. T., E. P. Eriksen, and R. N. Juliani, 1976. "Emergent Ethnicity: A Review and Reformation," *American Sociological Review* 41 (June), 391–402.

11. Contemporary Jewish Family Patterns in France: A Comparative Perspective

Sergio DellaPergola

Recent research in the United States shows that significant variation in the sociodemographic structure and dynamics of different ethno-religious groups is consistently related to the different family patterns that are characteristic of each group and that—beyond social class differentials—appear to be tied to their respective cultural traditions and normative systems.[1] If explorations in the United States yield a promising set of theories and empirical findings, there is still much for the social scientist to do in other regional contexts. In a number of countries lacking the North American tradition of mass immigration and (initial) cultural heterogeneity among the population, the ethnoreligious factor has generally been a less salient variable in analyses of sociodemographic processes. Yet in some of those countries—France among them—immigration has constituted a rather conspicuous component of modern total population growth.[2]

One basic analytic question, only seldom taken up in sociodemographic research, relates to the absorption and mobility histories of large groups of international migrants sharing one common place of

This paper was written during a fellowship at the Institute for Advanced Studies of the Hebrew University of Jerusalem in 1980/81, in the framework of the International Study Group on Demography of the Jews, headed by Prof. Roberto Bachi. I wish to thank the Institute's staff, Prof. Arieh Dvoretsky, Dr. Shabetai Gairon, Daliah Aviely, Bilha Gus, Annette Orrelle, and Shani Sivan, for their success in creating optimal working conditions.

origin but splitting between different places of destination. What kinds of selectivity processes develop between migrants and nonmigrants, and between migrants choosing different destinations? Do the migrants tend to maintain over time the common characteristics they had at the moment of emigrating, or do they rather tend to adopt sociodemographic patterns typical of the places of destination—which may significantly differ from place to place? In this perspective, too, family processes can be considered among the most sensitive indicators of the speed and direction of adaptation of newcomers into an absorbing society, and the starting point for further stages of mobility and assimilation.[3]

A further analytic track should consider sociodemographic changes affecting a migrant group in its transition from majority to minority status, and vice versa. While the way of operating of psychosocial factors in such environmental changes is hard to assess in the absence of appropriate attitudinal materials,[4] the effects of the structural changes involved may be substantial.[5] In particular, processes related to the choice of spouse are clearly affected by the size and composition of a population and of its constituting subpopulations, so that chances for homogamy or heterogamy can be quite different under a majority or minority status— other things being equal—with significant consequences for the subsequent sociodemographic development of a given group.

A comparativistic approach to population processes emerges as a research imperative from these considerations. While the primary aim of this chapter is to provide a general outline of selected family patterns among the Jewish population of France,[6] an attempt is made to consider French Jewry not only as another "case study" but rather as one segment within an interdependent and more complex system of Jewish populations scattered around the world. Because of the nature and direction of Jewish international migration over the last few decades, comparable population groups can be identified in France and in Israel. Comparative analysis of Jewish population processes in these two different contexts may not only sharpen our understanding of the specificity of the groups considered in a limited geographical framework, but may also contribute to a better and more systematic reading of processes occurring elsewhere in the larger Jewish population system.

In particular, the chapter examines how exposure to different societal environments affects the persistence of those traditional Jewish family patterns extant in some of the countries of origin of the migrants. Traditional Jewish family patterns have been characterized by very high proportions of persons ever married, relatively young ages at marriage, frequently arranged marriages, strong religious homogamy, frequent remarriage in case of divorce or widowhood, and centrality of the nuclear family (and in some casess of more extended family structures) in the social organization of the community.[7] Conformity and variation in these sociodemographic characteristics constitute important elements in the modern evolution of Jewish populations and societies.

Size and Structure of French Jewry

French Jewry emerged in the 1960s as the largest community in Western Europe and the fourth largest in the world—after those in the United States, Israel, and the Soviet Union. About 75,000 Jews immigrated to France from the three Maghreb countries (Morocco, Algeria, and Tunisia) during the 1950s, and about 145,000 during the 1960s, mostly following the 1962 Evian treaty and the accession of Algeria to independence. Another 80,000 Jews had come to France from other European and Middle Eastern countries between the end of World War II and 1970. The volume of Jewish immigration to France declined in the 1970s, reaching an estimated total of 20,000, but being offset by more visible emigration, including *aliyah* to Israel and some movements to Quebec. As a consequence of these population trends, French Jewry had developed into another instance of the "ingathering of the exiles," which—unlike the better-known Israeli case[8]— occurred in a general French context, lacking a tradition of linguistic, ethnic, or religious pluralism. Toward the mid- and late 1970s, there were an estimated 535,000 Jewish permanent residents in France. According to the population structure of Jews in the greater Paris metropolitan area—where over one half of the countrywide total live—46 percent were born in France and 54 percent were born elsewhere, of these 41 percent in North Africa[9] and 13 percent in other European countries.[10] Over one-half of the French-born were children and youngsters below the age of twenty. North African Jews constituted an absolute majority in each age class between twenty and sixty. Among Jews age sixty and over the weight of North African and European immigrants was balanced: roughly 40 percent for each group, the remainder being veteran French-born Jews. In assessing the different age structures of these basic origin groups, the disruptive effects of the Holocaust on the population of French and other European origin should be kept in mind.[11] Overall, out of one hundred Jewish immigrants, 20 percent had arrived in France up to 1939, 28 percent between 1940 and 1959, and 52 percent since 1960.

Israel itself had absorbed over the same periods of time substantial masses of Jewish immigrants from similarly heterogeneous countries of origin. Between 1948 and 1960, 981,000 new immigrants entered—

520,000 from North African and Asian countries, 402,000 from Eastern Europe, and 59,000 from Western countries. Another 608,000 immigrated between 1961 and 1976, with figures of 215,000, 236,000, and 157,000, respectively.

As a consequence of these relatively similar experiences between the late 1940s and early 1970s, French and Israeli Jewries shared three important demographic features: (a) they were the two fastest-growing of the world's large Jewish communities in the world, with a fivefold increase in the Jewish population of Israel between Independence Day and the end of 1976 and a threefold increase in France between 1944 and the mid-1970s; (b) both were quite recent populations, either by birth or by immigration, in the respective country of residence;[12] and (c) when considering together the continents of birth of the immigrants and of the fathers of the local born, both communities had a moderate majority of Jews of North African and Middle Eastern origin: 54 percent in France in the mid-1970s and 52 percent in Israel in 1976. By each of these criteria, the two communities significantly differed from any other large Jewish population. They differed radically from each other, however, on one basic dimension: one constituted about 1 percent of the total population of its country, while the other's share was about 84 percent. This combination of similar and dissimilar social structural features provides an appropriate backdrop for comparing the respective family patterns of Jews in France and in Israel.

Data

Any attempt to study Jewish demography must face the basic methodological issues of availability of sources of data on Jewish populations and their quality. Israel population trends can be analyzed in the light of a good systematic database that has developed over the past several decades.[13] With regard to Diaspora Jewish populations, one often has to confront the more complex analytic issues while at the same time attempting to create that very database. This concern is reflected in the data presented here, which are derived from a countrywide sample survey of French Jewish households jointly carried out by the Hebrew University's Institute of Contemporary Jewry and the Groupe de Sociologie des Religions of the Centre National de la Recherche Scientifique in Paris. For various technical reasons,[14] the survey had to be carried out in different, complementary stages between 1972 and 1976 in the metropolitan area of greater Paris and between 1976 and 1978 in selected provincial communities. The information collected has a unified character, however, and is consistently referred to one common point of time. The data reported here refer only to greater Paris. Preliminary analysis of the provincial returns points to a basic similarity of characteristics between Jewish populations in Paris and elsewhere in France.

The survey was developed out of two independent, though partially overlapping, sampling frames: (a) the general French electoral list and (b) a conglomerate list of persons associated with Jewish institutions. Sampling from the French electoral list was carried out after a basic typology of Jewish family names had been developed. Carriers of "typically Jewish" names were sampled more frequently than carriers of "doubtful" and "typically non-Jewish" names. Sample stratification also takes into account the estimated Jewish density of urban districts in the city of Paris and the size and distance from the city of suburban municipalities. Fieldwork was carried out through mailing the questionnaires, followed by direct interviewing. Present or past religious identification of each household member in the sample was ascertained through direct questions concerning individuals and their parents. Households with at least one Jewish member were retained for data processing. The final net sample for greater Paris included 1,256 Jewish households, or 3,808 individuals (about 10 percent of them non-Jews). After weighting the individual records to take into account different sampling fractions by type of name, and allocation for various factors of undercoverage in the survey, an inflated estimate of about 300,000 members of Jewish households in greater Paris—about 270,000 of them currently Jewish—was obtained for the mid-1970s.

Individual Family Patterns

Age at Marriage

Available data on singulate mean age at marriage (Table 1) allow for quite a systematic approach to differentials and changes in Jewish family patterns related to international migration. The significance of migrant selectivity for Jewish family formation is illustrated by a comparison of ages at marriage of persons who married in North Africa and the Middle East or in Europe, respectively, and subsequently migrated to France or to Israel. Age at marriage of North African (and Asian) Jews who moved to Israel was significantly lower than that of Jews from the same countries who went to France. The far more traditional marriage patterns of migrants to Israel are also indicative of other demographic, socioeconomic, and ideological migrant-selectivity processes. North African

Jews choosing to move to France featured an age structure with more favorable dependency ratios, a much higher proportion of university graduates and middle-upper-status white collars, and an overall greater degree of Western acculturation. These strong migrant-selectivity patterns must be kept in mind when interpreting the different mobility processes that characterized North African Jews during the early stages of their absorption in France and in Israel.[15] No such age at marriage differentials appear among Jewish migrants who married in European countries, where the transition to a "European" marriage pattern[16] had been already completed by the near totality of Jewish populations in the years between the two world wars.

The effects of immigrants' absorption on marriages performed in the countries of destination show up in higher ages at marriage among the

Table 1. MEAN AGE AT FIRST MARRIAGE AMONG JEWISH GROOMS AND BRIDES IN FRANCE AND IN ISRAEL, BY COUNTRY OF BIRTH, YEAR OF MARRIAGE, AND PLACE OF MARRIAGE[a]

	Country of Residence							
	France				Israel			
	Married Abroad		Married in France		Married Abroad		Married in Israel	
Country of Birth and Year of Marriage	Grooms	Brides	Grooms	Brides	Grooms	Brides	Grooms	Brides
Born in Europe-America								
Up to 1945	26.9	23.5	27.4	24.0	27.2	23.8	28.1	24.8
1946–60	29.6	24.7	31.4	26.5	29.4	24.7	28.9	23.8
1961–75	x	23.0	33.0	26.7	n.a.	n.a.	26.9	23.0
Born in North Africa								
Up to 1945	25.6	21.7	29.5	24.2	22.7	17.8	26.1	20.4
1946–60	28.3	23.9	28.2	23.4	24.2	19.4	25.3	21.1
1961–75	29.0	23.2	28.1	23.3	n.a.	n.a.	25.7	22.7
Born in country of residence								
Up to 1945			27.7	24.2			25.4	21.3
1946–60			27.5	24.0			24.5	21.2
1961–75			25.4	25.9			24.5	21.4

x = Not enough cases.
[a] Sources: France: Retrospective survey data. Israel: Israel Central Bureau of Statistics. Married abroad: Retrospective data from 1961 census. Married in Israel: Up to 1945, retrospective data from 1961 census; 1946 and after, current vital statistics, including also Jews born in Asia. It was assumed that persons born *and* living in a country also married in that country.

Table 2. PERCENT NEVER MARRIED AMONG JEWS IN FRANCE AND IN
ISRAEL, BY COUNTRY OF BIRTH, AND AMONG GENERAL FRENCH
POPULATION, BY SEX AND AGE

	Jewish Population						General Population France[d]
	France			Israel[c]			
Sex and Age	Total	Born in Europe[a]	Born in North Africa	Total[b]	Born in Europe-America	Born in Africa-Asia	
Males							
Total 20+	24	24	25	19	16	23	21
20–29	78	78	78	56	55	58	49
30–39	20	28	15	7	7	8	17
40–49	4	6	3	4	4	4	11
50–59	3	6	0	3	3	3	9
60–69	1	2	1	2	2	3	8
70+	4	6	0	2	2	2	6
Females							
Total 20+	19	19	18	11	10	13	14
20–29	69	73	65	34	35	33	32
30–39	9	8	10	5	5	4	10
40–49	6	8	4	2	2	2	8
50–59	3	5	2	2	2	2	8
60–69	3	5	1	3	3	2	9
70+	3	5	1	3	3	2	10

[a] Including French born.
[b] Including Israel born.
[c] 1972 census.
[d] January 1, 1974.

European and earlier North African immigrants to France. Similar mar-
riage-delaying effects accompany the exposure of North African immigrants to Israeli society. But while in Israel, age at marriage of different
origin groups rapidly tended to converge around intermediate values, in
France, marriages occurred at significantly older ages and Jewish ethnic
differentials were more persistent. Also the intergenerational unfolding
of family processes tended to follow quite different courses. Among
French-born Jews, males tended on the whole to marry at younger ages
than their foreign-born parents and age peers. Females, on the other
hand, married at somewhat older ages—which resulted in reduced
groom-bride age differentials. In Israel, age at marriage of the local born
tended to be lower than among immigrants marrying in the country, and
intermediate in comparison to age at marriage abroad of the main immi-

grant groups. The eventual result of these adaptation processes was the solid establishment in Israel of a much younger age at marriage than among French Jews, which may clearly affect other demographic variables such as fertility schedules,[17] population composition by marital status, and household structure.

Proportion Ever Married

While these trends refer to persons who ever married, the proportion ever married provides another sensitive indicator of the comparative dynamics of Jewish family patterns. Marriage has been in the past, and still tends to be, nearly universal in Israel, with only minor differences between major origin groups (Table 2). In France, on the other hand, rather high celibacy rates characterize the younger cohorts, probably masking some consensual unions. Cohort data (reported in Table 3) illustrate the growth in the frequency of celibacy in recent years, which also reflects changes in the perception of centrality of the family in the general society. Differences between Jewish immigrant groups were steadily narrowing, the French North African Jews rapidly adopting the behavior of their European counterparts. Table 2 also suggests that singulate mean age at marriage was higher among the Jews than among the general French population. However, the proportion never married among older French European Jews was significantly lower than among the general population. This remnant of the past greater marriage propensity of Jews, as compared to non-Jews in European societies, may perhaps be construed as an indicator of possible later marriages among the currently unmarried Jewish younger generation.

Mixed Marriage

Choice of partner is a most significant component of the overall redirection of French Jewish family processes. While in Israel the incidence of religious heterogamy is statistically insignificant among the Jews,[18] French Jewry witnessed a rapid increase in marital assimilation—especially since the late 1950s (Table 4). In the mid-1970s, 20 percent of all existing couples, and 28 percent of all couples formed in France, were mixed. The proportion of mixed marriages, out of all marriages performed in France, increased from less than one-sixth before 1955 to about one-third in 1956–65, and to one-half in 1966–75. Accordingly, about one-third of all Jewish grooms *and* brides outmarried in the late 1960s and early 1970s. The recent rapid increase in female Jewish outmarriage is quite remarkable and is partly stimulated by a relative dearth of Jewish males at the marriageable ages due to Jewish birthrate fluctuations during

Table 3. SELECTED COHORT MARRIAGE PATTERNS AMONG JEWISH
POPULATION IN FRANCE, BY SEX, AGE, AND COUNTRY OF BIRTH

Sex and Current Age	Born in Europe[a]				Born in North Africa			
	% Never Married[b] at Age:		% Out-Married[c] at Age:		% Never Married[b] at Age:		% Out-Married[c] at Age:	
	20–29	30–39	20–29	30–39	20–29	30–39	20–29	30–39
Males								
20–29	78		24		78		35	
30–39	63	28	13	32	54	15	30	23
40–49	72	11	8	26	53	14	8	12
50–59	78	14	6	8	63	9	0	2
60–69	73	28	4	10	73	25	4	3
Females								
20–29	73		19		65		18	
30–39	49	8	11	43	28	10	12	13
40–49	29	11	2	2	30	6	1	1
50–59	54	10	1	3	34	6	0	0
60–69	44	20	1	3	49	5	0	0

[a] Including French born.
[b] Based on first marriages.
[c] Out of ever married; based on current marriages.

World War II and in the postwar period. Additional cohort data (see Table 3) point to a general increase in the proportion of outmarried at later ages: later marriages are more frequently mixed.

The level of marital assimilation, by main origin groups, was still substantially different. The proportion of mixed couples was above 60 percent among more recent marriages involving European (including French-born) Jews, and about one-half that level among marriages involving North African Jews, whose rates too were rapidly increasing. Striking differences appear from more detailed data about the latter group. Between 1966 and 1975, less than 5 percent of mixed couples were recorded among Moroccan and Tunisian Jews marrying in France, as against 48 percent among Algerian Jews. There is evidence that mixed marriage was already spreading in Algeria since the 1950s: over 20 percent of couples formed in Algeria since 1955 were mixed. Very few Algerian Jews, virtually all of whom were French citizens, chose to emigrate to Israel at the time of mass migration, while a majority of the more traditional Moroccan and Tunisian communities did.

Interethnic Jewish Marriages

One may wonder whether the rapid increase of mixed marriage among the Jews of France is part of an integration process whose counterpart in Israel would be a higher proportion of marriages between members of different origin groups. Actually, one would expect that because of the selectivity of migrants involved in the buildup of French and Israeli Jewish communities, and because of various ecological, socioeconomic, and cultural determinants, Jewish ethnicity segregation in choice of partner would be somewhat more persistent in Israel. Internal socioeconomic status differentials were greater among Jewish immigrants to Israel; residential segregation of different origin groups in Israel was initially

Table 4. PERCENT MIXED MARRIAGES AMONG COUPLES[a] WITH AT LEAST ONE JEWISH SPOUSE, AMONG JEWISH GROOMS AND AMONG JEWISH BRIDES, BY YEAR OF MARRIAGE AND COUNTRY OF BIRTH OF SPOUSES

Year of Marriage	Total[b]	Thereof: Married in France	Born in France	Born in Other Europe			Born in North Africa		
				Total[b]	Married Abroad	Married in France	Total[b]	Married Abroad	Married in France
% mixed marriages among couples with at least one Jewish spouse[c]									
Total	20	29	34	18	6	20	12	2	32
1966–75	46	49	62	60	x	64	25	x	28
1956–65	29	35	25	49	x	51	27	2	41
1946–55	11	16	24	9	18	7	6	3	22
1936–45	8	17	19	14	5	17	2	2	21
up to –1935	7	11	11	7	0	10	4	2	
% mixed marriages among Jewish grooms									
Total	15	23	23	14	3	17	11	2	29
1966–75	31	34	41	21	x	23	25	x	28
1956–65	25	30	20	48	x	50	21	2	33
1946–55	9	14	21	7	10	6	6	3	22
1936–45	7	15	17	12	0	16	2	2	21
up to –1935	6	9	7	7	0	8	4	2	
% mixed marriages among Jewish brides									
Total	7	12	15	2	3	2	3	1	11
1966–75	28	32	44	11	0	13	8	6	9
1956–65	8	11	10	0	x	0	8	0	15
1946–55	2	2	3	1	3	0	1	1	0
1936–45	1	2	5	1	3	0	0	0	0
up to –1935	2	2	0	3	3	3	0	0	0

[a] Currently existing couples.
[b] Including unspecified place of marriage.
[c] Couples are classified according to the groom's birthplace. This may differ from the bride's birthplace.
[x] Not enough cases.

high because of the establishment of relatively homogeneous rural settlements and development towns; greater adherence to religious and other cultural traditions characterized significant strata of migrants to Israel, possibly slowing down the departing from traditional marriage patterns, including community homogamy. On the other hand, the residential resettling of Jewish migrants to France—though characterized by pockets of strong initial segregation[19]—mostly occurred in a large urban metropolitan environment in which Jews of different origins were accessible (to those interested) through the existing network of communal facilities. Above all, a large section of North African immigrants—mainly Algerians—identified themselves as French, with only a modest change in cultural perspective involved by migration. Minority status, total urbanization, and social mobility—leading to a growing structural similarity within the community—could support a common framework for French Jewish identity, whereas in Israel the process of cultural fusion was made more complex by the stronger superimposition of ethnic and socioeconomic differentials.[20]

In fact, the data in Tables 5 and 6 point to frequent interethnic marriage among French Jews who did not outmarry. The overall distributions by basic origin groups are affected by the changing composition of the French Jewish marriage market under the impact of immigration. While before World War II ethnically homogamous couples constituted about three-quarters of all Jewish in-marriages performed in France, after the war their share was reduced to about one-half of the total. Periodic shifts in Jewish population composition were a dominant factor in enhancing particular combinations of marital assortment, which points to the relative openness of each group to the others.[21]

Measures of association for cross-classifications allow us to control for the effect of size of subpopulations on the chance that a given marital assortment will occur. According to such corrected measuring, the choice of partner within French Jewish marriage cohorts rapidly tended to the distributions one would expect under the hypothesis of random mating. Among Jewish marriages performed in France in 1966–75, homogamy (according to the basic dichotomy: Europe—North Africa) was only 20 percent more frequent than otherwise expected. Comparable data for Israel during the same years yield a 65 percent excess of observed over expected community homogamy.[22] The amalgamation of different Jewish origin groups through marriage was speedier in France than in Israel. Yet, while in Israel virtually all the marriages were religiously homogamous, in France these constituted only a diminishing share of the whole Jewish nuptiality. The in-marrieds were part of a more reduced market in which an interethnic Jewish marriage could be preferred, at times, over permanent celibacy.

Divorce

A final dynamic aspect of Jewish family patterns relates to the dissolution of marriages through divorce. Table 7 shows the proportions of currently divorced persons, by sex and age, which can be affected by differential remarriage. Taken at their face value, these data confirm the general finding of less frequent divorce among the Jews as compared to general populations of Western countries. After controlling for age, current divorcees are comparatively rarer among North African Jews in France: overall, one-third of the corresponding level for the general French population aged twenty and over. Similar data from the 1972 Israel census indicate a slightly lower percentage of currently divorced Jewish males than in France, and a slightly higher proportion of females. These find-

Table 5. ALL EXISTING COUPLES AND JEWISH COUPLES[a] MARRIED IN FRANCE, BY COUNTRY OF BIRTH OF SPOUSES AND YEAR OF MARRIAGE

| | | Country of Birth of Spouses | | | | | | |
| | | Same Origin | | | Different Origin | | | |
Year of Marriage	Total	Total	Both France	Both Other Europe	Both North Africa	Total	France with Other Europe	France with North Africa	Other Europe with North Africa
All existing couples									
Total	100	74	23	14	38	26	11	12	3
1966–75	100	62	42	2	19	38	4	30	4
1956–65	100	65	27	3	35	35	14	19	2
1946–55	100	79	21	15	43	21	13	5	3
1936–45	100	86	12	24	51	14	10	3	1
up to –1935	100	80	15	31	34	20	14	2	4
Jewish couples,[a] married in France									
Total	100	68	29	22	17	32	15	14	3
1966–75	100	58	24	3	31	42	2	36	4
1956–65	100	54	51	0	3	46	17	28	1
1946–55	100	60	44	3	13	40	34	4	2
1936–45	100	77	25	49	3	23	17	4	2
up to –1935	100	70	27	43	0	30	24	3	3

[a] As distinguished from mixed couples.

Table 6. ALL EXISTING COUPLES AND JEWISH COUPLES[a] MARRIED IN
FRANCE—PERCENT DISTRIBUTION OF SPOUSES, BY COUNTRY OF BIRTH

Year of Marriage	Out of 100 Born in France			Out of 100 Born in Other Europe			Out of 100 Born in North Africa		
	France	Other Europe	North Africa	France	Other Europe	North Africa	France	Other Europe	North Africa
All existing couples									
Total	49	24	27	41	50	9	23	5	72
1966–75	55	5	40	40	20	40	57	8	35
1956–65	45	23	32	75	17	8	34	3	63
1946–55	53	34	13	42	48	10	10	6	84
1936–45	49	40	11	29	68	3	5	2	93
–1935	47	45	8	29	63	8	7	9	84
Jewish Couples[a] married in France									
Total	50	26	24	39	54	7	42	8	50
1966–75	39	3	58	23	35	42	50	5	45
1956–65	53	18	29	92	0	8	86	4	10
1946–55	53	42	5	87	7	6	23	12	65
1936–45	53	37	10	25	72	3	46	20	34
–1935	50	45	5	34	62	4	47	53	0

[a] As distinguished from mixed couples.

ings suggest further investigation of remarriage patterns of the previously divorced.

Household Size and Structure

Household Size

Not unexpectedly, the contemporary French Jewish family is typically a small, nuclear household unit. Jewish households of two to three persons are more frequent (see Table 8), with a substantial proportion of single-person households and relatively few large households (six persons and over). The main difference, in comparison to Jewish households in Israel, is the significantly smaller share of large households in France. These differences mostly persist after controlling for country of birth of household heads. North African- (and Asian-) born Jewish heads feature the larger household sizes (3.8 persons on the average in France versus 4.5 in Israel), and European immigrants do not differ substantially among themselves (2.9 persons in France versus 2.8 in Israel). A different model of longer-term intergenerational transformation of family structure emerges, however, in the French and Israeli Jewish populations. In Israel, households headed by native Israelis are intermediate in size (3.5) and are not the smallest ones (2.8), as in the case of native French Jews (Table 9). These differentials hold after controlling for age. Household size by age of household heads is affected by the unfolding of life-cycle events, and generally reaches its peak in Israel when the head is thirty-five to forty-four years old. In France, households headed by older persons tend to be larger, in connection with the generally later and less frequent transition of young Jewish adults from their families of birth to their families of procreation.

Table 7. PERCENT CURRENTLY DIVORCED AMONG JEWISH AND GENERAL POPULATION IN FRANCE, BY COUNTRY OF BIRTH, AGE, AND SEX

	Jewish Population						General Population[b]	
	Total		Born in Europe[a]		Born in North Africa			
Age	Male	Female	Male	Female	Male	Female	Male	Female
Total 20 +	2	2	2	2	1	1	3	3
20–29	1	0	1	0	2	0	1	1
30–39	3	1	3	1	3	2	2	3
40–49	1	3	2	3	0	2	3	4
50–59	2	2	3	3	2	1	4	5
60–69	1	2	1	2	1	2	4	5
70 +	2	1	4	1	0	2	3	3

[a] Including French-born.
[b] January 1, 1974.

Table 8. JEWISH HOUSEHOLD SIZE, BY COUNTRY OF BIRTH OF HEAD OF HOUSEHOLD, FRANCE[a] AND ISRAEL,[b] PERCENTAGES

	France, by Head's Birthplace				Israel, by Head's Birthplace			
Persons in Household	Total	France	Other Europe	North Africa	Total	Israel	Europe-America	Africa-Asia
Total	100	100	100	100	100	100	100	100
1	17	24	15	12	14	13	18	9
2–3	42	45	51	35	41	37	53	27
4–5	32	26	31	38	32	41	26	35
6 +	9	5	3	15	13	9	3	29

[a] Including non-Jewish members of the household.
[b] 1975. Source: Israel Central Bureau of Statistics, *Statistical Abstract of Israel 1976*, p. 49.

Table 9. AVERAGE JEWISH HOUSEHOLD SIZE, BY AGE AND COUNTRY OF
BIRTH OF HEAD OF HOUSEHOLD—FRANCE[a] AND ISRAEL[b]

Age of Head of Household	France, by Head's Birthplace				Israel, by Head's Birthplace			
	Total	France	Other Europe	North Africa	Total	Israel	Europe-America	Africa-Asia
Total	3.2	2.8	2.9	3.8	3.5	3.5	2.8	4.5
Up to 24	1.8	1.8	1.5	1.8	2.8	2.7	2.3	3.6
25–34	2.7	2.5	3.0	2.8	3.7	3.5	3.3	4.1
35–44	3.5	2.9	4.1	4.2	4.9	4.4	4.1	5.7
45–54	3.9	3.6	3.4	4.2	4.2	4.1	3.4	5.5
55–64	3.5	2.9	2.9	4.3	2.8	2.8	2.4	3.9
65+	2.5	2.0	2.4	2.8	1.8	1.8	1.8	2.1

[a] Including non-Jewish members of the household.
[b] 1975. Source: Israel Central Bureau of Statistics, *Statistical Abstract of Israel 1976*, p. 50.

Household Structure

A closer look at Jewish family structure in France, based on the relationship of individual members to the head of household (Table 10),
reveals the overwhelming dominance of "heads," "spouses," and "children." Other types of relations constitute only 3 percent of the population. Only among persons aged sixty and older do the "others"—
essentially mothers of other adults—become more frequent. On the
other hand, in connection with the relatively late age at marriage, and
high celibacy rates, of Jews in France, persistence of the family status of
"child" can be observed among young adults aged twenty to twenty-
nine, and—though less—at ages thirty to thirty-nine. About one-half of
these older "children" are currently married. The status of "head of
household" pertains to a majority of Jewish adults—regardless of sex—
after age forty. Sex differentials in household roles, however, are powerful, headship being a predominantly male prerogative in each age group.

More detailed data by country of birth of household members
illustrate the persistence of differentials in household structure by age,
sex, marital status, and degree of relationship to the head of the household (Table 11). Among North African Jews, somewhat more complex
household structures involving two generations of married adults under
one roof are twice as frequent as among households of European stock,
yet not very widespread. Similar findings obtain at the older extreme of
the age structure (Table 12). The proportion of "other" relatives is substantially higher among North African Jews. The more recent immigrant
status of North African Jews in France and its impact on housing and

living arrangements should be kept in mind when reviewing these data. The available evidence points, nevertheless, to a greater traditional familism among members of this immigrant group, and to moderately more extended families within its fold.

The "Conventional" Jewish Family and Some Alternatives

Some of the combined effects of the different family processes described so far are illustrated in Table 13, which shows the structure of French Jewish population by marital status and religion of partner (for the currently married). The changing weight of the Jewish family, as an ideal type, in contrast to alternative individual and family arrangements, can be evaluated across different sex, age, and origin groups. A rough index of "conventional" Jewish familism is the proportion of persons currently

Table 10. POPULATION IN JEWISH HOUSEHOLDS[a] IN FRANCE, BY SEX, AGE, AND RELATIONSHIP TO HEAD OF HOUSEHOLD

Age and Sex	Total	Head of Household	Spouse	Child	Other
Males					
Total	100	55	1	43	2
0–9	100	0	0	99	1
10–19	100	0	0	99	1
20–29	100	24	0	74	2
30–39	100	78	1	20	1
40–49	100	99	0	1	0
50–59	100	97	1	2	0
60–69	100	96	1	0	3
70+	100	90	0	0	10
Females					
Total	100	8	50	38	4
0–9	100	0	0	98	2
10–19	100	0	1	98	1
20–29	100	5	26	67	2
30–39	100	6	83	10	1
40–49	100	8	89	2	1
50–59	100	13	86	0	1
60–69	100	18	75	0	7
70+	100	32	34	0	34

[a] Including non-Jewish members of the household.

Table 11. PERCENTAGE OF CURRENTLY MARRIED JEWISH "CHILDREN"[a]
AGED 20–39, BY COUNTRY OF BIRTH AND SEX

Age of "Child"	Country of Birth			
	Europe[b]		North Africa	
	Male	Female	Male	Female
20–29	6	3	7	13
30–39	6	4	12	9

[a] Out of 100 individuals in each cell.
[b] Including French born.

Table 12. PERCENTAGE OF "OTHER"[a] JEWISH HOUSEHOLD MEMBERS AT
AGES 60 AND OVER, BY COUNTRY OF BIRTH AND SEX

Age	Country of Birth			
	Europe[b]		North Africa	
	Male	Female	Male	Female
60–69	3	5	4	11
70 and over	8	24	8	52

[a] Other than head of household, spouse, and child, out of 100 individuals in each cell.
[b] Including French born.

in-married, as contrasted with those *never, formerly,* or *out-*married. This proportion is steadily declining among the younger cohorts, Among the combined twenty to thirty-nine age groups, less then one-half—37 percent of Jewish males and 44 percent of Jewish females—were currently married to a Jewish partner. These levels were obviously lower than among older age cohorts measured at comparable ages. Significant differences still obtained by origin groups, especially among Jewish women: between ages twenty and thirty-nine, only 37 percent of the European born (including the French), versus 53 percent of the North Africans, were married to a Jewish partner in the mid 1970s.

Comparing French Jewish and Israeli data on the frequency of conventional Jewish familism—i.e., belonging to a nuclear, homogamous Jewish family—offers a further measure of the differences developing between the Jewish populations in these different environments (Table 14). Although based on individual records, the findings have household and community significance. While sociodemographic gaps that had existed between the different Jewish immigrant communities have greatly diminished, both in France and in Israel, a very substantial

Table 13. Jewish Population in France Aged 20 and Over, by Sex, Age, Country of Birth, Current Marital Status, and Religion of Spouse

Sex and Age	Total					Born in Europe[a]					Born in North Africa				
	Total	Never Married	Formerly Married[b]	Out-Married	In-Married	Total	Never Married	Formerly Married[b]	Out-Married	In-Married	Total	Never Married	Formerly Married[b]	Out-Married	In-Married
Males															
Total	100	24	4	11	61	100	24	4	14	58	100	24	3	8	65
20–29	100	78	1	6	15	100	78	1	5	16	100	78	2	7	13
30–39	100	20	3	19	58	100	28	3	22	47	100	15	3	17	65
40–49	100	4	2	18	76	100	6	2	24	68	100	3	1	12	84
50–59	100	3	4	9	84	100	6	4	15	75	100	0	3	3	94
60–69	100	1	6	7	86	100	2	7	9	82	100	1	5	3	91
70+	100	4	12	13	71	100	6	13	15	66	100	0	9	10	80
Females															
Total	100	19	12	5	64	100	19	14	8	59	100	18	11	2	69
20–29	100	69	0	5	26	100	73	0	6	21	100	65	1	6	28
30–39	100	9	2	26	63	100	8	2	39	51	100	10	2	10	78
40–49	100	6	4	1	89	100	8	6	2	84	100	4	4	0	92
50–59	100	3	11	2	84	100	5	11	5	79	100	2	10	0	88
60–69	100	3	22	0	75	100	5	19	1	75	100	1	25	0	74
70+	100	3	65	1	31	100	5	61	2	32	100	1	70	0	29

[a] Including French born.
[b] Divorced, widowed.

Table 14. PERCENTAGE IN CONVENTIONAL JEWISH FAMILY[a] AT AGES 20 TO
39 IN FRANCE AND ISRAEL, BY SEX AND COUNTRY OF BIRTH

Sex and Age	France, by Birthplace			Israel, by Birthplace		
	Total	Europe[b]	North Africa	Total[c]	Europe-America	Africa-Asia
Male						
20–29	15	16	13	43	53	48
30–39	58	47	65	91	91	92
Female						
20–29	26	21	28	64	71	71
30–39	63	51	78	91	91	92

[a] Jews currently married to a Jewish partner, out of 100 individuals in each cell.
[b] Including French born.
[c] Including Israel born.

gap emerges between Jews in the two countries. The split that has occurred appears in full among both European and North African immigrants. These different family processes and structures also significantly condition intergenerational community continuity, at least to the extent that existence of the family is the ordinary prerequisite for reproduction and child socialization processes to unfold.[23]

Discussion

This overview aims to constitute a first, necessary baseline toward future investigations of more complex questions concerning the causes and consequences of sociodemographic change and variation in the contemporary Jewish family, in France and elsewhere. Although the main focus of this chapter is on French Jewry, its concerns are geographically and thematically more extended. The general question raised is to what extent interaction between an initial population structure and alternative sets of marriage-market, socioeconomic, and cultural options and constraints may generate changes in a variety of family patterns. The answer is that variation may be overwhelming, and may cut across a large number of distinct, though related, family processes.

In this chapter, Jews in France have been frequently compared with their origin peers in Israel. Such elementary typologies do some violence to historical and sociological reality, and cannot substitute for more detailed analyses of smaller and more homogeneous subcommunities. Yet it is not uncommon that people are stimulated to identify themselves along such rudimentary community lines, under the impact of actions taken by institutions, or of debates unfolding in the media. In such a perspective, the parsimonious breakdowns suggested here constitute a meaningful working tool.

In a study focusing on migrants, different effects of environments in the places of origin and of destination on family variables should be kept in mind. Unlike migration to Israel, which at least in its mass stages often involved the transfer of entire and quite intact Jewish communities, several transitional processes had begun before migration among Jews who chose a French destination. These included socioeconomic modernization, some diffusion of marital assimilation, and some fertility control. But different "transformation matrices" to which the Jewish populations in France and in Israel were exposed during the last thirty years generated sharp contrasts in various dimensions of Jewish family life. This meant, for a typical cohort of Jews in France, fewer and later marriages, more frequent marriages with Jews of different geographical origins, more religious out-marriages, and possibly—though this is not proven conclusively here—somewhat more frequent divorce. In terms of living arrangements, this corresponds to smaller households composed of heads and/or spouses and children with a high proportion of primary individuals, and a gradual disappearing of the "other" relative. The ultimate result of these combined processes is a progressive diminution of the "Jewish family" in France, which may contrast with its persistence in Israel. Indeed, the high proportion of unmarried young adults implies a substantial erosion in the process of intergenerational replacement among French Jewry. The high frequency of mixed marriage leads to Jewish birth "losses" through the dominant identification of children of mixed couples with the non-Jewish side. Moreover, the findings of this study carry significant implications for the amount of total participation in Jewish community activities in France, in view of the known or expected lower activity rates among alternative family types, as contrasted to the conventional, homogamous, nuclear Jewish family.

On the other hand, analysts of sociodemographic change investigating the Jewish segment of Israeli society will not fail to recognize that whatever erosion processes may be now at work in family patterns there, they do not constitute anything comparable with the rapid decline of the traditional Jewish family that has characterized French Jewry over the last few decades, more significantly so since the mid-1960s. Considering that the demographic dynamics now typical of French Jewry closely resembles that of most Diaspora Jews, the innovative character of Israeli sociodemographic patterns cannot be understated in a worldwide perception of Jewish population trends.[24]

The more recent findings presented here point to two distinctly different modes of absorption among Jewish immigrants in France and in Israel. In France, the frame of reference into which immigrant Jews tended to assimilate was a general French population whose quintessentially Western European family patterns differed from those that had prevailed among Jews in North Africa. Changes in the Jewish family, such as postponing marriage or marrying out of the Jewish community, in part reflected the difficulty of finding suitable partners among members of a minority group, but also seem to have been consonant with the immigrants' upward-mobility desires and achievements. In Israel, while the range of social-mobility opportunities may have been more limited for the new immigrants, no homogeneous, dominant frame of reference existed for absorption. Each immigrant group constituted the "other" for another immigrant group. At least demographically, this was conducive to a convergence of previously different behaviors. While these different experiences are of interest in a general evaluation of assimilation processes, it clearly ensues that observation of demographic trends in the Israeli population microcosm does not provide an adequate proxy for evaluating current Jewish family patterns elsewhere in the world. The latter objective can only be obtained by a continuing effort of data collection and analysis in the various Diaspora communities themselves.

In a more localistic perspective, family patterns do not function at present as an agent of demographic self-support for the Jewish community of France. While the contemporary intellectual and communal vitality of French Jewry is witnessed by remarkable accomplishments,[25] the current erosion in centrality and Jewishness of the French Jewish family may be a prelude to a significant weakening of the community in the longer run. The historical model of Jewish population development in France has been one of successive immigration waves taking over from more veteran and assimilated strata and ensuring continuity if not actual growth of the community.[26] This stratification has included the Jews in the southern France papal domains (Avignon and Comtat Venaissin), the Sephardim in the French southwest, the larger Alsatian Jewish community, the immigrants from Eastern and Central Europe from the 1880s through the interwar period, and finally and more significantly—at least quantitatively—the largest ever immigration wave—from North Africa. But now the demographic impact of this last wave seems to be declining, and an intriguing question for further research is whether and how this centuries-long relay will continue.

Notes

1. See F. Kobrin and C. Goldscheider, *The Ethnic Factor in Family Structure and Mobility* (Cambridge, Mass.: Ballinger, 1978).

2. On immigration to France, see Institut National d'Etudes Démographiques, *La Population de la France* (Paris: 1974 World Population Year CICRED Series, 1974). For a comparison of recent fertility trends of immigrant groups in France, see M. Brahimi, "Chronique de l'immigration," *Population* 35:1 (1980), 173–88.

3. Examples of comparative studies of emigrant diasporas are: C. A. Corsini and E. Sonnino, "The CISP Survey on the Families of Italian Emigrants Abroad," in M. Livi-Bacci, ed., *The Demographic and Social Pattern of Emigration from the Southern European Countries* (Firenze: Dipartimento Statistico Matematico dell'Università di Firenze—Comitato Italiano per lo Studio dei Problemi della Popolazione, 1972), pp. 279–375; and J. Zubrzycki, "Polish Emigration to British Commonwealth Countries: A Demographic Survey," *International Migration Review* 13:4 (1979), pp. 649–72.

4. See discussions by C. Goldscheider, *Population, Modernization and Social Structure* (Boston: Little, Brown, 1971), chap. 10; F. D. Bean and J. P. Marcum, "Differential Fertility and the Minority Group Status Hypothesis: An Assessment and Review," in F. D. Bean and W. P. Frisbie, eds., *The Demography of Racial and Ethnic Groups* (New York: Academic Press, 1978), pp. 189–211; D. E. Lopez and G. Sabagh, "Untangling Structural and Normative Aspects of the Minority Status—Fertility Hypothesis," *American Journal of Sociology* 83 (May 1978), 1491–97.

5. C. Castonguay with C. Veltman, "L'orientation linguistique des mariages mixtes dans la région de Montréal," *Recherches Sociographiques* 21:3 (1980), 225–51.

6. For a more comprehensive treatment, the reader is referred to D. Bensimon and S. DellaPergola, *La population juive de France: socio-démographie et identité* (Jerusalem: The Hebrew University–Centre National de la Recherche Scientifique Paris, Jewish Population Studies series), 1984.

7. See J. Katz, "Family, Kinship and Marriage Among Ashkenazim in the Sixteenth to Eighteenth Centuries," *The Jewish Journal of Sociology* 1:1 (1959), 4–22; R. Bachi, "L'évolution de la nuptialité et de la fécondité chez les juifs de la Diaspora: influence de la tradition et de la modernisation," *Démographie et destin des sous-populations* (Paris: Association International des Démographes de Langue Française, 1983), 87–96; and J. Matras, "On Changing Marriage and Family Formation among Jewish Immigrant Communities in Israel: Some Findings and some Further Problems," in U. O. Schmelz, P. Glikson, and S. DellaPergola, eds., *Papers in Jewish Demography 1969* (Jerusalem: The Hebrew University, Jewish Population Studies series), 1973, pp. 265–76.

8. See R. Bachi, *The Population of Israel* (Jerusalem: 1974 World Population Year CICRED Series, 1977); and D. Friedlander and C. Goldscheider, *The Population of Israel* (New York: Columbia University Press, 1979).

9. This includes, throughout this chapter, a small minority of Jews born in Asia.

10. Inclusive of a few American-born Jews.

11. See D. Bensimon, "Mutations socio-démographiques aux XIXᵉ et XXᵉ siècles," *Histoire* 3 (1979), 199–200.

12. According to the 1972 Israeli census, the median length of stay in the country of foreign-born Jews was 21 years and the median age of the local-born 12.9 years. In France, in the mid-1970s, the corresponding values were 14.4 and 19.6 years. By combining the different figures for foreign and local born, a median estimate of 17.2 years of "exposure to country" obtained in Israel, versus 16.8 in France. These values are obviously lower than normally observed among the populations of developed countries.

13. Census, vital, and migration statistics are regularly published by Israel's Central Bureau of Statistics.

14. See S. DellaPergola, "The French Jewish Population Study: Progress Report and Evaluation of Research Problems," U. O. Schmelz, P. Glikson, and S. DellaPergola, *Papers in Jewish Demography 1973* (Jerusalem: The Hebrew University, Jewish Population Studies series, 1977), pp. 79–107.

15. See D. Bensimon-Donath, *Immigrants d'Afrique du nord en Israel* (Paris: Anthropos, 1970), *L'intégration des Juifs nord-africains en France* (Paris-La Haye: Mouton, 1971); M. Inbar and C. Adler, *Ethnic Integration in Israel: A Comparative Case Study of Moroccan Brothers Who Settled in France and in Israel* (New Brunswick, N.J.: Transaction Books, 1977).

16. See the detailed retrospective data on Jewish populations in U. O. Schmelz, "The Israel Population Census of 1961 as a Source of Demographic Data on the Jews of the Diaspora," *The Jewish Journal of Sociology* 8:1 (1966), 49–63; J. Matras, *Families in Israel, Part II,* Population and Housing Census, 1961, vol. 39 (Jerusalem: Israel Central Bureau of Statistics, 1968); and general discussions in J. Hajnal, "European Marriage Patterns in Perspective," in D. V. Glass and D.E.C. Eversley, eds., *Population in History* (London-Chicago: University of Chicago Press, 1965), pp. 101–43; and S. Cotts Watkins, "Regional Patterns of Nuptiality in Europe, 1870–1960," *Population Studies* 35:2 (1981), 199–215.

17. Fertility of Jews in France, not dealt with in this chapter, is discussed in this author's three other papers: "Contemporary Jewish Fertility: An Overview," *Papers in Jewish Demography 1981* (Jerusalem: The Hebrew University, Jewish Population Studies series), 1983, 215–38; "Comparative Trends in World Jewish Fertility, 1830–1980," paper presented at General Conference of the International Union for the Scientific Study of the Population, Session I, 10, Manila, Philippines, 9–16 December 1981; and "L'effet des mariages mixtes sur la natalité dans une sous-population: quelques problèmes et resultats concernant la diaspora juive," *Démographie et destin des sous-populations* (Paris: Association Internationale des Démographes de Langue Française, 1983), 223–36.

18. Religiously heterogamous marriages are not legally possible in Israel. Mixed marriages performed abroad are recognized as valid by Israel's legal system. See M. Roshwald, "Who Is a Jew in Israel?" *The Jewish Journal of Sociology* 12:2 (1970), 233–66. In Israel, conversions to Judaism (mostly by non-Jewish partners in mixed marriages performed abroad) largely outnumber conversions from Judaism. See D. Gotthold, "Converts in the State of Israel" [Hebrew], unpublished seminar paper, Jerusalem, The Hebrew University, 1969.

19. Mainly in Paris suburbs, but also in certain central city districts. See

C. Tapia, "North African Jews in Belleville," *The Jewish Journal of Sociology* 16:1 (1974), 5–23.

20. For an overview, see (e.g.,) S. Smooha, *Israel: Pluralism and Conflict* (London: Routledge & Kegan Paul, 1978).

21. After making allowance for certain differences in the classification of spouses by birthplace, our data for the 1950s and 1960s fit well with the current marriage statistics examined by E. Frischoff and A. Hattab, *Survey of Jewish Marriages Registered by the Consistory of Paris, January 1955 through June 1962* (Paris: Community, 1964).

22. Cross-classification of grooms and brides, by birthplace, gives in this case a 2 × 2 table, with homogamous marriage on one diagonal. Homogamy measure reported here (Benini index) is based on the ratio between actual cases on the diagonal and the number of expected cases based on the product of the table's marginals, corrected for the maximum possible number of homogamous couples given the distributions of grooms and brides. See L. A. Goodman and W. H. Kruskal, "Measures of Association for Cross-Classifications. II: Further Discussion and References," *American Statistical Association Journal* 54 (December 1959), 133–34.

23. On recent Jewish fertility trends in Israel, see D. Friedlander and C. Goldscheider, "Immigration, Social Change and Cohort Fertility in Israel," *Population Studies* 32:2 (1978), 299–317; and C. Goldscheider and D. Friedlander, "Jewish Fertility in Israel: A Review and Some Hypotheses," in P. Ritterband, ed., *Modern Jewish Fertility* (Leiden: Brill, 1981), pp. 232–54. See also n. 17 above.

24. See U. O. Schmelz, "Jewish Survival: The Demographic Factors," *American Jewish Year Book* 81 (1981), 61–117.

25. A revealing indicator is the 500 doctoral theses on Jewish topics in the social sciences and the humanities submitted in 1967–1976 or in preparation. See D. Bensimon, "Sociologie des judaïcités contemporaines: Bilan et perspectives de la recherche française," *Revue Française de sociologie* 22:1 (1981), 33–50.

26. See B. Blumenkrantz, ed., *Histoire des Juifs en France* (Toulouse: Privat, 1972); P. Hyman, "Jewish Fertility in Nineteenth Century France," in P. Ritterband, ed., *Modern Jewish Fertility* (Leiden: Brill, 1981), pp. 78–93.

12. Family Patterns Among the U.S. Yiddish-Mother-Tongue Subpopulation: 1970

Frances Kobrin Goldscheider

Family patterns in the United States have been undergoing rapid change in the second half of the twentieth century. Some changes represent a return to older patterns interrupted by the "baby boom"—especially declining fertility, increases in age at marriage, and proportions never marrying. In addition, other, newer trends have emerged which, each in its own way, also contribute to a decline in the centrality of family in people's lives. Most frequently noted is the rapid increase in rates of divorce leading to an increasing number of one-parent families. Equally dramatic is the rapid increase in the proportions living in one-person households, formed by adults moving away from family altogether. Whereas one-person households amounted to but 9 percent of total households in 1950 (Kobrin 1976), in 1980 their share had reached 24 percent.

In this context, it is important to consider the extent to which American Jews are participating in these changes. Research to date on American Jewish family patterns has suggested that Jews differ in significant ways in their family-building patterns and the structures that result. Based on data primarily from a series of community studies, Jews in the United States in the twentieth century have been shown to have low fertility and late ages at marriage. But very high proportions marry, and those marriages have been very stable relative to the general population (Mindel and Habenstein 1981; Goldstein and Goldscheider 1968; Kobrin and Goldscheider 1978).

This chapter focuses on the extent to which these patterns persist in national data, and includes a consideration of household size and structure. Specifically, for 1970, what were American Jewish marriage and fertility patterns, and how did they compare to the U.S. total? How did levels of voluntary separation and proportions of one-parent families compare? Were Jews more or less likely to be living altogether away from family? The data to be used were collected by the 1970 U.S. census on the Yiddish-mother-tongue population.

Data

This is an unusual data set for the study of American Jewry. U.S. census data normally used for ethnic analysis have been restricted to race and country of origin, both useless for isolating Jews after the earliest decades of the twentieth century, and the census has never included a question on religion. As a result, analysis of the American Jewish community depended on a series of local studies, and national-level analyses were only pursued using the very small numbers of Jews turned up by general national samples, such as the 1957 Current Population Survey and the general social surveys of the National Opinion Research Council (NORC), and specialized surveys focusing on, for example, family issues such as the national fertility surveys which were restricted to women and until recently included only the ever married.

The need for national data with breadth of information and enough cases to allow depth of analysis was so great that a national survey of American Jews was designed and executed in 1971—the National Jewish Population Survey (NJPS). At the same time, however, the Bureau of the Census decided to include on the 15 percent sample schedule a language question which, for the only time except for 1940, was not restricted to the foreign-born. And to the question "Was a language other than English spoken in the home when you were growing up?" large numbers of American Jews, most of them native-born, replied "Yiddish."

A secondary purpose of this chapter is to suggest that the census Yiddish-mother-tongue data provide valuable national information for the study of American Jewry. Thus there are really *two* national data sets for essentially the same date which, if comparatively analyzed, will give us more confidence and clues to the appropriate use of both.

The data on Yiddish mother tongue have been little used for the study of American Jewry. (A valuable exception is Rosenwaike 1971.) In general, scholars have been concerned that data on Yiddishists are increasingly unrepresentative (Goldstein and Goldscheider 1968), and there has been no way to evaluate this bias. The totals reported are always well below estimates of the American Jewish population; 1.6 million Yiddishists were counted in 1970 compared to the estimated 5.7 million Jews in the United States. Further, little detail has appeared in published tabulations. The availability of sample census files, however, has made possible much more detailed analysis. All of the questions included on the 15 percent sample can be used and the numbers of cases can be very large. Even on the 1/1,000 P.U.S. there are 1,600 Yiddishists, and by merging the state and neighborhood 1 percent samples, 32,000 cases are available. This technique has been used to study Jewish fertility in California (Watts 1980). The problem of representativeness can also be addressed much more productively. The existence of the NJPS makes possible a direct examination of the representativeness of the U.S. Yiddish-mother-tongue subpopulation.

One can also examine the characteristics of the non-Yiddish household members of the Yiddish-mother-tongue households. The 1.6 million Yiddishists live in households containing between 3.5 and 4 million people, most of whom are Jews and could be identified as such based on household relationships (children of Yiddishists) and background characteristics (parent's country of birth).

As a preliminary step in such an analysis, Table 1 compares the census Yiddish-mother-tongue subpopulation with those in NJPS who answered the broadest Yiddish-knowledge question on that survey. (Regrettably, the designers of the NJPS thought so little of the census mother-tongue question that it was not asked.)

The characteristics of the two groups are strikingly similar. For each, just over 70 percent were native-born, and the age distributions are nearly identical. Both are more likely to be foreign-born than the weighted[1] NJPS total population and, of course, much older. The major difference arises, however, because of the presence of third and higher generations in the NJPS. Preliminary analysis suggests that foreign-born mother-tongue Yiddishists are quite similar to total foreign-born in NJPS, and the second generation is even more so. (A more detailed analysis of these issues can be found in Kobrin 1981.) Adding in the children in the census file will render the total even more representative.

The issue of representation, however, is one that can never be fully resolved. In contrast to a count of citizens, or residents of an area, counts of geographically dispersed ethnic groups depend on a concept which is much more difficult to operationalize. The designers of the NJPS struggled with the problem of defining "what is a Jew," and aimed for flexibility both in the questions asked and in the sampling strategy. The data presented in the next sections are based on one fairly unconventional definition of the American Jewish population. But it is a valuable sub-group of Jews, and analyses to date show that 1970 census data on the mother-tongue-Yiddish subpopulation, and their families, totaling up to 4 million (and the Hebrew speakers and their families, which total up to 250,000), represent a valuable resource for the study of American Jews in the late twentieth century.[2]

Family Patterns

Three family processes can be studied on a general level in the data available on Yiddishists in the 1970 census. The questions asked on marital status and on children ever born allow an assessment of fertility, age at marriage, and the extent of marriage and separation. (Unfortunately, the better questions on marriage were asked only on the 5 percent sample.)

Table 2 indicates the numbers of children that had ever been born to married women of various ages by 1970. Women over thirty in 1970 in the Yiddish subpopulation had somewhat over two children each, compared to the about two and three-quarters borne by all U.S. women past thirty at that date. Moreover, Yiddish women started bearing later.

Table 1. COMPARISON OF U.S. YIDDISH SUBPOPULATION SAMPLES: NJPS 1971 AND U.S. CENSUS, 1970

	Total NJPS	Yiddish Subpopulation	
		NJPS	U.S. Census
Number	—	—	1,600,000
Percent of total	—	41.6	—
Percent native-born	83.7	70.1	70.9
Age distribution			
0–9	12.4	1.1	1.4
10–19	17.8	5.7	4.2
20–29	13.2	9.1	8.2
30–39	8.4	7.3	9.4
40–49	15.7	18.5	18.2
50–64	19.9	34.2	34.8
65+	12.5	24.2	23.8
Total	100.0	100.0	100.0
n	~6,000	~2,500	32,000

Sources: National Jewish Population Survey, 1971; combined 1% state and neighborhood P.U.S. files.

Table 2. CHILDREN EVER BORN TO WOMEN BY AGE IN 1970: YIDDISH
MOTHER TONGUE AND TOTAL U.S. WOMEN

Age	U.S. Total	Yiddish Mother Tongue
<19	.09	.05
20–29	1.26	.77
30–39	2.90	2.22
40–49	2.93	2.22
50–64	2.45	1.74
65 +	2.55	2.07

While few in either group had borne children before age twenty, barely
half as many Yiddish women had become mothers by such a young age.
Similarly, while all women twenty to twenty-nine had borne 43 percent
as many children as women thirty to thirty-nine, for Yiddish women the
number of children ever born by age twenty-nine was only thirty-four
percent of the level reached by women of thirty to thirty-nine, another
indication of the concentration of births at older ages. Both groups show
evidence of the "baby bust" of the 1930s and subsequent baby boom.
More detailed data are required to measure the relative family-building
progress of the younger women since the baby boom, but analysis of
NJPS data indicates that young Jewish women, even more extremely
than the total U.S. pattern, are not bearing children at replacement levels
(DellaPergola 1980).

One factor in late childbearing for the Yiddish subpopulation is their
later age at marriage. Although data on age at marriage are not available
on the 15 percent schedule, the marital status by age distribution allows
an estimate of marriage age by assuming that the decline in single
proportions with each older cohort reflects the experience of the separate
real cohorts as they aged. Table 3 indicates that the Yiddish of both sexes
marry somewhat later than the total U.S. population. Both men and
women marry more than one and a half years later than average, with
women not marrying until nearly age twenty-three and men waiting
until after reaching age twenty-five. Less than one-third of Yiddish men
had married by age twenty-five compared to nearly half the U.S. total;
similarly, nearly two-thirds of total American women had married by
age twenty-five while barely half the Yiddish women had married by
that age.

At the older ages, however, the proportions never married are lower
for the Yiddish subpopulation than for the U.S. total. Although Yiddish-

speaking Jews marry late, more eventually marry, particularly among women. The most extreme examples are the cohorts aged forty-five to forty-nine and fifty to fifty-four in 1970. Five to 6 percent of all American women in these cohorts had not married by 1970, compared to but 3 percent of Yiddish women.

Table 4 indicates that not only are Yiddish-speaking men and women more likely eventually to enter the married state; they are also less likely to leave it. Although the data are not as precise as is needed, since there is no information on remarriage, it seems that Yiddish marriages are less likely to be broken voluntarily, and are ended rather later by death as well. By age thirty, both Yiddish men and women are more likely to be currently married than the U.S. total. The differences are consistent, with levels 5 to 10 percent higher among the Yiddish. By contrast, the U.S. total population includes much higher proportions separated or divorced than does the Yiddish subpopulation, reaching levels often twice as high or more. The differences are most dramatic for men under forty. This reflects in part the earlier marriages of the U.S. total, which have been longer at risk of dissolution, but this factor cannot account for much of the difference observed.

Finally, similar contrasts can be observed among the widowed. For both sexes and all ages, the Yiddish subpopulation is less likely to be widowed than the average for the United States as a whole. Lower mortality has been observed for Jews relative to the general population

Table 3. PERCENTAGE NEVER MARRIED BY AGE IN 1970: YIDDISH MOTHER TONGUE AND TOTAL U.S. ADULTS

	Males		Females	
Age	U.S. Total	Yiddish	U.S. Total	Yiddish
15–19	95.9	95.6	87.5	96.1
20–24	54.6	69.6	36.8	46.2
25–29	21.1	30.0	12.7	18.2
30–34	10.0	11.2	7.6	5.5
35–39	10.5	6.5	4.8	6.1
40–44	6.7	6.5	5.4	5.5
45–49	5.9	5.1	5.1	3.0
50–54	7.1	5.1	6.4	3.2
55 +	5.8	4.2	6.6	5.9
Singulate mean age at marriage	23.5	25.1	21.0	22.8

Table 4. Marital Status by Age in 1970: Yiddish Mother Tongue and Total U.S. Adults

Age in 1970	Total	Never Married	Married, Spouse Present	Separated/ Divorced	Widowed
			Males		
<20					
U.S. Total	100.0	96.5	2.7	0.6	0.2
Yiddish	100.0	95.2	3.8	1.0	—
20–29					
U.S. Total	100.0	39.2	54.9	5.7	0.2
Yiddish	100.0	49.4	49.0	1.6	0.0
30–39					
U.S. Total	100.0	10.2	81.1	8.3	0.4
Yiddish	100.0	8.6	86.1	3.4	0.0
40–49					
U.S. Total	100.0	6.3	85.9	7.0	0.9
Yiddish	100.0	5.7	89.6	4.5	0.2
50–64					
U.S. Total	100.0	5.7	83.4	7.6	3.3
Yiddish	100.0	4.4	89.1	4.4	2.2
65 +					
U.S. Total	100.0	6.7	70.3	6.7	16.3
Yiddish	100.0	4.5	78.8	5.0	11.7
			Females		
<20					
U.S. Total	100.0	89.7	7.8	2.1	0.4
Yiddish	100.0	96.6	3.4	0.0	0.0
20–29					
U.S. Total	100.0	25.7	63.5	9.7	1.2
Yiddish	100.0	33.3	62.1	4.2	0.4
30–39					
U.S. Total	100.0	6.2	81.5	10.3	2.0
Yiddish	100.0	5.8	85.0	7.9	1.4
40–49					
U.S. Total	100.0	5.3	78.8	10.6	5.3
Yiddish	100.0	4.0	87.9	5.3	2.8
50–64					
U.S. Total	100.0	6.5	65.6	10.5	17.5
Yiddish	100.0	5.1	77.6	4.3	12.9
65 +					
U.S. Total	100.0	6.7	35.5	5.7	52.2
Yiddish	100.0	5.9	42.6	4.6	47.0

(Goldstein 1981), which would lead to the longer survival of marriages, but the size of the differences observed would seem to suggest a higher probability that remarriage following widowhood must be present as well.

All of these differences—in proportions marrying, remarrying, separating voluntarily, or experiencing widowhood—operate together to lead to a highly married population. The couple culture has strong roots in the marriage patterns developed through 1970 among this Yiddish subpopulation. If the recent cohorts, which are marrying even later, become less likely to eventually marry, as has been documented in total U.S. marriage patterns, this will represent a much greater break with older generations.

Household Structure and Living Arrangements[3]

The final concern of this chapter is household structure and living arrangements. Major changes in living arrangements have occurred for the total U.S. population, characterized by increases in one-parent families and single-person households. The first has occurred as a consequence of the rise in divorce, which affects marriages at an early stage and is thus more likely than widowhood to disrupt children's lives as well. The increase in single-person households results from a more complex set of processes, but can be most simply understood as a decrease in the probability that unmarried adults who are not the parents of minor children will join the family of some relative—i.e., a decline in family extension. The extent to which the American Jewish family structure is similar to the U.S. total is not known.

Table 5 addresses the question of one-parent families and single-person households (90 percent of primary individual households consist of only one person). The data presented for the Yiddish-mother-tongue subpopulation have been restricted to household heads so that the structures of large households will not be overrepresented in the distributions.

In general it is clear that the differences seen in the analysis of marital status carry over to differences in household type. Overall, more Yiddish households are husband-wife (71.4 percent versus 69.1 percent) and fewer are single-parent (7.6 percent versus 11.3 percent). Differences by age, however, suggest some convergence on this dimension for women. (Male levels are low and have been declining over time in the U.S.) The largest differences are for older women, where Yiddish women are considerably less likely to head families; among younger women (discounting the youngest group, which is distorted most by differences in age at marriage) the Yiddish level more closely approximates those of the

Table 5. HOUSEHOLD TYPE BY AGE OF HEAD: YIDDISH MOTHER TONGUE*
AND TOTAL U.S., 1970

Age	Total	Husband-Wife Households	Other Male Family Head	Female Family Head	Primary Individual Male	Female
Total						
U.S. Total	100.0	69.1	2.6	8.7	7.3	12.2
Yiddish	100.0	71.4	2.2	5.4	6.3	14.7
14–34						
U.S. Total	100.0	75.3	2.5	8.5	7.9	5.8
Yiddish	100.0	71.4	1.2	4.1	12.4	10.9
35–44						
U.S. Total	100.0	79.5	2.7	9.8	4.8	3.2
Yiddish	100.0	82.0	1.9	7.2	5.5	3.5
45–64						
U.S. Total	100.0	71.7	2.8	8.4	6.0	11.1
Yiddish	100.0	78.1	2.3	5.7	4.4	9.5
65+						
U.S. Total	100.0	46.3	2.8	8.3	10.8	31.8
Yiddish	100.0	55.3	2.4	4.5	7.9	30.0

*Includes only Yiddish household heads.

total population. So although among Yiddish families the husband-wife type predominates relative to the total population, similar forces of change may be at work.

In terms of single-person households, however, the Yiddish group appears to stand less clearly on the side of traditional family values relative to the total population. Overall, in fact, a higher proportion of Yiddish households consist of a solitary woman (15 percent) than for the total U.S. (12 percent). At this point, such a difference simply reflects the different age distributions of the two populations, since the Yiddishists disproportionately include widowed women. Controlling for age, proportions are lower for all Yiddish women but the youngest. On the other hand, the higher proportions married among the Yiddish-mother-tongue subpopulation greatly reduces the pool of those eligible for heading a separate household.

Table 6 presents the proportion living as primary individuals and thus away from family among the restricted group of people who are neither currently married nor the parent of a resident minor child. Other groups of Eastern and Southern European origin have been included for comparison. The variation in proportion married is thus removed, and the next question becomes: Given that an adult has neither immediate family tie—spouse or minor child—does he or she live with other family members, or not? For the Yiddish-mother-tongue subpopulation in the United States in 1970, the answer is that such adults are considerably more likely to live away from family (and the vast majority alone) than is the case for other similarly situated adults in the total U.S. population (61 percent versus 54 percent). At every age, Yiddishists are as or more likely not to join a relative to make a home. This contrasts even more sharply with the Polish- and Greek-mother-tongue subpopulations, where extended family living is much more prevalent. The only group which approaches the Yiddish level of independent living are Russians, and this occurs primarily because more are first generation, and, particularly among the young, have fewer relatives among whom to live.

In terms of living arrangements, then, the Jewish reputation for familism results primarily from its emphasis on marriage, and not on family extension. Data not presented indicate that part of the difference reflects the greater affluence of Jews relative to other members of society, since separate living quarters are expensive. But most of the difference remains, suggesting a greater avoidance of family extension, and a lower pain threshold for the problems of "two women in the kitchen."

Discussion

The Jewish family in America, at least as represented by the Yiddish-mother-tongue subpopulation in the 1970 census, differs in many ways from the U.S. total population, or from several of the other origin/language groups arriving from the same general geographic area at about

Table 6. AGE PATTERNS OF NONFAMILY LIVING ARRANGEMENTS, U.S. TOTAL AND SELECTED MOTHER-TONGUE ETHNIC GROUPS, 1970

Age	U.S. Total	Yiddish	Russian	Polish	Greek
		% Living Away From Family			
25–44	42	53	60	37	42
45–64	57	57	57	49	27
65–74	65	70	71	56	55
75+	54	62	59	46	45
Total	54	61	61	48	41
n	1922	809	222	1228	225

Sources: 1970 U.S.P.U.S. 1/10,000 sample for totals; 1/50 for mother-tongue ethnics (both 1/100 samples, pooled).

the same period of history. The extent and duration of marriage is clearly greater, while fertility is lower. Couple bonds are strong, relative to the U.S. total. Other bonds are less strong, at least in terms of residential decisions, and thus family extension is rarer. Although relationships can be very strong without coresidence, it seems likely that issues of privacy and independence in the relationships between parents and children might be more acute in Jewish households.

Notes

1. Cases with weights above 10, however, were excluded.

2. This value is to be enhanced further when computer files of the 1940 census become available. Soon thereafter, records for 1910 will become public.

3. A preliminary version of this portion of the material was presented at the 1979 annual meeting of the Population Association of America (Kobrin and Goldscheider 1979).

References

DellaPergola, S. 1980. "Patterns of American Jewish Fertility." *Demography* 17:3, 261–74.

Goldstein, S. 1981. "Jews in the United States: Pespectives from Demography." *American Jewish Yearbook 1981* (Philadelphia: Jewish Publication Society), pp. 3–59.

Goldstein, S., and C. Goldscheider. 1968. *Jewish-Americans: Three Generations in a Jewish Community.* Englewood Cliffs, N.J.: Prentice-Hall.

Kobrin, F. E. 1976. "The Fall in Household Size and the Rise of the Primary Individual in the United States." *Demography,* February.

———. 1981. "National Data on American Jewry, 1970–71." Paper presented at the Eighth World Congress of Jewish Studies, Jerusalem.

Kobrin, F. E., and C. Goldscheider. 1978. *The Ethnic Factor in Family Structure and Mobility.* Cambridge, Mass.: Ballinger Publishing Co.

———. 1979. "Primary Individuals and Family Extension: Economic, Demographic and Ethnic Factors." Paper presented at the Annual Meeting of the Population Association of America, Philadelphia.

Mindel, C., and R. Habenstein, eds. 1981. *Ethnic Families in America: Patterns and Variations.* New York: Elsevier Publishing Co.

Rosenwaike, I. 1971. "The Utilization of Census Mother Tongue Data in American Jewish Population Analyses." *Jewish Social Studies* 33: 141–59.

Watts, R. 1980. "Jewish Fertility Trends and Differentials: An Examination of the Evidence from the Census of 1970." *Jewish Social Studies.*

CHANGE AND CONTINUITY IN
CONTEMPORARY JEWISH FAMILIES

13. Persistence and Change in the Hasidic Family

William Shaffir

In recent years, Hasidic Jewry has attracted the interest of Jews and Gentiles as never before. Academics and novelists have made the public increasingly aware of the life and behavior patterns of the Hasidim, while some Hasidic groups have deliberately drawn attention to themselves.[1]

Since the publication of Kranzler's *Williamsburg: A Jewish Community in Transition* (1961), many sociologists and anthropologists have examined the dynamics of Hasidic life (Gutwirth 1970; Mayer 1979; Mintz 1968; Poll 1962; Rubin 1972; Shaffir 1974).[2] The central question has been how the Hasidim are able to maintain a distinctive lifestyle while in North America and Western Europe, where they live mostly in urban situations and are surrounded by a larger society with dramatically different values and norms. Generally, the authors have described an astonishing religiocultural stability and have attempted to account for it by analyzing the community institutions that support the distinctive lifestyle. All agree that an important factor is the Hasidim's relatively successful efforts to isolate themselves from larger societal influences. Yet despite their insulation, the Hasidim are affected by changes in the larger society.

This chapter focuses specifically on the impact of outside secular influences on the Hasidic family, and represents a preliminary effort to analyze data from a larger project investigating stability and change

I would like to thank McMaster University for the financial assistance received for the fieldwork phase of this project. Appreciation is extended to Steven Cohen for valuable comments on an earlier draft of this chapter.

within the Hasidic family. Data for this paper are primarily from twenty informal interviews conducted with members of several Hasidic communities, including Lubavitch, Satmar, Tash, and Klausenberg, in Montreal and Toronto between January and April 1981. I have also used data collected during the course of my research on Hasidic communities in Montreal between 1969 and 1973.

The Hasidic Perception of Secular Influences

Current changes within the Hasidic family are so subtle—particularly in contrast to those in the larger society—that they can be seen only against the background of the groups' tradition and self-understanding. Certainly Hasidim do not desire change, particularly change that equals assimilation to the outside world. Indeed, their communities are actively organized to shield their members from the impact of surrounding secular influences.

Although Hasidic Jews are quite willing to incorporate most of the modern world's technological innovations into their lives, they perceive many of its cultural values as disruptive to the lifestyle they wish to observe. Generally speaking, they cast the outside world in a negative light and believe that its forces can only be detrimental unless carefully scrutinized and filtered. They are particularly aware of a need to shelter the young from what they see as undesirable secular influences. A Lubavitch woman captures a view shared by all Hasidim:

> Everyone today is so nutrition conscious. There are many tempting foods available, but we know they are really junk foods. . . . We cannot be any less aware of what we allow to enter our children's minds. We must be aware that what we give them provides the best nourishment for their souls—full of spiritual vitamins and minerals, not superficially tasty yet full of harmful chemicals and additives.
>
> To expect to stop all secular activity is unfortunately unrealistic. But at least we should be more aware of the potential harm involved, of how vigilantly we must supervise all of our children's activities. (*Di Yiddishe Heim* 20:21).

While Hasidim acknowledge that contact with the outside world cannot be avoided completely, they believe it can be controlled. Such control, they reason, can best be achieved by educating the young to realize the distinction between the precepts, values, and beliefs underlying their lifestyle and the norms and values of the secular culture. A Tasher and a Satmarer reflect this view:

That's made very clear to them that there's an outside world which we're not supposed to follow. . . . Of course they are aware [of the outside world]. They see things and they're taught that these are not the right things. . . . In cases where *boocherim* [older Yeshiva students] were not taught and they came out to the outside world, they . . . didn't know how to deal with it. I mean everybody is going to end up in the outside world to a certain extent.

The environment is polluted and there's no getting away from this. We breathe the air and we are affected. But it's especially dangerous for the children. Children are repeatedly taught that what is out there is not for them. [This is achieved by] *chinukh*—[education]—teaching them, talking to them, reminding them.

Formal education, in fact, offers a key example of both the Hasidim's awareness of the assimilative forces in the larger society and the length to which they go in their attempts to maintain a balance between insulation from and participation in it. They accept the laws that mandate provision of a secular education for boys and girls (in contrast to their tradition, which allows for an almost exclusively religious education for boys only); but all their schools use extreme caution in efforts to prevent the content and organization of the secular programs from conflicting or interfering with the goals of the religious studies programs. The following remarks by a Tasher reflect the measures taken to avoid possible detrimental influences from secular studies:

We would check the story. . . . Or sometimes we would photocopy stories from a regular reader in which there is a story that has nothing in it that could harm. [Can you give me a few examples of a very modern type of story which could harm?] . . . I would say that a modern story would be *cheder* [primary school] boys who would go to play baseball. . . . There are stories that have sex in it and things like that which is totally out. . . .

In spite of such efforts to guard against the intrusion of undesired outside influences, assimilative secular forces have greatly changed much of the environment in which Orthodox Jews function in North America (Kranzler 1977; Mayer 1979). It is precisely for this reason that a growing number of Hasidic communities are attempting to create their own enclaves in suburban and semirural locations.

The Tasher Hasidim of Ste. Therese, Quebec, are a case in point. Having identified the urban setting as less than desirable for the pursuit of a Torah lifestyle, the Tasher *rebbe*, in 1964, moved his followers from Montreal to an isolated setting some eighteen miles north of the city. A Tasher comments:

The trick is to isolate as much as possible. . . . The idea of isolation is brought by the Rambam [Maimonides] that a person is very much influenced by his surroundings. Our main success is because we are a community out of town, isolated in technical terms. It helps a lot. I mean it would never be so successful had we lived in town and chosen a certain street. . . . That would not help. That would not be as successful.

By using insulating mechanisms, the Hasidim have achieved a high degree of success in offsetting the assimilative tendencies of the larger society. Nevertheless, they do remain in contact with it and hence are exposed to and influenced by external forces beyond their control.

The Role of the Traditional Family

It has been claimed that the survival of the Jewish faith, as well as of the Jewish nation, depends on the strength and cohesion of the family as the carrier of tradition (Kranzler 1961).[3] Wirth (1928, 37, 109) expresses the same thought in his classic study of the ghetto: "The real inner solidarity of the ghetto community lay in the strong family ties"; and negatively: "To the extent that the solidarity of the family has been affected by modern life has the community been weakened and the allegiance to the old heritage been periled."

Certainly the family is a key to the Hasidim's efforts to ensure conformity to a prescribed lifestyle because it is the first and most enduring locus of the socialization process, the mediator or communicator of social values. The Hasidic family serves as an intermediary agent for the community, linking the individual to the larger social structure within the particular Hasidic group. In this capacity, it becomes one of the cornerstones of community cohesion, continuity, and survival. No other institution plays so crucial a role in the socialization process.

Although the family in the general society has recently experienced dramatic changes, respondents claim the Hasidic family has undergone far less turbulence. The relative stability of the family unit is attributed to the range of social and institutional supports available to the Hasidic community which enable the family to cushion the effects of outside pressures for change.

To what do the Hasidim attribute the family's success in maintaining the tradition and heritage? The most critical element, they claim, is that the parents serve as effective role models for the younger generation, displaying consistent behavior after which the children may pattern their own.[4] Pointing to the larger world, Hasidic Jews say that it is precisely the dramatic discrepancy between what parents say and what they do that leads to the confusion and disillusionment of the younger generation. They assert that there are few possibilities for observing hypocritical behavior in the Hasidic family. For the most part, the parents' observance of religious beliefs is consistent with what is expected of the children:

> In our community, children watch their parents and grandparents and their relatives, and they see that there are things that a Jew must do. They are taught that this is the way it must be and they are ready to do it too. They watch their parents. The example is set by the parents, in the family, and the children follow naturally.

Respondents claim that unlike groups in which different generations acquire different views of the world, they experience few intergenerational conflicts. A Lubavitch woman asserts:

> We didn't have a generation gap, I think, because of Torah. Torah held us together. . . . We're following the same line, that's the Torah line. You know, it isn't as if I'm the old-fashioned mother and this is the old-fashioned father. . . . The Torah has kept us so that my children and I have the same values. We think the same.

In brief, the family remains Hasidim's primary transmitter and maintainer of core values. Thus, it continues to serve, as it has traditionally, as the most important vehicle for the socialization of the young and as the central institution of the community, encouraging conformity and discouraging assimilation.

However, outside influences have begun infiltrating the Hasidic community. Their effect is reflected in certain deviation by the younger generation from expected and taken-for-granted norms, thus raising suspicion about Hasidim's contention that their communities are devoid of intergenerational conflicts:

> So ideas come in, like foreign ideas come in, women's liberation, it's a whole mentality. It's very subtle. It comes into every place. It comes in and it's a challenge (Lubavitch woman).

The Hasidic communities' boundaries are not impregnable to secular forces, some of which undoubtedly affect the family. In at least four separate yet interconnected areas—women and work, the desire for material possessions, separation and divorce, and family planning—respondents claim to detect the effects of worldy influences on the behavior and values of the Hasidic family.[5]

Women and Work

The phenomenon of Hasidic women entering the work force is reported in the social science literature on Hasidic communities. As recently as 1962, Poll could write of the Hasidic division of labor: "The freedom of the woman is limited. . . . She may not take an active part in the labor force, and she is not prepared for any career" (1962, 53). Rubin's (1972) findings, based on research conducted approximately one decade later in the same community as studied by Poll,[6] showed that the situation of women's participation in the work force had altered dramatically:

> Expectations concerning division of labor between husband and wife are undergoing radical change. At their root is the emerging view that, unless confined to the home by pre-school children, women share with their husbands the responsibility of providing for the family (1972, 106).

Rubin found that 52 percent of the women whose youngest children were six years or older were employed outside the home (also see Mayer's (1979) work on the Orthodox of Boro Park, a community with a sizable Hasidic population).

Respondents confirm increases in the number of women in the labor force. Today, for example, many Lubavitch women are employed, usually in part-time positions and often as teachers in religious schools.

Respondents typically offer two, mainly practical considerations to account for the phenomenon. First, they say, general economic pressures, coupled with the traditionally large Hasidic families, may require the wife to supplement her husband's income. As a Lubavitch woman remarks: "People, kein aine horeh [may no evil eye befall them], have large families, and with the current economic situation, women sometimes have to help out and they fully expect to do their share." A second, somewhat more idealistic justification centers around the shortage of religious teachers. Given the importance of a proper Orthodox education to the Hasidim, many feel a woman should, if possible, offer her services for this purpose in a religious girls' school, especially if she is specifically trained for it.

Desire for Material Possessions

The value of conspicuous consumption is closely connected with the phenomenon of working wives. In the case of Satmar, for instance, Rubin (1972, 218) clearly establishes a strong link between the two: "The acceptance of working wives in Satmar seems to have been the value of conspicuous consumption. . . . The quest for new sources of income led the majority to send their wives to work." Most Lubavitch respondents agreed that today's Hasidim, especially the younger generation, put a greater emphasis on material goods than did those of the past:

> There's a difference between the generations. Our parent's generation had only one thing in mind and that was survival. . . . These kids, thank God, they've survived and they want a little more now. They're into more material things than the previous generation. . . . You'll notice the eigh- teen- and twenty-year-old girls and young women are much more fashion- able . . . than their parents were. . . .
>
> Like to go to New York, to be dressed, is not to have a $50 dress anymore. To be dressed, for a girl, is to have a $150 dress. That's in Lubavitch where the materialism is not supposed to take a place. . . . The modern aspect of having is very much in Lubavitch as well.

Not all respondents identified conspicuous consumption as a prac- tice that has increased in recent years. Some tied the phenomenon to a particular stage in a person's life cycle; others were unable to detect any shift, either in their lives or in those of the other Hasidim around them. All agree, however, with the concern voiced by one person: "We have to make sure that these [material goods] are not the main things in life and we must impress this on the young people."

Separation and Divorce

My findings on the incidence of and attitudes toward separation and divorce show some variations from those of previous researchers. (Again, the passage of time may account for differences.) In 1962, Poll claimed that, among the Hasidim of Williamsburg, "Marriages are for life. Divorce is almost nonexistent" (p. 55), and concluded his chapter on the family with a list of seven binding ties that held marriages together. Ten years later, Rubin agreed that divorce was rare; he believed it worth noting, however, that a divorcée, "once a stigmatized person, seems to have lost her stigma and has no apparent difficulty remarrying" (1972, 132). My more recent findings suggest that the once accepted norms for separation and divorce may be undergoing change. As a Lubavitcher said: "At one time, divorce? It was a disgrace. There was a pressure that kept people together. Today, it's much more accepted."

Despite the absence of statistics, students of Hasidic communities have documented the ostensibly low divorce rate among the Hasidim (Mintz 1968; Poll 1962; Rubin 1972). Notwithstanding this conviction, all respondents agreed that hearing about cases of divorce or separation is increasingly common among the Hasidim. Few doubt that such talk reflects an actual upsurge in the incidence of divorce in the larger Lubavitch community, but more are able to cite actual cases as evidence that the rate is, in fact, growing. One Lubavitcher recounts:

> Take my daughter, she's getting married. . . . Her friends were engaged. I mean they're two Lubavitchers and she just heard yesterday . . . a week before the wedding, it was called off. Another one of her friends was married two months and now is separated. A third friend broke her engagement two weeks after the engagement. I mean these are three friends. . . . You never heard it like that. I mean if you heard it once in three years, it was too many.

Some respondents attribute the growing frequency of divorce largely to the recent growth of the larger Lubavitch community. They claim that the many newcomers to the Hasidic movement are increasing the group's divorce rate statistically, and that this rise in actual numbers accounts for the more frequent discussion of the topic. Others, however, say that the growing incidence and acceptance of divorce in the larger society have left their mark even on the long-standing Lubavitch community. For example:

> I think it [the higher divorce rate] is, unfortunately correct. . . . I think it's generally a sign of the times. . . . And where the divorce rate among other groups has risen, I think that our divorce rate has also risen, but not in the same surge of growth as others have had.

Family Planning

My findings also suggest that some Hasidim may be affected, at least to an extent, by the larger society's acceptance of birth control. Traditionally, the most highly valued function of the Hasidic family has been procreation, the first commandment given by the Torah. In fact, having children is of such great importance to the Hasidim that infertility is one of the major grounds for divorce; the practice of birth control, except for medical considerations, is religiously forbidden.

Although few statistics are available, there is considerable evidence that many Hasidim continue to hold their traditional views. For example, a Tasher describes the current birthrate:

> One kid per year per family. . . . We expect that every family will go up to ten, twelve kids, unless there's a medical problem. . . . We have a chart of each family here, and we have a chart of the kids and you see '71, '72, '73, '74, '75.

A Belzer echoes this view:

> Thank God the size of families is always going up. The idea is to have as many children as you can. You always hear of someone who has just become a father or is about to.

Nevertheless, in my most recent conversations with Lubavitcher, I came across suggestions to the contrary. Respondents, without exception, spoke about the rebbe's recent remarks relating to family size and birth control. While all believed that the rebbe emphasized this particular topic out of concern for the state of world Jewry, specifically its declining birthrate, some also offered that he was also particularly concerned with his own immediate followers' intentions regarding family size.

In 1980, in his address to the twenty-fifth annual convention of Neshei Ubnos Chabad (Women and Daughters of Chabad), the Lubavitcher rebbe chose to impress upon his followers the importance of avoiding the use of birth control:

> The Yetzer Horah [evil inclination] is very clever. If he would present himself openly no Jew would even listen to him. Therefore, he puts on "Jewish clothes,"—a silk kaftan—and tries to persuade the Jew that it is a Mitzvah not to have children. "This way," he will say, "you will have more time to devote to valuable projects, etc." However, we must realize that despite these devices, the arguments are those of the Yetzer Horah, and there is nothing that the Yetzer Horah wants that is good for a Jew.
>
> If someone has questions about this matter, they can resolve them by looking at what has happened to couples who have limited the number of their children. This program has been called a very diplomatic name, "family planning." Its proponents maintain that since every aspect of a person's life should be planned out in advance, a plan must also be developed concerning how many children to have and at what stage of life to have them. . . .
>
> When the normal process of marital life, as decreed by God in the Torah, is altered, and altered radically, the peace of the household is bound to be disturbed. "Family planning" is opposite not only to a Torah approach to married life, but to a normal human approach to life. It has caused couples to seek psychotherapy, marriage counseling, etc. Instead of bringing order into their lives, family planning has disturbed the order established by God in the Torah. Torah law shows us how to live a normal day-to-day life, a true life. The greatest Mitzvah called for by the lifestyle is having children—as many as God wants. (1980)

The impact of this *seecheh* (discourse) was considerable. As one Lubavitch woman says, it "has really shaken up the whole community. People talk about it and don't stop." Said another:

The seecheh really has changed things. The rebbe spoke to all Jews, he always does, but the rebbe's message was also meant for all of us in the Lubavitch community. They were meant especially for the younger people. You can't imagine what a positive difference it has made in people's attitudes toward children and especially large families.

The entire incident seems worth consideration. The rebbe's position on birth control has not altered over the years; the fact that he chose an important public occasion to restate it so forcefully may imply that he had been sensing some weakening in his followers' views. And although the women's reaction to his words may indicate surprise at hearing the topic addressed in such a direct manner, it may also suggest that they struck a sensitive point, at least for some of them.

Conclusion

The data indicate that trends in the larger society are having a rippling effect on the Hasidic family. Respondents stress, however, that adaptation to these changes has not significantly altered the raison d'être of the family unit—the inculcation of religious principles and their incorporation into daily life. A Belzer and a Lubavitcher:

> You see, the family hasn't changed, really. The *brooches* [blessings] are the brooches and the kids have to be taught. So far as raising children is concerned, there isn't a change.

> Of course there are some changes. After all, we are living in a different society and there are different methods for raising and disciplining children. At a different level, there are no differences because what is important to a family doesn't change from the religious point of view. In other words, the laws of Shabbes (the Sabbath), Tahres Hamishpoche [family purity], and Yiddishkayt [Orthodox Judaism] in general don't shift over time.

Many agree that the family cannot help but adapt to various political, economic, and social shifts and changes within the larger society, but they continue to view it as the cornerstone of organizing a proper and successful way of life. As a Tasher remarks:

> The family has changed over the years. There's more education today, there's the surrounding society that you can't isolate yourself from so easily. So the responsibilities of the family have changed somewhat. But basically, it is within the family that the child is taught a way of life. Here is where the foundation is laid, here is where the roots begin to grow, and this has not changed over the years. Show me the parents and I can tell you a lot about their children.

Finally, as Hasidic communities respond to social and economic changes in the world around them, the family's efforts to screen and control secular influences will require examination and reassessment. So may its social control mechanisms for ensuring conformity with tradition. Hasidim believe they must be vigilant to ward off the polluting influences of the larger society. Some of these—such as evidenced in greater materialism and female labor force participation—pose less of a threat and therefore require less of a response than others. In general, maintaining maximal feasible isolation is the official rhetorical strategy for containing the more pernicious aspects of recent trends. Other trends, such as some signs of increasing divorce and lower birthrates, occasion much greater concern. The very expression of that concern demonstrates that even Hasidim only partially succeed in shielding themselves from the influences of the larger society.

Notes

1. For example, the Lubavitcher Hasidim have organized a series of highly visible institutions, events, and activities aimed at intensifying other Jews' identification with and commitment to Orthodox Judaism. Neon billboards in shopping centers that draw a predominantly Jewish clientele remind women and girls to observe the lighting of Sabbath candles. Circulars announce that Lubavitch will provide up to 50 percent of the cost of making a kitchen kosher.

In a somewhat similar, but less dramatic, vein, the Tasher Hasidim have also garnered considerable public attention since 1978 through their efforts to convince the Quebec government to grant their community full municipal status, including the authority to convert their religious rules into municipal bylaws. In mounting their unsuccessful battle, they made considerable and effective use of the mass media, gaining both local and national publicity.

2. Several master's theses and doctoral dissertations have been written about Hasidic life. See, for example, Berger-Sofer 1979; Levy 1973; Shaffir 1969; and Sobel 1956.

3. Considering the importance of the family in Jewish life in general and in Orthodox and Hasidic communities in particular, Mayer's assertion that "there is a surprising absence of actual research on the nature of the Jewish family" (1979, 98) prevails.

There are some exceptions. Kranzler's study of Williamsburg analyzes the process of change in this predominantly Orthodox community. Although he offers excellent insights into the dynamics of Jewish family organization and everyday life, he provides no close-up examination of the Hasidic family. His chapter titled "The Structure of the Family" does, however, explain how the patriarchal structure of the Old World gradually disintegrated soon after the first wave of immigration, then revived; the author credits Hasidim for this reversal, claiming that their "religio-cultural value system proved to be a force capable of overcoming the factors working for disintegration in the changing structure of the Jewish family in Williamsburg" (1961, 138).

Poll's (1962) well-known study of the Hasidic community of Williamsburg includes a six-page chapter on the pattern of Hasidic family life, including selection of a mate, the husband's authority in making family decisions, expectations for women and children, the role of youth in the Hasidic community, and the norms, regulations, and expectations surrounding marriage and procreation.

Rubin's (1972) study of the Satmarer Hasidim includes a detailed appreciation of the norms and practices underlying courtship and marriage ceremonies, a tracing of the young couple's entry into a new stage of the life cycle, and a consideration of the responsibilities accompanying marriage (including sexual fulfillment, earning a livelihood, and managing a household). Rubin also examines other phases of the family life cycle: the socialization of children, adolescence, divorce, and death, burial, and mourning.

Gutwirth's (1970) study of the Belz Hasidic community in Antwerp contains no specific section on the family. However, it does examine, in careful detail, the socialization of youth in the community, the respective community positions of males and females, and the cultural, social, and religious patterns surrounding marriage.

4. Weinberger emphasizes the importance of role models in his analysis of Orthodox Jewish life: He writes:

> Quite often they [young people] far surpass the level of piety they experienced at home, and even when the gaps in their learning are filled in a yeshiva, they lack *shimush,* the exposure to mature religious personalities at close hand, leaving them with a lack of religious sophistication. It is such young people who are at a disadvantage in confronting the kind of conflict resolution that marriage makes all the more imperative (1976, 14).

5. Most of the data I have collected on these subjects are from conversations with Lubavitcher Hasidim. Data based on discussions and conversations with members of other Hasidic communities are, at this point, less systematic. It is my strong impression, however, that data about other Hasidic communities will reveal that the Lubavitch patterns are not unique. Clearly, additional research is required to confirm, modify, or disconfirm this impression. For a related discussion, see Shaffir 1978.

6. Both Poll's and Rubin's studies focus on Williamsburg, Brooklyn, the largest concentration of Hasidic Jewry in North America. Rubin's analysis is only of the Satmarer; Poll's presumably includes many of the other sects in the area.

References

Berger-Sofer, R. 1979. "Pious Women: A Study of the Women's Roles in a Hasidic and Pious Community: Meah Shearim." Doctoral dissertation, Rutgers University.

Di Yiddishe Heim. New York, Council Neshai Ubnos Chabad.

Gutwirth, J. 1970. *Vie juive traditionnelle: Ethnologie D'une communauté hassidique.* Paris: Les Editions de Minuit.

Kranzler, G. 1961. *Williamsburg: A Jewish Community in Transition.* New York: Philip Feldheim.

———. 1977. "The Changing Orthodox Jewish Family in the Context of the Changing American Jewish Community." Paper delivered to the 1977 convention of the National Council for Jewish Education, Washington, D.C.

Levy, S. 1973. "Ethnic Boundaries and the Institution of Charisma: A Study of the Lubavitcher Hasidim." Doctoral dissertation, City University of New York.

Mayer, E. 1979. *From Suburb to Shtetl: The Jews of Boro Park.* Philadelphia: Temple University Press.

Mintz, J. 1968. *Legends of the Hasidim.* Chicago: University of Chicago Press.

Poll, S. 1962. *The Hasidic Community of Williamsburg.* New York: The Free Press.

Rubin, I. 1972. *Satmar: An Island in the City.* Chicago: Quadrangle Books.

Shaffir, W. 1969. "The Montreal Chassidic Community: Community Boundaries and the Maintenance of Ethnic Identity." Master's thesis, McGill University.

———. 1974. *Life in a Religious Community: The Lubavitcher Chassidim in Montreal.* Toronto: Holt, Rinehart and Winston.

———. 1978. "Witnessing as Identity Consolidation: The Case of the Lubavitcher Chassidim." In Hans Mol, ed., *Identity and Religion: International, Cross-Cultural Approaches* (Beverly Hills, Calif.: Sage Publications), pp. 39–57.

Sobel, B. 1956. "The M'lochim: A Study of a Religious Community." Master's thesis, New School for Social Research.

Weinberger, B. 1976. "The Growing Rate of Divorce in Orthodox Jewish Life." *Jewish Life* (spring), 9–14.

Wirth, L. 1928. *The Ghetto.* Chicago: University of Chicago Press.

14. Coming of Age in the Havurah Movement: Bar Mitzvah in the Havurah Family

Chava Weissler

The Emergence of Havurot

Labeled as "an idea whose time has come" (Reisman 1980, 561), the havurah has firmly established itself on the American Jewish scene. Contemporary havurot originated in the late 1960s with young Jews who were unhappy with the Conservative and Reform congregations in which they had been raised. Influenced by the counterculture, they were dissatisfied with contemporary Jewish institutions, both religious and communal, which they regarded as sterile, impersonal, hierarchical, and divorced from Jewish tradition.

Basing themselves in part on ideas presented by Jacob Neusner (1972) in his discussion of religious fellowships in ancient Palestine, these young Jews sought warm personal ties in close-knit communities, and deepened religious experience in less formal, more participatory styles of prayer. They have founded and maintained "independent havurot" (i.e., those unaffiliated with any Jewish institution, although some use the

The field work on which this paper is based was conducted in the "Dutchville Minyan" in 1978 and 1979. The research was supported in part by a Doctoral Dissertation Fellowship from the National Foundation for Jewish Culture, to whom I wish to express my gratitude. My thanks go as well to Barbara Kirshenblatt-Gimblett, Martha Himmelfarb, Steven Weiss, Solomon Mowshowitz, and Norman Newberg for comments on earlier drafts of this paper.

facilities of such institutions) in most large cities in the East, Midwest, and West.

An independent havurah typically has between twenty and one hundred members, most of them between twenty and forty years of age. These havurot were at first made up primarily of single people, including many students, but as time passes they include a higher proportion of couples and families. Most independent havurot hold their own Sabbath services, which are usually their emotionally central activity. They also sponsor Jewish study groups, and occasions, such as kiddushes and potluck dinners, for informal social interaction. True to their counter-cultural roots, independent havurot are committed to an egalitarian and participatory Judaism. Opportunities for all members to fill religious and communal leadership roles and for women and men to participate equally in religious activities are hallmarks of havurah communities. There is also commitment to Jewish tradition: a high incidence of some form of Sabbath and dietary law observance is found among havurah Jews.

As independent havurot proliferated, the idea of the synagogue havurah began to take shape. Religious and communal leaders, notably Rabbi Harold Schulweis of Encino, California, saw in the idea of the havurah a way to strengthen the synagogue and answer the Jewish needs of their congregants. Synagogue havurot are usually, although not always, founded on the initiative of the rabbi or some other staff member of the synagogue or, more recently, of the Jewish community center. The goal, however, is for the members of the havurah themselves to take responsibility for group leadership, and joining the group is seen as a commitment. Such groups meet regularly (usually at least once a month) in informal settings such as private homes. (Elazar and Monson 1979, 67). However, they rarely sponsor regular Sabbath services, so as not to compete with the synagogue in which they are based. Wasserman describes this type of havurah as follows:

A modern synagogue-based Havurah typically consists of about ten couples who meet on a regular basis for the purpose of becoming more informed and sentient Jews. Although there is no universal prescription for Havurah activities, theorists generally agree that a combination of study, prayer, and celebration should be pursued—if not immediately upon formation, then as goals to be achieved. The degree to which each component is emphasized varies widely according to the desires and needs of each Havurah (1979, 169).

The synagogue havurah "has emerged as a tool for repersonalizing the synagogue as an institution and reactivating members so that their

Judaism is no longer simply something to be delegated to the rabbi" (Elazar and Monson 1979, 68). As such, these havurot have proliferated rapidly. A survey undertaken by Elazar and Monson showed that by 1975, 20 percent of American synagogues had at least one havurah. On the West Coast, perhaps because of the influence of Rabbi Schulweis, perhaps because California represents what Elazar terms the "metropolitan-technological frontier," the percentage was more than double, 43 percent (Elazar and Monson, 1979, 70–71).

Havurot as Extended Families

In attempting to account for the success of havurot, recent articles report that these groups fill many of the functions of extended families. The authors use a variety of terms for these functions: "Jewish support networks" (Reisman 1980), "psychosocial kinship systems," or "modified extended families" (Wasserman, Bubis, and Lert 1979), or simply "extended families" (Weiss 1977). By these terms, the researchers do not intend to compare havurot to such full-fledged corporate extended family structures as joint families or lineages, which are described in anthropological literature. Rather, they define extended families, or psychosocial kinship systems in terms of the affective bonds and ties of mutual assistance that may exist between individuals and between nuclear families.[1] Thus, as Reisman reports:

> The creation of havurot within the synagogue is, in effect, an attempt to develop surrogate extended families within the synagogue community. Here people are afforded the opportunity to have a continuing intimate association—to feel a sense of belonging, to be linked with people they know personally and who care about them, and to have people with whom to share happiness and sorrow—bar mitzvahs, Passover seders, sickness, death, etc. (1975, 207).

Since the articles cited all deal with synagogue or community center havurot, it will be useful to examine the validity of their findings for an independent havurah. However, it will be of more substance to look at some of the underlying assumptions of these reports, and to try to fill in some significant omissions.

Many of these articles contain statements about the mobility, alienation, and anomie that result from industrialization, and the toll this has taken on the contemporary Jewish community:

> Clearly the sense of anomie which Durkheim discovered almost a century ago has not abated. In fact as our society has further industrialized, there has been a concomitant atrophy of the two major social institutions which

have traditionally provided support to people over the course of their lives—the family and the neighborhood. This process has been particularly acute for the Jews whose historic pattern has been so dependent upon the direction and nourishment provided by the all-encompassing Jewish community (*kehillah, shtetl,* or ghetto) and the extended family. Today most Jews no longer live in Jewish neighborhoods and the extended family has been replaced by the nuclear family (Reisman 1975, 206).

Because of the widespread atrophy of extended kinship networks, the authors tend to assume that havurot arise to substitute for missing kin. That is, they assume that the "real" extended families are actually absent (Weiss 1977, 135; Reisman 1980, 562). One question we shall ask is, How absent are they? and whether other factors than their absence might contribute to the functioning of havurot as extended families. In this connection it is especially interesting to examine events, such as life-cycle rituals, at which the "real" extended family is likely to be present.

In addition, most of the reports do not deal with the stresses and strains that are part of the extended family nature of havurot; rather, they "accentuate the positive" and emphasize the opportunities for community, intimacy, and autonomy in havurot. Only Wasserman says explicitly: "The promise of an extended family through Havurah is too often understood as an instant renaissance at its most ideal, with all of the implicit warmth and none of the strains and conflict" (1979, 177). Not only may there be strains within the havurah, but at those events at which the havurah and the "real" extended family come into contact, there is almost certain to be conflict. By examining this conflict, we may clarify the functions of family and havurah in the lives of members.

Finally, to the extent that any of these articles are concerned with the Jewish, or more explicitly religious, aspects of havurot, they are concerned with their effects on the Jewishness of the adults. The studies of synagogue havurot undertaken at the UCLA School of Social Welfare (Wasserman, Bubis, and Lert 1979, 41) seem to indicate that these havurot were primarily peer support groups which placed little emphasis on interaction with children. Reisman, in discussing the adult-centered quality of havurot, remarks in passing:

> Paradoxically, this adult orientation may contribute more to the children's positive Jewish attitudes than the more typical avowedly child-centered synagogue-sponsored programs. In the chavurah, children see direct evidence of their parents' Jewish commitment and interest, which often is less obvious when the parents "drop off" the children to be "made Jewish" by Jewish professionals (1980, 569).

Apart from these few comments, little attention is paid to the children of havurot.

Thus, although extended families have historically functioned as prime agents of enculturation, there has been no serious discussion of the extent to which this is also a function of havurot. I propose to investigate the role of the havurah in the enculturation of the next generation, looking not only at the success in the passing on of Jewishness, but also in the passing on of Havurah Judaism, the particular vision of Jewish life developed by the adults through their participation in the havurah.

This chapter will explore all of these questions—the functioning of an independent havurah as an extended family, the presence or absence of "real" kin, the conflict between havurah and "real" kin, and the role of the havurah in enculturation—within the context of an ethnographic examination of a single event. The event selected is a Bar Mitzvah celebration which occurred in a group I shall call the Dutchville Minyan, an independent havurah in a large East Coast city, in early September 1979.

The Dutchville Minyan

The Dutchville Minyan was founded in 1974 on the initiative of a dozen people, about half of whom had had previous experience with other havurot or minyanim. The founders wanted a more informal, participatory service than that offered by the Dutchville Jewish Center, a Conservative congregation to which some of them belonged. The Center gave the Minyan space for services, first in the library and later in a classroom. Minyan members took turns leading the services, conducting the Torah discussions, and filling other necessary roles. Saturday morning services have remained the focal activity of the Minyan.

It is apparent that the formation of the Minyan filled a need, for the membership grew rapidly. By the time of the Bar Mitzvah under discussion (1979), there were about ninety adult members, 70 percent of them in the twenty-six to forty age range. Half of the members were married, there were a few single parents, and there were eighteen families with children, twenty-eight children in all. (There has been a marked upward trend in marriage and fertility: in 1981, of the 120 adult members, two-thirds were married, and thirteen children were born since 1979).

By 1979, the strains of large membership had already taken their toll. For much of 1978, the Minyan had been wracked by conflict; finally, in the spring of 1979, it had split into two "davening groups." However, during the summer, the two groups had joined forces once again, and at the time of the Bar Mitzvah, everyone was attending a single service. (There have been subsequent splits: in 1981 there were three separate Saturday morning "davening groups" which came together for holidays, life-cycle celebrations, and other occasions. The term "Dutchville Minyan" when used by members of any of these groups refers to the entire collectivity.)

Most of the Minyan's membership lives in the neighborhood of Pleasant View, and about half are homeowners. Thus, most members live within walking distance of each other. The Dutchville Jewish Center was one of the few synagogues that remained in Pleasant View when the neighborhood began to change, some twenty years ago. Pleasant View is now stably integrated, and attracts left-liberal, professional, middle-class residents. The Minyan's membership reflects this. The majority of members work in social services or education, with a sprinkling of lawyers, academics, civil servants, graduate students, and others. Many members are employed by the organized Jewish community. And although during the first few years of the Minyan's existence there was much tension between Minyan and synagogue, 60 percent of the Minyan's membership now belongs to the Dutchville Jewish Center.

The Minyan holds Sabbath and holiday services, study groups, potluck dinners on Friday nights, kiddushes, picnics, and parties. But in addition to these structured events, Minyan members do engage in many of the extended-family activities described for synagogue havurot. Members borrow each other's cars, look after each other's children, have each other over for Sabbath and holiday meals, cook for each other's Brit Milah and Bar/Bat Mitzvah celebrations, help to make up a minyan when a member must say kaddish for a deceased relative. (Because the Minyan is so large, such activities often, but not always, occur within social subgroups.) All this goes on in spite of the fact that nearly a third of the membership has extended family right in the same city. Nor are members who have extended family close by any less tied into the Minyan social network than other members.

The Kleins (all names are fictitious) are one such family. Saul Klein, a journalist, has parents and siblings living in the same city, while Joan Klein, a public school teacher, has parents and a brother in a neighboring town (her sister and brother-in-law live in Israel). The Kleins' sons, Mark and Daniel, have grown up interacting with grandparents, aunts, and uncles. If real kin are present, and the Kleins choose to interact with the Minyan as with a surrogate extended family, there must be reasons for the choice, and the two groups must fulfill different functions in their lives. To better understand these functions, we shall turn directly to an account of the Bar Mitzvah itself.

Preparations for the Bar Mitzvah

Preparations began long before the actual day of the ceremony. A full syntagmatic description is unnecessary, but certain events must be noted. For many years, Mark had been a student at the Dutchville Jewish Center. During the year immediately preceding his Bar Mitzvah, however, he attended a local Hebrew day school, which did not provide Bar Mitzvah preparation. When it came time for his parents to choose a Bar Mitzvah tutor for him, they turned to Ian, a Minyan member who had prepared a number of other youngsters, most of them unaffiliated with synagogues or havurot, for Bar Mitzvah. For three and a half months Mark and Ian studied together, meeting informally at each other's homes. The Kleins' most important goal for Mark was that he learn to read Torah. With Ian he learned the cantillation of the Torah and *haftarah,* and studied the content of his biblical portion.

During that same summer, Joan (who as a teacher was on vacation) began to sound out her friends who had celebrated their children's Bar or Bat Mitzvah, to find out what she could about appropriate menus, quantities of food, ways to set up the auditorium for the lunch. Although her mother pressured her to have the food catered, she insisted on home-prepared food. Her one splurge, she said, was to hire a few people to help with the serving.

A few weeks before Mark's Bar Mitzvah, she baked and froze all the cake for the lunch and party, and recruited friends to help bake kugels, cut up vegetables, and make up the platters a day or two before the ceremony. She also embroidered a needlepoint bag and *'atarah* (decorated collar strip) for Mark's new *talit,* sewed individual challah covers for each of the tables for the lunch, hemmed a new white cloth to cover the Torah scroll, and assembled a booklet containing thoughts and poems that Mark and his parents had written for the occasion, as well as the Torah reading, some of the songs for the service in transliteration, and the Grace after Meals. This booklet was printed up (by Joan's father, a printer) to be distributed at the Bar Mitzvah.

A week and a half before the ceremony, Mark, Saul, Joan, and Ian sat down together to plan the service. It was very important to Mark, as it was to his parents, that the service be as much like a regular Minyan service as possible. As Mark told me later, "I felt very strongly that my Bar Mitzvah is no different than any other Minyan Shabbes. The only difference is that Ian's leading davening and I'm leyning for the first time." This meant of course that although the Kleins were members of the Dutchville Jewish Center, the Bar Mitzvah would not be held in the main sanctuary, with rabbi and cantor officiating. Mark was only the second Minyan youngster to celebrate a Bar Mitzvah in the Minyan: two slightly older teenagers had insisted, to the chagrin of their parents, on having the ceremony in the main sanctuary.

In upholding the norms of the Minyan, Mark went perhaps a little too far. Because dress in the Minyan is informal, he insisted that he wanted to wear, for his Bar Mitzvah, what he usually wore to shul: jeans and a T-shirt. This led to an entire family quarrel about what Mark should wear: Joan's parents felt that the only appropriate dress was a three-piece suit. Saul's parents thought that a sport jacket and slacks would be sufficient. Joan's Israeli relatives thought Mark should wear a white shirt and navy blue slacks. Saul and Joan wanted him to wear all white, and in the end they won out, or as Mark said, "So we compromised, and I accepted it." He wore white slacks, a white shirt with multicolored Mexican embroidery, and a Persian embroidered *kipah* (skullcap). Saul wore a similar outfit, Daniel wore a blue polo shirt and dark pants, and Joan, as she said, decided to be nice to her mother, and wore a dressy plum-colored outfit with heels and a necklace.

The Bar Mitzvah could not be exactly like a Minyan service, in spite of Mark's wishes, for several reasons. Most important, there would be two to three times the usual number of people there. The Kleins had invited 250 people, but were hoping only 200 would show up. Therefore, the service could not be held in the usual small room in the Dutchville Jewish Center, but rather in an auditorium upstairs. In addition, most of the guests would be unfamiliar with the Minyan service, some of them unfamiliar with services and Hebrew altogether, others of them Orthodox. Mark was afraid that no one but the regular Minyan members would know the tunes and sing along, which was his favorite part of the service.

The Wednesday, Thursday, and Friday before the Bar Mitzvah, both Joan and Saul spent most of the day at the synagogue, setting up the room, cutting up vegetables, making lox and cream cheese molds, and in general getting ready. (Saul took those days off work, and Joan had the summer off in any case.) Both of their mothers came to help them, as well as a number of friends from the Minyan. On Thursday afternoon Mark came with Ian to rehearse reading of the actual Torah scroll.

By Friday afternoon, all was ready. The upstairs auditorium had been partitioned into two sections, the smaller one for the service and the larger one for the lunch. The smaller section had 200 chairs arranged in a wide oval several rows deep around a table on which lay the Torah scroll, covered with the white cloth Joan had prepared for the occasion. In the larger section there were about twenty round tables, each covered with a white cloth and set with pretty paper plates and plastic flatware. On each table would be placed a bottle of wine for kiddush, and a challah covered with the white, gold, and black challah covers Joan had sewn for the occasion. There were also long tables on which to set up the food as a buffet.

The Day of the Bar Mitzvah

The service was called for ten o'clock on Saturday morning. Minyan members and relatives began to arrive early. Members, excited about the big event, were much more dressed up than usual. One woman remarked that "we're all in our dress-up-go-to-meetin' clothes." Twenty of Mark's classmates were invited, and all the boys were wearing suits. Minyan members tended to sit together in groups, a little lost in the sea of relatives. Extra chairs had to be set up.

The service began as Daniel, Mark's nine-year-old brother, led the introductory blessings *(birkhot ha-shahar)*. Then Ian, sitting in a chair placed near the Torah table, led the service, including the singing of some of Mark's favorite songs during the first part of the service *(pesuke de-zimrah)*. He paused before beginning the morning service proper *(shaharit)* to speak briefly. Ian talked about the reasons this Sabbath was special to him. First, he mentioned that it was Elul, a time of preparing for the High Holidays. Next, he said that because people are away during the summer, this Sabbath, the first one in September, was a time when the community reassembles. Finally, he talked about the Bar Mitzvah. He indicated that he was not going to say much about Mark in particular, because Mark had asked him not to embarrass him. But he did say, "I prepare a lot of students for Bar Mitzvah, and the special thing about this Bar Mitzvah is that it's taking place in the context of a community. Mark can come back next week and read Torah again if he wants to. He can be part of a community."

Ian then continued with the service. Immediately after he took out the Torah scroll, the Klein family—Saul, Joan, Mark, and Daniel—came to the center of the room. Saul and Joan put Mark's talit on him, Mark recited the blessing inaudibly, and Saul and Joan said the *she-heḥiyanu*[2] blessing out loud. The talit, handwoven with multicolored stripes, was much too big for Mark, even though Joan had hemmed it up. "He'll grow into it," Joan had said. Mark struggled with it all during the service.

Next, Ian asked both sets of grandparents and Mark's one surviving great-grandmother to come to the center of the room. The entire family came and stood around the Torah table, in generational order, with Mark at the end of the line. The Torah scroll was passed from the great-grandmother on down to Mark, "to symbolize the chain of tradition," as Ian explained. Then Mark, holding the Torah, sang the *Shema,* and the service continued.

From the Torah scroll, Mark read seven sections *('aliyot)* which were selected from the biblical portion of the week *(parashah).* He read extremely well. Those honored by being called to the Torah were both sets of grandparents, Mark's parents and brother, his aunts and uncles, his teacher Ian, and two sets of dear friends from the Minyan. Joan's sister and brother-in-law, who are Orthodox, refused to accept an *'aliyah.*

When Mark had completed the selection from the Prophets *(haftarah)* and the blessings that follow it, the entire congregation threw candy at him, shouted *"Mazel tov!"* and sang *"Siman tov u-mazal tov"* (a good omen and good fortune), clapping and dancing. All of the children, Mark included, ran around picking up the candies, little wrapped caramels.

After things had quieted down, Mark began the Torah discussion. He spoke briefly about how the verse in his parashah, "Parents shall not be put to death for children, nor children be put to death for parents: a person shall be put to death for his own crime" (Deut. 24:16), was seemingly contradicted by another biblical verse, "For I the Lord your God am an impassioned God, visiting the guilt of the fathers upon the children, upon the third and fourth generation of those who reject Me" (Exod. 20:5). Several people made comments, and Mark responded. The discussion lasted five or ten minutes, shorter than usual, but understandably so with such a large crowd and eventful morning. Mark concluded the discussion by saying that he wasn't sure how religious he would be in his adult life, but he was grateful to have had the opportunity to learn about Judaism.

Ian finished up the service, omitting the additional service *(musaf),* as the Minyan usually does. Joan announced that everyone was invited to lunch, and asked people to carry the chairs over to the other section of the room and put them around tables. Mark led kiddush, Daniel said the blessing over the bread *(ha-motsi,)* and then people were called up table by table to the buffet, which included assorted noodle kugels, rolls, bagels, and black bread (from the bakery of a Minyan friend), whitefish, herring, egg salad, cheeses, chickpea salad, and cream cheeses and lox spread. Most of the food was prepared by Joan. There was also a salad bar, and for dessert, platters of assorted little pieces of cake of various kinds, from miniature cheese cakes to mandel bread. There was a large Bar Mitzvah sheet cake with Mark's name on it on display, but this was saved for the evening party.

During lunch, everyone seemed in a very good mood. A number of people remarked on how nice the service was, how much they liked Ian's davening, how well Mark had done. For the Minyan, it was a com- munity high—it was something to which many of them had contributed, a joyous occasion on which they could all come together despite the conflict and factionalism of the past year, a time when the community could exhibit itself to outsiders, who were by and large duly impressed.

Lunch was concluded by Mark's Israeli, Orthodox uncle leading the grace after meals *(birkat ha-mazon)*, the only role he would consent to take in this non-halakhic service. On Saturday night there was a party at the Kleins' home, not for the family but for Mark's friends, and for Saul and Joan's friends, from Minyan, synagogue, and work.

This is not quite the end of the story. The next morning, at Mark's request, the Kleins invited ten people from the Minyan to their home for a plain weekday morning service at which Mark would lay *tefillin* (phy- lacteries) for the first time. Ian showed him how to do it, and helped him follow the weekday service, led by one of the friends. At the end of the service, because it was Elul, Mark blew the shofar, a skill he had recently acquired. Afterwards, there was a brunch with the leftovers from the previous day's lunch. It was a quiet little ritual, meaningful to Mark in affirming his commitment to continuing his Jewish involvement.

And in spite of his disclaimer at the end of the Torah discussion, it became apparent during the succeeding weeks and months how seriously Mark took that commitment. He blew shofar on Rosh ha-Shanah, was called to the Torah on Yom Kippur, read Torah regularly in the Minyan, in spite of the fact that the first time he tried it after the Bar Mitzvah he didn't prepare well enough and made many mistakes. Minyan members joked away his embarrassment, encouraged him to persevere, offered him help in preparing. He still reads Torah regularly, and recently tried the role of *gabbai*[3] for the first time.

Analysis

In the context of the foregoing account, we can now try to answer some of the questions posed at the outset. It is, first of all, apparent that the Dutchville Minyan does fulfill many of the support functions reported for synagogue havurot: friends from the Minyan helped Joan prepare food, and the entire Minyan shared in the celebration—the *simḥah*—of the Bar Mitzvah. Because the Minyan is so much larger than most syn- agogue havurot, only a subgroup were really close to the Klein family. Not all members were invited to the Saturday night party, for example.

But the Kleins took care to invite the entire Minyan to the service and to the lunch, and the entire Minyan took pride in Mark and in the event.

A Clash of Values

When we turn to questions of the Minyan as extended family versus the "real" extended family, and of the enculturation of the next generation, the issues are more complicated. At this Bar Mitzvah celebration, where both "real" and Minyan extended families were present, we can discern a clash of values. To a large extent, this is played out in terms of esthetics: in the argument over appropriate clothing for Mark, for example, each suggested outfit carries with it an entire vision of what a Bar Mitzvah ought to be. The grandparents' demand for more formal dress, as well as for a catered lunch, also implies a preference for a more conventional Bar Mitzvah service in a regular synagogue with a rabbi and cantor officiating, and a more passive role for the congregation. Interestingly, this was not the preference of the oldest generation. When I asked Mark how his relatives had liked the service, he said, "My great-grandmother said, 'This is the first service that I've been to since I came to America that reminded me of the old country.'" Mark continued, "I think both sets of grandparents liked the service and the way it was done, but I'm not sure how much they would have preferred it to be downstairs (i.e., in the main sanctuary of the synagogue)."

The outfit preferred by Saul and Joan implies another view of the Bar Mitzvah: informal, yet special. These themes are carried through in the home-cooked food served for lunch and the communal singing that was part of the service. The Kleins, Mark included, wanted a Bar Mitzvah that would be representative of havurah Judaism, in which the service would be led, not by a professional, but by a member of the community; in which the community would participate actively in the service and the celebration. That this is not what the extended family wanted is evidenced by the fact that during the weeks before the ceremony, Joan talked repeatedly about the difficulty she was having in accommodating her family in the arrangements for the Bar Mitzvah. She finally concluded, "Saul and I know we can't please everybody, so we're mostly trying to please ourselves." Saul and Joan preferred the Minyan's homemade and informal esthetic about celebrations, along with the Minyan's assumptions of competence and participation on the part of the congregation. The "real" extended family did not share this vision of Jewish life.

Thus, that the Kleins interact with the Minyan as with extended family, at least in the Jewish arena, represents a positive choice in terms of values. They have found a group with a view of Judaism congruent to their own. The Minyan becomes, in effect, a "Jewish extended family."

This being the case, it is particularly interesting that the primacy of the "real" family received so much symbolic expression in the ceremony. For example, it was chiefly family members who were called to the Torah. Most strikingly, the Torah scroll was passed down through the family chain of generations to Mark. Powerful as this was as a symbol of the biological continuity of Mark's family, it was peculiarly inappropriate as a symbol of the origins of Mark's own sense of Jewish identity.[4]

In referring to the Minyan as a "Jewish extended family," I am in fact using Mark's own term. When I asked him about the roles of his extended family and of the Minyan in his life, he said that for his Jewish education, for religious things in general, the Minyan is much more important, because neither side of his extended family is, as he put it, particularly religious. For other things, like birthdays, the family is more important. He was clear that the Minyan does function to an extent like family. He talked about two "second mothers," both women in the Minyan, and said that going to a seder at the home of some Minyan friends was like a family seder. He then began to list adults in the Minyan he felt close to, and finally said, "almost everyone in the 'home minyan' [the 'davening group' which he and his parents attend]."

The Minyan as Agent of Enculturation

Mark also remarked that he feels that the Minyan is a particularly good place for him to grow Jewishly. This brings us to a discussion of the role of the Minyan in enculturation.

It is evident from what Mark said about his Bar Mitzvah, as well as what he did in preparation for it, how closely he identifies with Minyan values. Unlike some of the other youngsters in the Minyan, Mark wanted his Bar Mitzvah to be celebrated at a Minyan service. As he said, he wanted it to be "no different than any other Minyan Shabbes," with a lot of congregational singing and participation and the usual informality of dress. When I asked Mark how he thought his Bar Mitzvah compared with those of his classmates, he said, "Last year, every kid in my class except one had a Bar or Bat Mitzvah, and I got to go to a lot of shuls. And there was only one I could live with—it was in a small synagogue, sort of like the Minyan. It met in someone's house. I don't like it when someone like a cantor or rabbi leads, and you have the people in the *kahal* (congregation) just sitting and doing nothing."

Having absorbed the ideal that Judaism should be an active, not a passive matter for members of a congregation, Mark had the goal to learn a skill which would enable him to participate actively. He wanted to learn to read Torah, not just memorize his portion. He recognized the importance of personal commitment to maintaining the religious life of the community.

This commitment, though felt and acted upon in the Minyan, is rarely as clearly articulated as is a certain ambivalence about Jewish tradition. Ambivalence is most typically expressed in the Torah discussion, in which Minyan members articulate their "problems" with the text, with the authority of halakhah, or with some other aspect of Judaism. It was important to Mark that there be a Torah discussion—that quintessentially participatory havurah movement innovation—as part of his Bar Mitzvah. The body of his discussion did not conform to the typical havurah movement format, but rather harked back to an earlier Jewish model, the reconciling of two contradictory texts. However, the conclusion of his remarks is of particular interest: Mark took care to disavow any definite future commitment to Jewish life and practice. In implying that commitment to Jewish life is based on somewhat ambivalent personal preference, Mark once again demonstrated how thoroughly he had absorbed the Judaism of the Minyan.

If individual preference and ambivalence toward tradition form the basis of Minyan and havurah Judaism, serious questions are raised about its transmissibility. And in fact, although the sample is too small to be statistically significant, it is worth noting that of the seven Minyan children who have celebrated Bar or Bat Mitzvah, two are strongly involved in the Minyan, two are partially involved, and three are completely uninterested (although one of these is active in a Zionist youth group). These youngsters (almost all of whom have attended Jewish day schools for varying lengths of time) have been affected by several factors. The level and type of parental involvement in the Minyan and the nature of the parent-child relationship are important in determining the child's relationship to the Minyan and its vision of Judaism. In addition, because it contains such a small peer group of teenagers, the Minyan provides a more comfortable atmosphere for the youngster who is oriented toward adults rather than toward his or her peers. But beyond these factors, if adult Minyan members justify their own Jewish involvement by saying that they find it personally meaningful, and make no bones about their ambivalence about some aspects of Jewish tradition, they have nothing much to say to a child who passes Bar Mitzvah age—the age of Jewish responsibility—and says that he or she doesn't like participating in Jewish activities, or doesn't find them personally fulfilling.

Thus, for the Minyan successfully to enculturate a child into Havurah Judaism, it must make his or her participation personally fulfilling. In Mark's case, this was done remarkably well. Over the years of attending Minyan services, Mark witnessed the importance davening had for his parents and other Minyan adults. He also had the opportunity to try out his own religious experiences in a relaxed atmosphere, one in which he could get up and walk around, or leave the room and play with other children in the hall if he felt like it. For a year or two, the Minyan held special Torah discussion for the children, during which they could discuss the text at their own level, with the help of a rotating group of Minyan adults.

During the months before his Bar Mitzvah, Mark developed close personal relationships with several Minyan adults other than his parents, notably Ian, his teacher. Thus, Mark had a variety of role models with whom to identify, all representing somewhat different, but committed, approaches to Jewish life. Immediately after the Bar Mitzvah, Mark was provided with many opportunities to participate in Minyan activities: to read Torah, to blow shofar, to be called to the Torah, and even to fill out a questionnaire on his preferences about services sent out to the membership by one of the Minyan's committees. Finally, he has received much gratifying recognition from the Minyan for his continued active participation. As Ian remarked during the ceremony, Mark had indeed celebrated his Bar Mitzvah in a community he could become part of.

Conclusion

Unlike most of the members of the synagogue havurot described in the literature, the Kleins, and many other members of the Dutchville Minyan (and of other independent havurot), chose to found and participate in the Minyan out of a clear sense of the centrality of Judaism in their lives, and of the type of Jewish lives they wanted to lead. This framework for Jewish life was not offered by their "real" extended families, and for this reason, they chose another group of people, the Minyan, which did provide the opportunity for them to live Jewishly in the way they wished. Thus, the important thing was not whether or not their "real" extended families were present, but whether or not the values and way of life their families offered were what they wanted. It was to the group that shared their values that the Kleins turned to socialize their son to Jewish adulthood. It was from the Minyan, rather than from his grandparents, that Mark learned what it meant to be a Jewish adult, and it is within the Minyan's framework that he continues to learn to take on that role. It might, then, have been symbolically more appropriate if, in the course of his Bar Mitzvah, the Torah scroll had been passed, not from his great-grandmother to his grandparents, to his parents, to him, but rather from Minyan member to Minyan member, including his parents, to him. This would more accurately have expressed the sources of Mark's Jewish identification.

Notes

1. Wasserman, Bubis, and Lert (1979) apply a number of different theoretical formulations to the havurah. One of the most interesting is a discussion of "psychosocial kinship systems" taken from Pattison et al. (1975), who define the functional kin of the individual—those with whom there are significant interpersonal relationships—on the basis of five variables:

1. The relationship has a relatively high degree of interaction, whether face to face, by telephone, or by letter. In other words, a person invests in those with whom he has contact.
2. The relationship has a strong emotional intensity. The degree of investment in others is reflected in the intensity of feeling toward the others.
3. The emotion is generally positive. Negative relationships are maintained only when other variables force the maintenance of the relationship, such as a boss or a spouse.
4. The relationship has an instrumental base. That is, not only is the other person held in positive emotional regard, but he can be counted on to provide concrete assistance.
5. The relationship is symmetrically reciprocal. That is, the other person returns your strong positive feeling and may count on you for instrumental assistance. There is an affective and instrumental quid pro quo (Pattison et al. 1975, 1249).

This will give the reader a sense of the type of definition the authors of the cited articles are working with. Interestingly, this model describes relationships within the "Dutchville Minyan" with a high degree of accuracy.

2. "Blessed are you, Lord our God, Ruler of the Universe, who has kept us in life, and preserved us, and caused us to reach this season." This prayer is said when important milestones in the life cycle or liturgical calendar are reached.

3. The gabbai calls people up to say the blessings over the Torah reading, and follows the reading to correct any mistakes the reader makes.

4. The primacy of the biological family is often reasserted at life-cycle events. (This is not surprising, since in some sense what these rituals are about is the biological continuity of life.) This primacy can be asserted in two ways: symbolically, by giving the "real" extended family ritual prominence, and organizationally, by celebrating the event in accordance with the extended family's

presences and wishes. The symbolic prominence of the family (*'aliyot* at a Bar Mitzvah, the role of a *sandak* at a Brit Milah, for example) usually provokes little conflict, although Minyan members have been known to complain when only family and not Minyan members are honored with *'aliyot* at a Bar/Bat Mitzvah. The attempt by the extended family to influence the style of the celebration, however, may lead to much tension.

Interestingly, different events provoke varying amounts of tension, and differ in terms of who determines the esthetic of the celebration, the nuclear family (who desire a havurah-style celebration) or the extended family (who desire a more conventional American Jewish celebration). Birth celebrations (Brit Milah or Brit Banot) provide the least controversy and are most under the control of the nuclear family, and thus the havurah esthetic. This may be in part because these are the least elaborate of the major life-cycle events, to which the smallest number of guests are invited.

Bar/Bat Mitzvah celebrations and weddings, as large-scale events, provoke more conflict. Bar/Bat Mitzvahs are usually celebrated as the nuclear family wishes, weddings as the extended family wishes. To some extent this is a function of the different ages of the havurah members in either case: the parents of the Bar or Bat Mitzvah are in a position to arrange the event according to their own desires, since they are the ones who are making the celebration. The young couple who are getting married (the incipient nuclear family), however, are frequently *not* making the celebration, and thus must bow to their parents' wishes. Older couples, who make the wedding arrangements, often have weddings more in keeping with the havurah esthetic: home-cooked or at least dairy food, Jewish music and dancing, participation in the ceremony by havurah members.

Interestingly, the *ufruf* ceremony (calling of the bride and groom to the Torah on the Sabbath before the wedding) has been developed in the Dutchville Minyan to a peak of elaboration previously unknown in Jewish life. This is probably because the wedding is in so many ways a family event, with only a limited number of Minyan members invited. The couple also want to have a celebration which is more in keeping with their own esthetic, and to which the entire Minyan can be invited.

References

Elazar, Daniel J., and Rela Geffen Monson. 1979. "The Synagogue Havurah—An Experiment in Restoring Adult Fellowship to the Jewish Community." *Jewish Journal of Sociology* 21:67–80.

Neusner, Jacob. 1972. "Qumran and Jerusalem: Two types of Jewish Fellowship in Ancient Times." In *Contemporary Judaic Fellowship in Theory and Practice,* Jacob Neusner, ed. (New York: Ktav Publishing House), pp. 1–11.

Pattison, E. Mansell et al. 1975. "A Psychosocial Kinship Model for Family Therapy." *American Journal of Psychiatry* 132:1246–51.

Reisman, Bernard. 1975. "The *Havurah:* An Approach to Humanizing Jewish Organizational Life." *Journal of Jewish Communal Service* 52:202–9.

————. 1980. "The Chavurah: A Jewish Support Network." *American Behavioral Scientist* 23:559–73.

Wasserman, Harry. 1979. "The Havurah Experience." *Journal of Psychology and Judaism* 3(3):168–83.

Wasserman, Harry, and Gerald B. Bubis, with Alan Lert. 1979. "The Concept of Havurah: An Analysis." *Journal of Reform Judaism* 26:35–50.

Weiss, Avrum N. 1977. "The Havurah as an Extended Family." *Journal of Jewish Communal Service* 54:135–37.

EPILOGUES

15. Vitality and Resilience in the American Jewish Family

Steven M. Cohen

Today, in Jewish communal circles in the United States, it is commonplace to hear that, at best, the American Jewish family is threatened, and at worst, it is in shambles. Those with a pessimistic view of the future of the American Jewish family cite the growth in four types of families: the Singles, the Childless, the Intermarried, and the Divorced, as if to suggest that the American Jewish family is on the SCIDs *(sic)*.

A close examination of some of the most recent evidence, though, largely contradicts the pessimistic view. Using the crude "health-and-illness" metaphor, the American Jewish family is nowhere near as sick as some have suggested, but it is certainly undergoing (or has recently undergone) significant changes. Young adult Jews indeed are staying single and childless longer, divorcing and intermarrying more frequently. But, surprisingly, none of these trends holds out serious dangers for Jewish continuity in demographic terms, even though they may well affect the quality of Jewish family and communal life. One can readily marshall both data and interpretations that counterbalance the unduly pessimistic perspective which has become current of late.

Later Marriages, Not More Lifetime Singles

We may begin with the issue of growing singlehood. Like Americans generally, and like highly educated Americans in particular, Jews have been marrying much later than their parents of the postwar years did: the recent Jewish population studies report that about two thirds of Jewish men in their early twenties have never married. Nevertheless, something like 95 percent of Jews aged thirty-five to forty-four have married. The pessimistic perspective would contend that many Jews, in contrast with their elders and predecessors, will never marry. But such an inference leaps far beyond the available evidence. There is simply no reason to believe that the decline in marriage of those in their twenties today is not limited to those in their twenties today. A more plausible interpretation of the recent data would conclude that young American Jewish adults may not be getting married as early as their parents did, but the vast majority are getting married.

Children Later in Life, But Probably Not Fewer of Them

The data on recent Jewish fertility also lend themselves to differing interpretations. The most widely circulated projection is that today's young Jewish women will bear, on average, no more than 1.6 or 1.7 babies. That estimate assumes that they will have children at the same young age as their mothers did. In fact, today's Jewish women are not only marrying later, they're having babies later, too. (The two trends are obviously related.) The issue turns on whether Jewish women now in their thirties will, in the next five to ten years, have enough babies to offset the smaller number of children they thus far have had in their twenties.

The recent data are by no means clear on this point. The 1981 Greater New York Jewish Population Study (directed by Paul Ritterband and Steven M. Cohen) offers some encouraging signs (from a survivalist's perspective). The study area includes not only heavily Orthodox Borough Park but also the trendy Upper East Side and Greenvich Village, as well as Westchester and Long Island, communities very similar to suburban areas throughout the United States. In all, it is a region that encompasses nearly a third of American Jewry. Our preliminary analyses find that the birthrates for women thirty-five to forty-four in this area are at the replacement level. Those who are now married have had 2.2 children; while all women in that age group—married, never married, and formerly married—have had an average of 2.1 children. There has been a dramatic upturn in childbirth in the later years among American women, and apparently Jews are no exception to this trend; in fact, they may even be leading it. We simply don't know whether today's women age twenty to thirty-four will have as many babies as those slightly older than they are; we can say that they'll have them later in life.

Insofar as Jewish women do have just as many children as their mothers did, but later in life, the Jewish population does not figure to shrink considerably. However, not all consequences of delayed childbearing are neutral for group continuity. Later childbearing does, over time, contribute to some population shrinkage unless it is compensated for by extended life expectancy. Moreover, since Jewish communal affiliation and ritual observance jump following the attainment of school age by the first child, the delay in childbearing means that many more Jews are living longer parts of their young adulthood outside conventional Jewish family life. In short, the fertility trends, as best we understand them, are not particularly beneficial for Jewish continuity (however defined), nor are they disastrous (as some have portrayed them).

A Slow Rise in Divorce

Yet another constituent element in the popular, conventional, and pessimistic view of the Jewish family is the purported rise in the Jewish divorce rate. In actuality, the Jewish divorce rate has risen (and probably has stopped rising) in line with the increase (and the recent downturn) in the overall American divorce rate. The only national comparative data we have demonstrate that the Jewish divorce rate has remained at around half of the white Protestant rate, and it shows no signs of significantly surpassing that ratio. The little data we have also suggest that Jews who divorce remarry faster than others. In short, fewer Jewish Americans than others experience divorce, and those who do are better able to establish second marriages.

Intermarriage: Far from a Disaster

And last, the pessimistic view also incorporates the belief that not only is the frequency of intermarriage rising, but that intermarriage inevitably brings about Jewish population erosion either in the current or in the next generation. Here, too, the evidence is far from conclusive and what little we have bodes neither very well nor very ill for the continuity of the American Jewish population in the medium term.

Most active researchers in the field have now called into question the widely publicized outmarriage rate of 32 percent for marriages contracted by born-Jews in 1965–71, reported by Fred Massarik and Alvin

Chenkin in their preliminary analysis (1973) of the 1970–71 National Jewish Population Study. (In fact, since an individual rate of 32 percent works out to a couple rate of almost 50 percent, some reports in the popular press speak of an intermarriage rate of "one half"; that is, if one Jew in three marries a non-Jew, half the marriages involving Jews also involve non-Jews.) In 1983, two Hebrew University demographers, U. O. Schmelz and Sergio DellaPergola, published their more detailed and careful analyses of the same data. They reported that 22.5 percent of Jews of all ages who married between 1965 and 1971 married a nonconverting Gentile. Sociologist Bernard Lazerwitz of Bar-Ilan University, analyzing the same data, reported that fewer than 10 percent of Jews under thirty-five married a nonconverting Gentile. In the 1981 Greater New York Jewish Population Study, about 11 percent of those who married in the 1970s married a non-Jew who did not convert.

Probably the most pertinent and comprehensive analysis to date has been undertaken by Charles Silberman in his recently published study of American Jewry. Silberman examined the recently conducted community studies; these have covered about 60 percent of the American Jewish population. He then estimated the intermarriage rates for communities which were not recently surveyed by assuming that unsurveyed cities and regions could be paired with regionally and demographically similar surveyed communities. (For example, he assumed the Baltimore intermarriage rate approximates that of Philadelphia, and that Detroit's is similar to Cleveland's.) By weighting the various communities and regions to take into account population size, he constructed an overall estimate of the rate of outmarriage (the proportion of Jewish individuals marrying someone not born Jewish). For the entire country, using both low and high estimates for the unsurveyed regions, Silberman arrives at an outmarriage rate of only 24–26 percent.

As a result, many specialists in the field find little to substantiate the fear so often expressed in Jewish communal circles that intermarriage is, in effect, "going through the roof." Instead, we believe the late 1960s constituted a distinctive period of growth in intermarriage, just as the period also witnessed vast changes in many aspects of family life—among Jews, among other Americans, and throughout the West. If so, then the rate of intermarriage may have leaped sharply upward in the late 1960s, but then plateaued thereafter.

To the extent that intermarriage has increased, not all its consequences adversely affect Jewish continuity. First, Jews who intermarry—and especially those who assimilate upon doing so—come disproportionately from weak Jewish backgrounds. Meanwhile, outmarriage is also the immediate cause for conversion to Judaism of about one sixth of the born–Gentile spouses (mostly women). They typically turn out to be as committed to Judaism, especially to its religious rather than ethnic features, as the average American Jew who marries another born-Jew. Thus, intermarriage may serve as a salutary escape and entry vehicle—allowing less committed Jews to leave the community, and a smaller number of newly committed Jews to enter. In all, it seems that the number of people in the current generation (that is, the generation of marriers) who identify as Jews is not significantly diminished by intermarriage, and may even be slightly enhanced by it.

But even if intermarriage has little impact on the current Jewish population size, it may very well affect the size of the next generation of Jews. Unfortunately, here our data are even skimpier than those on the current Jewish identity of adult intermarriers. We have no way of knowing the extent to which children of intermarried couples will identify and behave as Jews. We can reason only from the current behavior and statements of parents who have intermarried.

In the New York area study, we found that the levels of ritual observance and Jewish institutional affiliation in intermarried homes where the born–Gentile spouse converted equaled those of in-married homes. In the mixed married homes, where no conversion followed outmarriage, most of the Jewish parent-respondents in our study claimed that their children were being raised as Jews. This is the case in about three quarters of the homes where the mother is Jewish, but in only about a third of the cases where the father is Jewish.

As a result of conversions and of the triumph of Jewish identity in the contest over the group affiliations of the offspring of mixed marriages, we estimated that intermarriage actually may be serving to increase the number of Jewish children. In our estimates, we defined the children of mixed marriages as Jewishly identified only when their parents said they were Jewish, and only when they were being raised in homes where the parents met some minimal standards of ritual observance, communal affiliation, or in-group (Jewish) friendships.

For the sake of argument, we then made new calculations on the assumption that half of the mixed married homes that claimed to be raising Jewish children and were affirmatively Jewish in some way were, in fact, raising children who would emerge as effectively non-Jewish adults. Even with such an assumption, according to our best estimates, the net effect of all outmarriages—including that of adding the children of the conversionary marriages to the population—was to produce a probable loss of only 3 percent per generation nationwide, or half that in New York. (That figure assumes a 25 percent outmarriage rate and a net loss to the Jewish population amounting to roughly 15 percent of the outmarriers.) Thus, as with singlehood, divorce, and fertility, intermarriage trends also seem to hold out no immediate threat to the continuity of a large American Jewish population as involved (or as uninvolved) in Jewish life (however one defines involvement) as in the recent past.

The Sources of Pessimism

If the recent available evidence does indeed contravene the disaster scenario so often circulated among Jewish communal professionals and volunteer leaders, their pessimism about the state of the American Jewish family in particular, and the fate of American Jewry in general, itself merits some explanation. In other words, putting matters colloquially, if things are so good, why do so many people think they're so bad?

Aside from a cultural predisposition to worry about survival, there are, I believe, at least four reasons why many observers see the Jewish family and American Jewish life as not simply changing—as they always have—but as on the road to serious deterioration.

One explanation might derive from the high, elite standards found among those who typically interpret the state of American Jewry to the organized community. The men and women who are in the business of observing American Jewry—rabbis, educators, community workers, and Jewish studies professors—hold their subjects up to the highest standards, standards which the masses of American Jews have never met, despite idealized and romanticized notions about the good old days.

Second is the matter of institutional advocacy. Those who head institutions devoted to enhancing Jewish knowledge and identity are very struck by the enormity of the social problem they are addressing. Insofar as they are committed to changing the quality of American Jewish life, they tend to focus their attention and perceptions on shortcomings rather than on examples of revival and renewal. Moreover, consciously or not, they may feel an incentive to demonstrate the weaknesses in American Jewish educational, intellectual, and cultural life so as to ensure and expand the support of philanthropic activists. In so doing, they may be contributing to exaggerated perceptions of the problems they are addressing in their professional endeavors.

The third source of pessimism for the American Jewish future is found in what may be called "folk Zionism." Many Israelis learn from their youth that after the founding of the Jewish State in 1948, the Diaspora is peripheral to the unfolding of Jewish history, and, in light of inevitable assimilation and anti-Semitism, it is also inherently unstable.

These ideological perceptions may well color the interpretation of anecdotes and more rigorous evidence by the many communally influential observers of American Jewry who also are committed Zionists—be they Israeli officials or immigrant intellectuals who comprise a hefty segment of Israeli commentators on Diaspora Jewish life.

Finally, as in all fields, once accurate but now outmoded conceptual models may be structuring our thinking. At one time, the Jewish contact with modernity meant severe disruption of family life and communal ties (turn-of-the-century Western Europe certainly provides a ready example). At one time, it meant that some Jews saw their group ties as a social handicap and fled their Jewishness. At one time, it meant massive dislocations in so many spheres of life. However, modernity may have come to mean, for most American Jews, none of these adverse consequences. Instead, it appears American Jews have successfully adapted to the pluralist, voluntarist society in which they live. Not only have they made extraordinary achievements in the political, economic, and cultural arenas, but they are preserving their group identity and community as well.

Younger Jews: Less "Jewish" or Just Less Married?

To illustrate how anecdotal evidence and first impressions can often be deceiving, we may review another piece of analysis we recently completed of the Greater New York Jewish Population data. We focused our attention on differences in Jewish identity between today's older and younger adults, as well as between people in different family statuses. In so doing, we found that young adults, those under thirty-five, were indeed very uninvolved in Jewish life. For example, the majority belonged to no Jewish institutions as compared with only less than a quarter unaffiliated among those fifty-five to sixty-four. Only half of the young adults said that all their closest friends were Jewish, as opposed to more than four fifths of the middle-aged Jews. Data such as these, and the qualitative impression the conditions they represent leave upon lay observers, have led many to conclude that the younger generation of Jews is simply less committed to Jewish life than its elders.

Before accepting such an inference, we compared the never-married with couples with school-age children. In so doing, we found the same sorts of huge differences. Over a third of the never-married said they failed to celebrate Passover and Chanuka as opposed to only 10 percent of the couples with children; almost three fifths of the singles belonged to no Jewish institution in contrast with less than a quarter of those with children; and most of the never-marrieds said they had a Gentile close friend as opposed to only a quarter of the parents.

When we compared people in different age groups, all of whom were married parents, we found virtually no differences in Jewish identity between the old and the young. In other words, the reason that young people seem less Jewishly committed is that they have yet to start the families that once led their own parents, and now many of their contemporaries, to the types of activities that most observers recognize as the hallmarks of visible Jewish commitment. When today's young adults marry and have their own children, they too may well attain the same levels of Jewish commitment as did other married parents in the past and in our current time. In short, today's young adults who have yet to marry and have children are in no way permanently alienated from conventional Jewish life; but they are currently on the periphery of the organized community.

Thus, the Jewish family remains central to Jewish commitment and continuity. Yet, its shape and its relationship to Jewish continuity may well be changing.

Policy Implications for Organized Jewry

The many trends in Jewish communal and family life noted in the foregoing have prompted a vigorous effort by organized Jewry to try to halt or reverse recent demographic changes. In the last few years, the Jewish community has organized numerous conferences and issued scores of reports and recommendations so as to design ways to get large numbers of Jews to change their family-related decisions—that is, to marry young, marry each other, stay married, and have many children. Unfortunately, in the face of the massive influence of the larger society, and as far as we know from other such endeavors, efforts at demographic jawboning in a voluntarist society are doomed to frustration and ultimate failure. Even whole governments have vainly sought to influence the demographic behavior of their citizenry with only minor effect, if any. How much less can be expected in this regard of a voluntary community?

But just because it is unrealistic to expect organized Jewry to seriously influence the demographic behavior of large numbers of individual Jews, some may still believe it is morally necessary for that community to exemplify certain values and to conduct itself in a caring and sensitive fashion. Singles looking for Jewish marriage partners, parents who bear the expense of time, money, and intergenerational conflict to send their children to Jewish schools but who are nevertheless left wanting, couples under strain in need of counseling, and mixed-married families searching for ways to conduct their Jewish lives—all, some would argue, deserve a community that attends to their legitimate Jewish needs for their own sake and not merely because communal leaders are concerned, rightly or wrongly, with the demographic numbers. Thus, to take only one area, the decisions to support quality day care and low-cost effective Jewish schooling and camping could be made on a sound value basis, and not because of an ill-advised attempt to raise the Jewish birthrate. In short, the nature of relations between Jews and Jews, and between Jews and their institutions, are all within communal leaders' control; but the ability to influence millions of personal decisions about marriage and childbearing probably is not.

American Jewry may well include large numbers of singles, childless, intermarried, and divorced individuals for some time to come. The realistic challenge to organized Jewry is to redesign schools, synagogues, agencies, associations, and their programs so as to accommodate not only married couples with children (who already heavily utilize institutional facilities), but members of alternative families as well. In fact, today, almost all married Jewish parents of school-age children affiliate with some Jewish institution at some time, even if these affiliations are perfunctory or unrewarding. For those concerned with the quality of American Jewish life, efforts to reach the few who remain totally unaffiliated may be less than optimally effective. Instead, a more productive approach from their point of view may be efforts to adjust programs and institutions to the emergence of vast constituencies of Jews who will live for many years in family situations far different from the conventional model.

16. Afterword

Paula E. Hyman

A new field of inquiry, such as family history, reshapes the way we conceptualize human experience. It raises to significance elements of the past whose meaning had previously escaped formal notice and definition. It asks new questions and seeks new sources to answer them. Family history, for example, has held that the very structure of private life within households is of intrinsic interest, that the personal behavior and attitudes of ordinary men and women are of importance in our quest to understand the cultural, political, and economic development of our world. It has posited a link between the family and larger social institutions, with the family often operating as an independent variable. Since the family has served as the principal sphere of women, whose public lives were routinely circumscribed, family history has also provided an opportunity to explore the consciousness and activity of women as well as their impact upon other family members, the economy, and the larger society.

As this volume of essays has tentatively suggested, Jewish family history can also rescue from oblivion the collective experience of ordinary Jews. It can illuminate how the family mediates between the individual, the Jewish community, and the larger society. Studying the Jewish family enriches our understanding of such critical phenomena of modern Jewish history as acculturation, Jewish identity, and social mobility.

Much remains to be investigated. While family historians have delineated the nature of the modern Western bourgeois family and have explored the reasons for its emergence,[1] Jewish family historians have yet to ascertain the structure of the Jewish family in medieval Europe, in nineteenth-century Eastern Europe, in early modern Islamic countries, or in much of Western Europe. Nor have they begun to compare the Jewish family with the Gentile families among whom Jews have lived.

Preliminary evidence suggests, for example, that Jews may have exhibited some "modern" family traits before such characteristics were widespread in the larger population. Did Jewish families display a close emotional attachment to their children earlier than was the case for the majority population? Goitein's work certainly points to a strong measure of concern demonstrated by medieval Jewish parents for their children in a time when family historians posit a relatively low level of emotional attachment among family members.[2] While Philippe Ariès notes that "indifference to small children is characteristic of all traditional societies,"[3] the memoirs of Glückel of Hameln, a seventeenth-century traditional German Jewish woman of the mercantile class, reveal an intense involvement with her large family. Her lament upon the death of her two-year-old daughter Mata, the first of the two of her fourteen children to die in childhood, reflects a grief and sense of loss as appropriate to the twentieth as to the seventeenth century.[4] If one accepts the thesis that high childhood mortality inhibited the formation of powerful ties with young children, it is possible that lower child mortality rates among Jews may have accounted for a different texture of sentiment within the traditional Jewish family. Further, the existence of close bonds with small children may then have promoted behavior that facilitated the survival of infants and children. Thus, while the practice of sending infants to the countryside for wet-nursing was common among the bourgeoisie and the urban lower classes, particularly in France in the eighteenth and early nineteenth centuries, it was not accepted by European Jews of similar class background. When wet nurses were hired by Jews, they were brought into the household. The avoidance of wet-nursing doubtless saved the lives of Jewish infants, for the mortality rate of the small charges of wet nurses was notoriously high.[5] It is not clear to what extent religious norms governed the use of wet nurses nor to what degree the ritual behavior of Jews contributed to their lower death rate. However, some aspects of the Jews' religious and cultural practice probably did help to reduce their mortality. For example, the mandated practice of washing the hands before eating, if scrupulously observed, offered some small measure of protection from disease.

Jewish norms may also have promoted more cordial relations between spouses than was the case in premodern Europe and North Africa. Jewish law considered sexuality to be a divine gift, which need not lead to sin if it were properly regulated within marriage.[6] Medieval Jewish treatises on sexuality urged consideration for the wife's sexual needs and suggested consultation between spouses to determine what sexual expression was pleasing to both.[7] At a time when wife beating was acceptable in Christian Europe, rabbinical courts issued sharp denunciations of instances of wife beating that were brought to their attention and compelled recalcitrant husbands to divorce their wives and provide for their support.[8]

If Jews may have been modern in the intensity of the emotional bonds within the family circle even in premodern times, they were also in the vanguard among European populations in controlling their fertility. Numerous studies have indicated that Central European and American Jews in the past two centuries have had lower birthrates than the general populace, even when such social characteristics as level of education, urbanization, and profession are held constant.[9] The causes of the precipitous decline in Jewish fertility are a subject of vigorous debate, and the connection between Jewishness and family size has not yet been fully elucidated.

While the European and North African Jewish family may have diverged from its surroundings in the Middle Ages and the early modern period by exhibiting certain modern characteristics, the contemporary Jewish family differs from other Western families in its conservation of certain "traditional" traits. For example, American Jews experience a low, although rising, divorce rate; they divorce less than half as often as white Protestants.[10] Likewise, endogamy among Jews, while in decline, is still more frequent than in any other white ethnic group in America.[11]

While much research has been conducted in the area of demography, particularly with regard to fertility, many questions have yet to be answered. The basic outlines of Jewish household composition across time remain to be established, especially in comparison to the local non-Jewish population. As members of a minority group whose legal status was often precarious, did Jews keep more boarders within their household in order to provide more persons with rights of residency? Did Jewish adolescents, both male and female, leave home more or less frequently than their Gentile compatriots? How much impact did Jewish communal regulations have upon household composition?

As for the affective dimensions of family life, our knowledge remains fragmentary. We need scholarly investigation of responsa literature, memoirs, child-raising manuals, and belles lettres to explore attitudes toward children, incidence of deviance in relations between the sexes as well as child-parent relationships, and the roles of women and men within the family circle. How have migration, acculturation, and adaptation to modern industrial society changed the internal workings of the Jewish family in different places? While Jewish families in the Diaspora still differ demographically from non-Jewish families, do they differ in their psychological dynamics as well?

Insofar as the Jewish family has retained distinctive features even as it has adapted to new social, cultural, and economic conditions, its role in the development of modern Jewry comes to the fore. In particular, the contribution of the family, both nuclear and extended, to the extraordinary social mobility of Jews in the modern period has yet to be investigated. While it is often noted that Jews invested in education to a greater extent than other immigrant groups, the economic strategies that Jewish families devised in both Europe and America to take advantage of the opportunities offered by industrializing societies call for close scrutiny. Similarly, the psychological function of the family in stimulating and supporting both the ambitions and self-denial necessary for attaining economic success deserve serious analysis. It was the family, after all, which instilled norms and values in its young and first defined success for them. Yet family historians and sociologists have left to novelists such questions as how the Jewish family selectively legitimated values from the larger society, how it perpetuated a measure of assertiveness among its women, how it secularized its values, and how it succeeded in sending forth its children to do battle in the world while keeping them closely attached, not the least by guilt, to the parental hearth.

Since extensive mass migration characterizes the modern Jewish experience, the ability of the Jewish family to adapt to new social and cultural circumstances is a subject of some interest. Was the Jewish family able, for the most part, to serve as a buffer between its members and the demands of a new society while preparing its children for integration? If so, what were its special strengths? Are there similarities between Jewish and other immigrant families accommodating to new societies? Which immigrant settings were most conducive to the stability of the Jewish family? What has been the impact of migration upon the Jewish family, and particularly upon intergenerational relations within the family circle?[12]

We have yet to explore all of the ramifications of the interaction of family and community, of family and Jewish identity. While family cohesiveness and Jewish communal affiliation often go hand in hand, there are also occasions when dedication to community proves detrimental to the biological family. Chava Weissler has demonstrated how the contemporary havurah family in America prefers community to its biological extended family. In a very different historical context, the prolonged sojourns of Hasidic men at the rebbe's court in the eighteenth and nineteenth centuries physically divided the Hasidic nuclear family. Opting for Hasidism could also split members of the extended family. The relationship between family and community is, therefore, more complex than popular notions would lead us to believe.

Finally, we need to know more about the acculturated modern Jewish family. What does it preserve of traditional Jewish norms of family life and traditional Jewish patterns of behavior? How, if in any fashion, do secularized Jews differ from their Gentile counterparts? How resistant are family patterns to change?

This is a long and ambitious agenda for the community of Jewish scholarship, yet its fulfillment promises to reveal and interpret to us fundamental aspects of Jewish culture throughout history.

Notes

1. For extended discussions of the emergence of the modern Western family, see Lawrence Stone, *The Family, Sex, and Marriage in England 1500–1800* (New York, 1977); and Edward Shorter, *The Making of the Modern Family* (New York, 1975) and his "Female Emancipation, Birth Control, and Fertility in European History," *American Historical Review* 78 (June 1973), 605–40.

2. Ibid.

3. Philippe Ariès, *The Hour of Our Death,* trans. Helen Weaver (New York, 1981), p. 447.

4. *The Memoirs of Glückel of Hameln,* trans. with notes by Marvin Lowenthal (New York, 1977), pp. 87–89.

5. For one account of wet-nursing in France, see George D. Sussman, "Parisian Infants and Norman Wet Nurses in the Early Nineteenth Century: A Statistical Study," in Robert I. Rotberg and Theodore K. Rabb, eds., *Marriage and Fertility: Studies in Interdisciplinary History* (Princeton, 1980), pp. 249–65.

6. For an overview of Jewish attitudes toward sexuality, see David M. Feldman, *Marital Relations, Birth Control, and Abortion in Jewish Law* (New York, 1974), pp. 21–105; and Jacob Katz, "Marriage and Sexual Life among the Jews at the End of the Middle Ages" [Hebrew], *Ziyon* X (1944), 40–43.

7. See, for example, Rabad of Posquières, *Ba'alei ha-Nefesh* (Jerusalem, 1955), pp. 135–40.

8. S. D. Goitein, *A Mediterranean Society,* vol. 3, *The Family* (Berkeley and Los Angeles, 1978), pp. 184–89; and Irving Agus, ed., *Rabbi Meir of Rothenberg,* 2nd ed. (New York, 1970), pp. 326–27.

9. See Paul Ritterband, ed., *Modern Jewish Fertility* (Leiden, 1981), passim; John Knodel, *The Decline of Fertility in Germany 1871–1939* (Princeton, 1974), pp. 137–38; and U. O. Schmeltz, *Jewish Population Studies* (Jerusalem, 1970).

10. Steven M. Cohen, "The American Jewish Family Today," *American Jewish Yearbook* (1982), pp. 136–54.

11. Steven M. Cohen, *Patterns of Interethnic Marriage and Friendship* (New York, 1980).

12. For preliminary research on the immigrant Jewish family in America, see Irving Howe, *World of Our Fathers* (New York, 1976), pp. 169–83; Charlotte Baum, Paula Hyman, and Sonya Michel, *The Jewish Woman in America* (New York, 1976), pp. 98–112, 116–20, 182–97, 214–33; and Thomas Kessner, *The Golden Door* (New York, 1977), pp. 71–103.

Index

Sabbath, German-Jewish women
maintaining, 69–70, 71
Schmelz, U. O., 224
Schulweis, Harold, 201
Scott, Sir Walter, 102–3
Separation (marital), Hasidim and, 193
Sexuality: Eastern European Jewry and, 51;
Jewish law on, 231–32; maskilim and,
55–57; Polish Jewry and, 21. *See also*
Marriage
Shadkhan, maskilim and, 53, 54
Shakespeare, William, 100
Silberman, Charles, 224
Singer, Isaac Bashevis, 114, 115
Singer, Israel Joshua, 111–12, 114, 115
Single-person households, among
American Jewry, 179–80
Sirkes, Joel, Rabbi, 21, 23
Smollet, Tobias, 101
Stern, Fritz, 71
Stone, Lawrence, 5
Synagogue havurah, 201–2

Temerlin, Maurice, 123–24
Thackeray, William Makepeace, 103
Trollope, Anthony, 103

United States, Jewish family patterns in,
172–82
Usurer, literature portraying Jew as, 100–
101

Variation, among Israeli ethnic groups,
131–46
Victorian novels, Jews portrayed in, 101–8
Villages, Moroccan Jewish family in Israel
settling in, 82–93

Way We Live Now, The, 103
Wengeroff, Pauline, 52
Wet-nursing, Jews and, 231
Widowhood, among American Jewry, 177,
178, 179
Wife beating, rabbinical courts on, 232. *See
also* Women
Women: in American-Jewish family, 222–
23; commerce and, 55; fertility among
Israeli, 139–42; in German-Jewish
family, 62–76; Jewish mother image
of, 118–27; *maskilim* and, 55; in
Moroccan Jewish family, 32–38, 87–
88; wife beating and, 232. *See also*
Childrearing; Marriage

Yeshivot: Eastern European Jewry and, 52;
Polish Jews and, 19
Yiddish literature, family portrayed in
family saga of, 110–16
Yiddish mother tongue, American Jewry
studied with, 172–82
Young adults, commitment of to Judaism,
227–28

Zelmenyaner, 113–14, 115

Contributors

David Biale is Associate Professor of History and Judaic Studies at the State University of New York at Binghamton. He is the author of *Gershom Scholem: Kabbalah and Counter-History* and will be publishing a second work on the theme of power and passivity in Jewish history with Schocken Books.

Steven M. Cohen, co-editor of this volume, is Professor of Sociology at Queens College, CUNY. He is the author of *American Modernity and Jewish Identity,* and is co-author of two forthcoming monographs, *Family, Community, and Identity: The Jews of Greater New York* and a study of modern Orthodoxy in the United States. He has published widely on several topics in American Jewish life, including the family, political attitudes and behavior, and changing patterns of communal affiliation and religious behavior.

Sergio DellaPergola is Senior Lecturer, Institute for Contemporary Jewry, the Hebrew University, where he is also Associate Director of the Division of Demography and Statistics. Among his many publications on the demography of Diaspora Jewry is *La population juive de France: socio-demographie et identité,* of which he is co-author, and *Anatomia dell'ebraismo italiano: Caratteristiche demografiche, economiche, sociali, religiose e politiche di una minoranza.*

Shlomo Deshen is Professor of Anthropology and Sociology, Bar-Ilan University. Much of his prolific scholarly activity has focused on the adjustment of North African immigrants and their children to Israeli society. He is the co-author of *Jewish Studies in the Middle East: Community, Culture, and Authority* and (with Moshe Shokeid) *Distant Relations: Ethnicity and Politics among Arabs and North African Jews in Israel.*

Calvin Goldscheider is Professor of Judaic Studies and Sociology and associated with the Population Studies and Training Center at Brown University. He was also Professor of Sociology and Demography at The

Hebrew University, Jerusalem. He has recently published a book on American Jews *(Social Change and Jewish Continuity)* and coauthored a comparative-historical analysis *(The Transformation of the Jews)*.

Frances Kobrin Goldscheider is Associate Professor and Chair, Department of Sociology, Brown University. She has published extensively on family change in the United States, as well as among Jews, both in the United States and in Israel.

Gershon David Hundert is Associate Professor of History and chairs the Jewish Studies Program at McGill University.

Paula Hyman, co-editor of this volume, is Dean of the Seminary College of Jewish Studies and Associate Professor of Jewish History at the Jewish Theological Seminary of America. She is the author of *From Dreyfus to Vichy: The Remaking of French Jewry, 1906–1939* and co-author of *The Jewish Woman in America*. She has published widely in European Jewish history and Jewish women's history and is completing a book entitled *Emancipation and Social Change*.

Marion Kaplan is Associate Professor of History at Queens College. She is the author of *The Jewish Feminist Movement in Germany: The Campaigns of the Juedische Frauenbund, 1904–1938,* editor of *The Marriage Bargain: The Dowry in European History,* and co-editor of *When Biology Became Destiny: Women in Weimar and Nazi Germany.* She is preparing a book on Jewish women in Imperial Germany.

Anita Norich is Assistant Professor of English, the University of Michigan, where she also teaches Yiddish language and literature in the Jewish Studies Program. She is writing a book on I. J. Singer.

Gladys Rothbell, at the time of this writing, was a doctoral candidate in the Department of Sociology, SUNY at Stonybrook, and was completing her dissertation on the stereotype of the Jewish mother. She will be co-authoring a book on Jewish and Italian immigrant women.

William Shaffir is Professor of Sociology at McMaster University, in Hamilton, Ontario Canada. His published work has focused upon field work methods and the study of Hassidic communities.

Moshe Shokeid is Professor of Anthropology and Sociology at Tel-Aviv University. Among his extensive writings is the volume, *The Dual Heritage: Immigrants from the Atlas Mountains in an Israeli Village.*

Susan A. Slotnick received her Ph.D. in Yiddish literature, linguistics, and folklore from Columbia University in 1978. She is now an assembly language programmer living in Pittsburgh who writes about Yiddish in her spare time.

Chava Weissler is Assistant Professor of Religion, Princeton University. She received her Ph.D. in folklore from the University of Pennsylvania. She is completing a book on ambivalence and tradition in a havurah community and has begun research on Jewish women's piety in the eighteenth and early nineteenth centuries.